SIENA

Watercolours MADE EASY

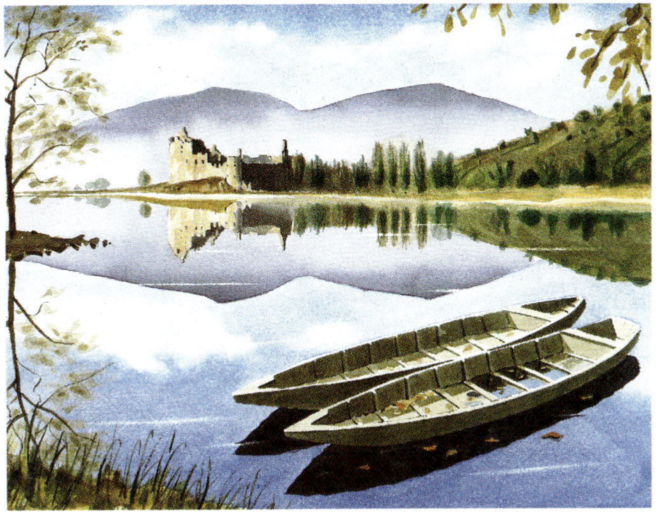

MIRANDA FELLOWS

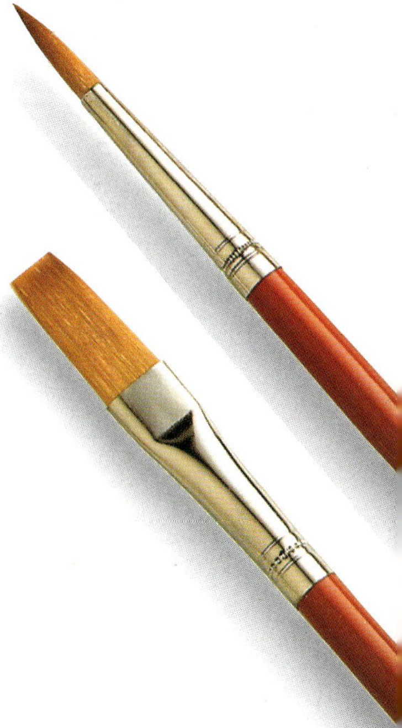

This is a Siena Book
Siena is an imprint of Parragon

First published in Great Britain in 1995 by
Parragon
13 Whiteladies Road
Clifton, Bristol
BS8 1PB

This edition published 1998

ISBN: 0-75252-634-0

Produced by Haldane Mason, London

Acknowledgements
Art Direction: Ron Samuels
Editor: Helen Douglas-Cooper
Jacket Design: Ron Samuels
Series Design: Paul Cooper
Page Design: Simon Wilder
Photography: Joff Lee
Styling: John Lee Studios

Artwork
All artwork by Louise Allison with the exception of the following:
Pages 40–1 and Projects 1, 6, 7 and 11 by Steve Dew;
and Projects 5 and 9 by John Palmer.

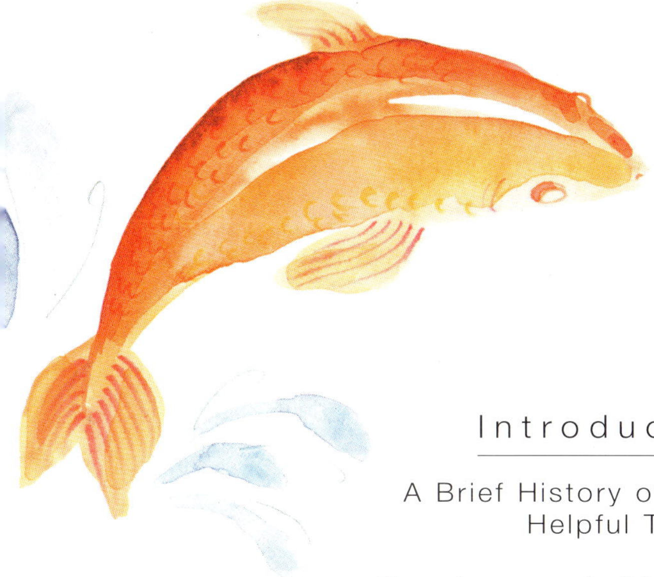

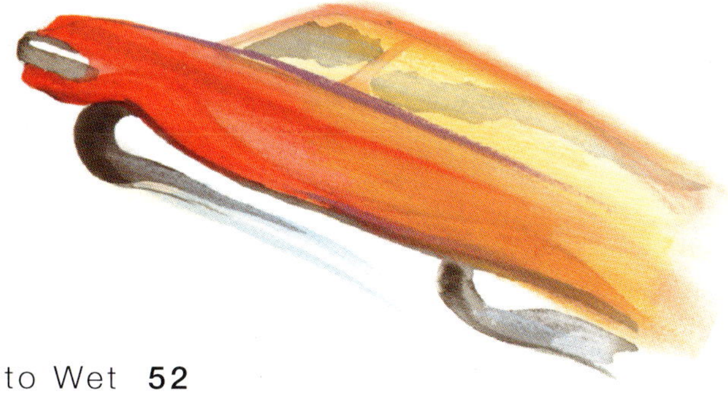

Contents

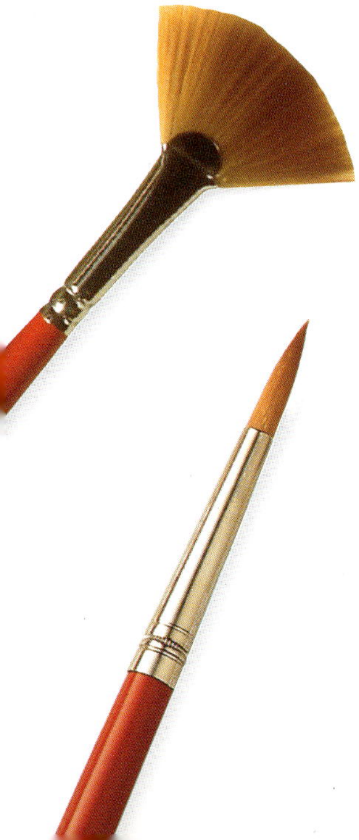

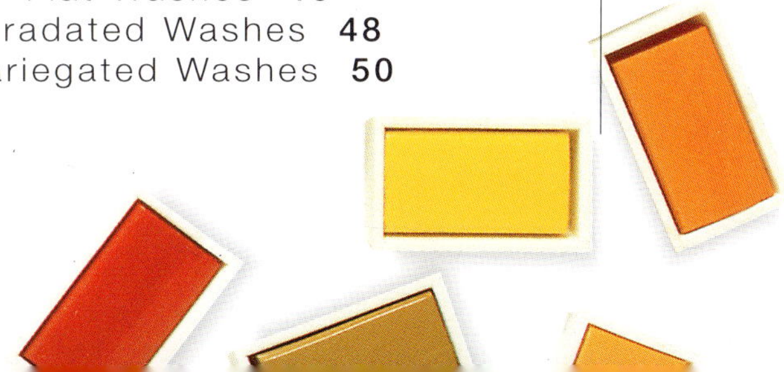

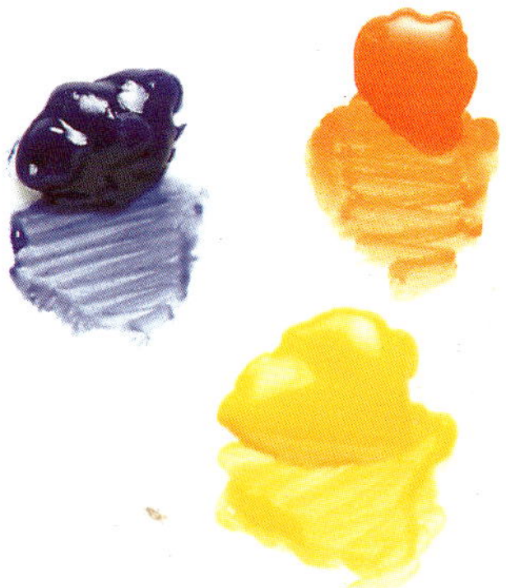

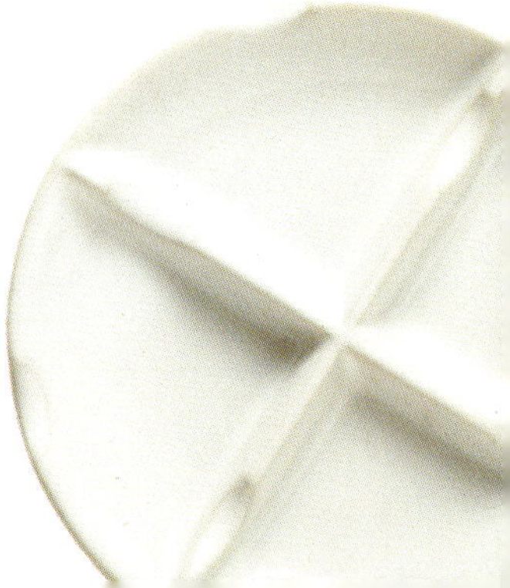

Introduction

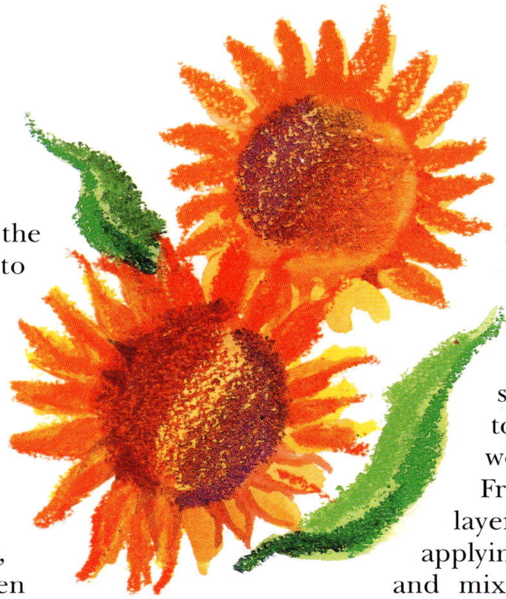

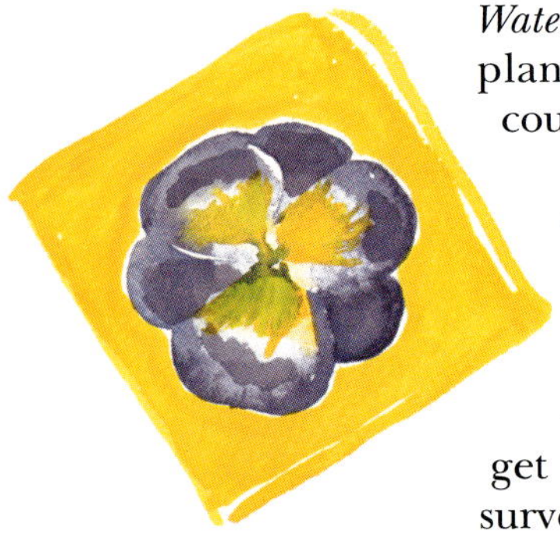

Watercolours Made Easy is the perfect introduction to painting with this wonderful medium, even for the most cautious beginner. The book is clearly and concisely written, and contains over 100 fresh and exacting illustrations that will bring watercolour painting to life before your very eyes. Split into three easy-to-follow sections, *Watercolours Made Easy* has been planned as a complete beginner's course in this exciting medium.

Section One, Tools and Materials, concentrates on describing the materials, helping to demystify the lofty realms of the artist as well as the art shop. Clear definitions of terms such as wash, translucency and dry brush will get you off on the right footing, while a survey of the materials available to paint with will help simplify your shopping trips.

In Section Two, Techniques, the fundamental skills essential to good watercolour practice are simply explained and illustrated. Each technique is shown as a swatch, and most are then developed into simple pictures to show how they work in context. From laying flat layers of paint to applying masking fluid and mixing media, the section provides an excellent grounding in watercolour techniques. Helpful hints and tips provide answers to all the additional questions you could possibly wish to ask.

The third section contains 12 exciting watercolour painting projects. Each covers a different range of applications and subjects – landscape, figures and still life. The final two projects consider more unusual and challenging subjects, encouraging you to begin to develop abstract images and to discover your own style. However, before becoming embroiled in such complex issues, let's see how watercolour can be made easy.

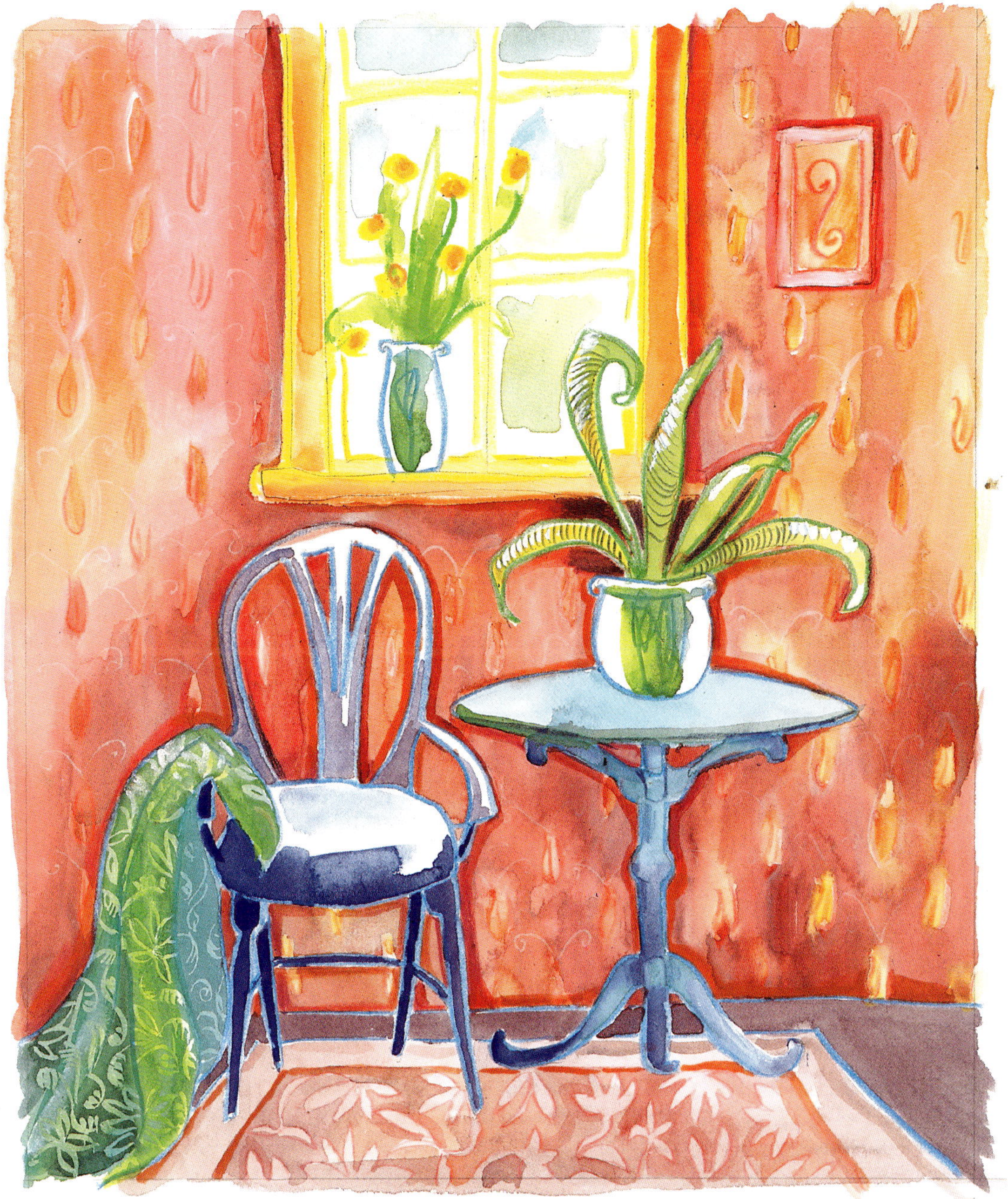

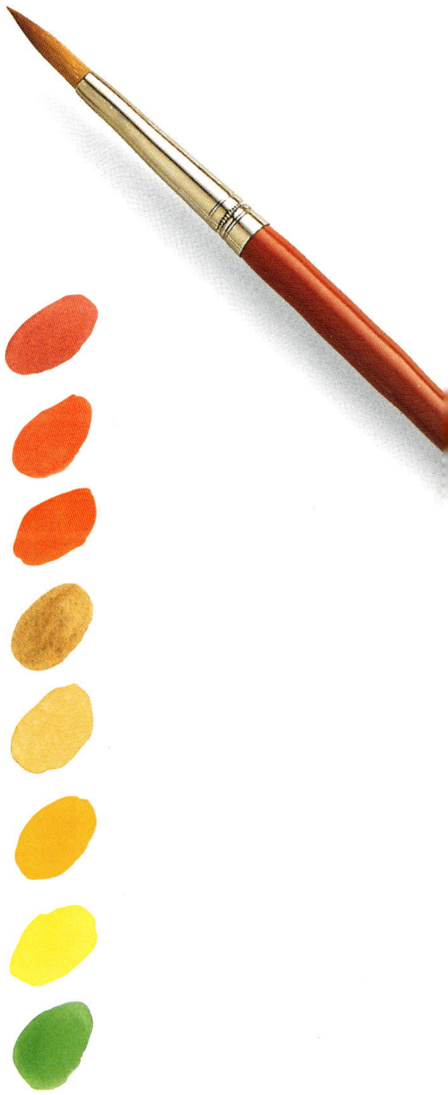

A Brief History of Watercolour

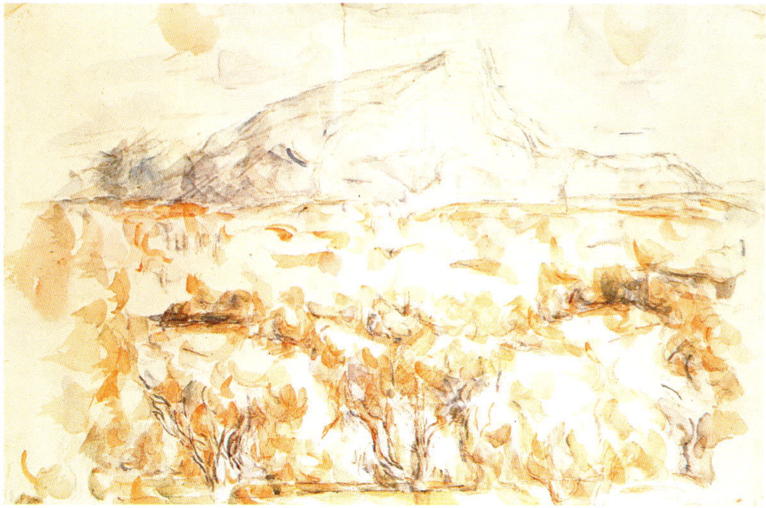

LEFT Cezanne's *Mont Sainte Victoire* is a loose sketch, using a limited palette.
RIGHT In *Fountains Abbey,* J.M.W. Turner has used watercolours like oils to produce strong colours and detailed work.

Watercolour is a medium that can boast a history as proud as it is long. When you pick up a brush to apply your first watercolour wash, you will be joining an artistic heritage that embraces many centuries and countries, not to mention legacies and styles. Of the many artists who have employed watercolours, one of the earliest was Leonardo da Vinci (1452–1519), the famous Renaissance master. Many of his anatomical studies were executed in watercolour. Slightly later and further north, the German artist Albrecht Dürer (1471–1528) often exploited watercolour's qualities in his landscape sketches and botanical studies. Other artists of great merit who used watercolour included Peter Paul Rubens (1577–1640), in paintings of light over landscape, and Anthony van Dyck (1599–1641), who was both Rubens' student and a court painter to Charles I of England.

Of the British contingent, William Blake (1757–1827) expounded the use of watercolour for illustrations, used in conjunction with pen and ink. John Sell Cotman (1782–1842), and Thomas Girtin (1775–1802), by contrast, were more fascinated by watercolour's ability to distil the atmospheric qualities inherent in nature. Both were active during the same period as J.M.W. Turner (1775–1851), the most famous watercolourist in history. No other artist had experimented with the medium as Turner was to. Without his works to learn from, the medium may not be as revered as it is today. From large expanses of pure wash, to fine details added with touches of intensely coloured pigment, Turner determined to exploit watercolour paint to its full potential – and then push it a little further. He was not afraid to experiment, and his work never conformed to rules. Thus he would spray and spatter the paint, rub it in with his thumb nail, spit on it to make it more fluid – employing whatever method he felt was necessary to produce the desired effect. This is as invaluable a lesson today as it was during Turner's time – don't be afraid to experiment. Watercolour allows you to play lots of games – the paint does not like to sit still until dry, preferring to run and drift, merge and melt on the paper. You need to get used to its fluid and erratic nature in order to enjoy yourself, but once you have, there is no other pleasure quite like painting in watercolour.

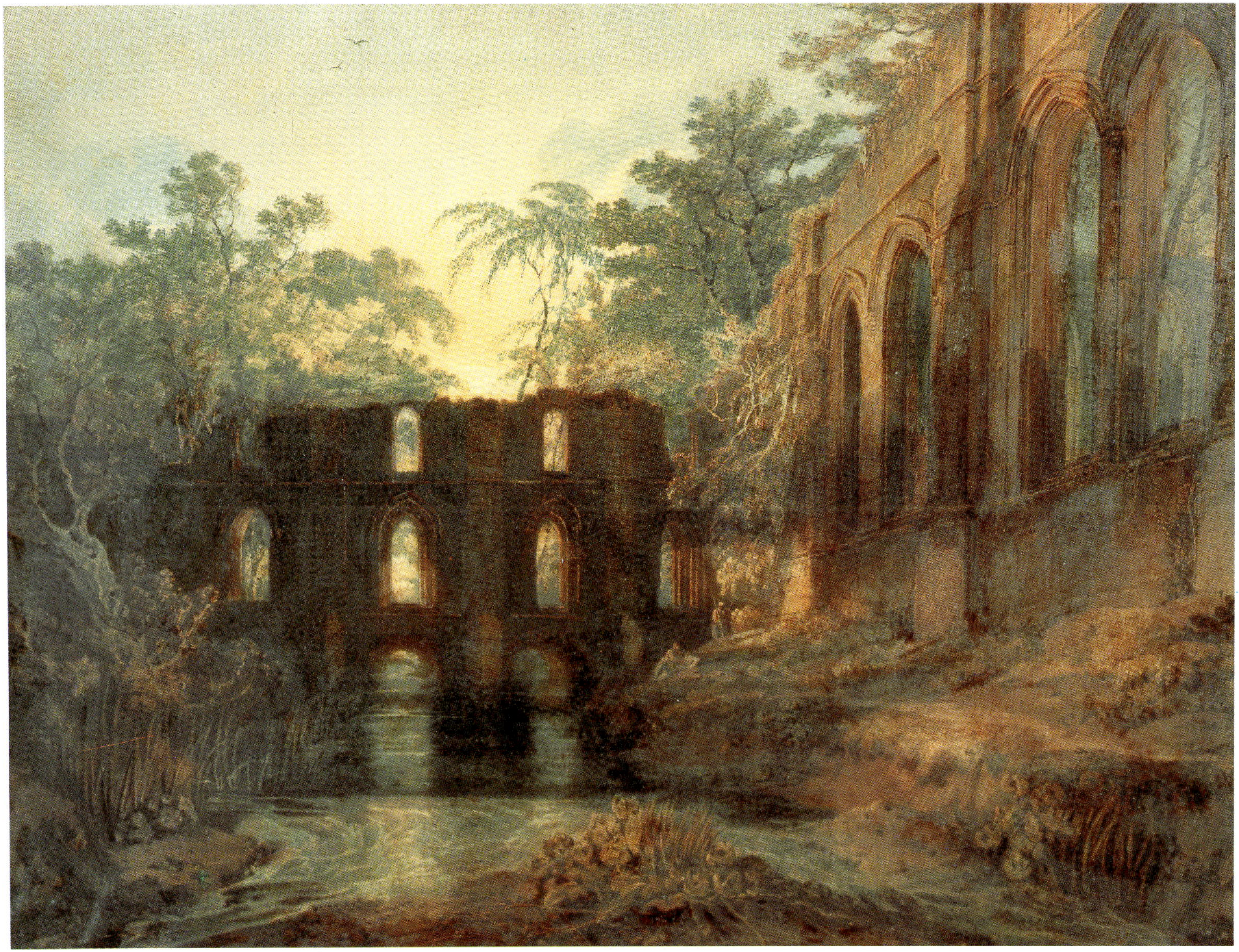

Helpful Terms

Additives
A range of painting media that can be mixed with watercolour to change its consistency or surface quality.

Board
A surface to which you attach your watercolour paper before starting to paint. You should be able to adjust the angle of your board when working, to alter the movement of wet watercolour paint as desired.

Colour wheel
The colour wheel is a circle of colours that includes the three primaries, and the secondary colours achieved by mixing each of the two primaries together. It is a useful colour-mixing aid and a quick reference for finding complementary pairs of colours.

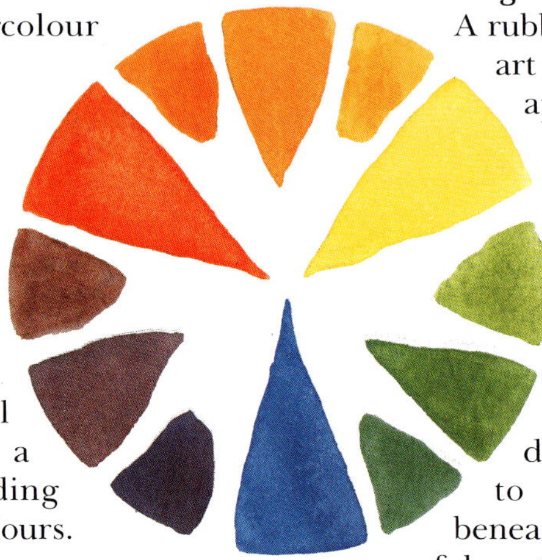

Complementary colours
Colours that sit opposite one another on the colour wheel are called complementary. The complementary pairs are red and green, blue and orange, and violet and yellow. Each pair consists of all three primary colours.

Composition
The process of arranging the elements in your picture into a cohesive design that contains a centre of interest.

Hue
The colour of a particular paint, such as red, yellow or green, is known as its hue.

Masking fluid
A rubberized fluid available from art materials' shops, which is applied to the surface of watercolour paper with a brush and allowed to dry before watercolour paint is applied over the top. Its purpose is to mask the paper from succeeding applications of paint. Once the overlaid paint is dry, the fluid is rubbed away to reveal the clean paper beneath. This is a particularly useful method for producing bright highlights.

Mixed media
When you combine two or more painting media, the result is called mixed media. It does not matter which media you choose to combine.

Neutral colours
To produce a range of greys and browns, mix complementary pairs of colours. These will produce clean neutral tones, whereas other colour combinations will produce muddy mixes.

Opacity
Paints that are not translucent are known as opaque. Opaque paints will block any colour that lies beneath them. Watercolourists often incorporate Chinese white body colour into their paintings, because it is an opaque water-based paint that can be mixed with watercolour to produce opaque and semi-opaque pictures.

Pan
A small tablet-shaped block of watercolour paint that is softened with a little water to make the paint usable. You can purchase whole or half pans, so called because of their comparative sizes.

Primary colours
The three primary colours are red, yellow and blue. They are the three colours in your palette that cannot be produced by mixing any other colours together.

Secondary colours
Each of the three secondary colours is

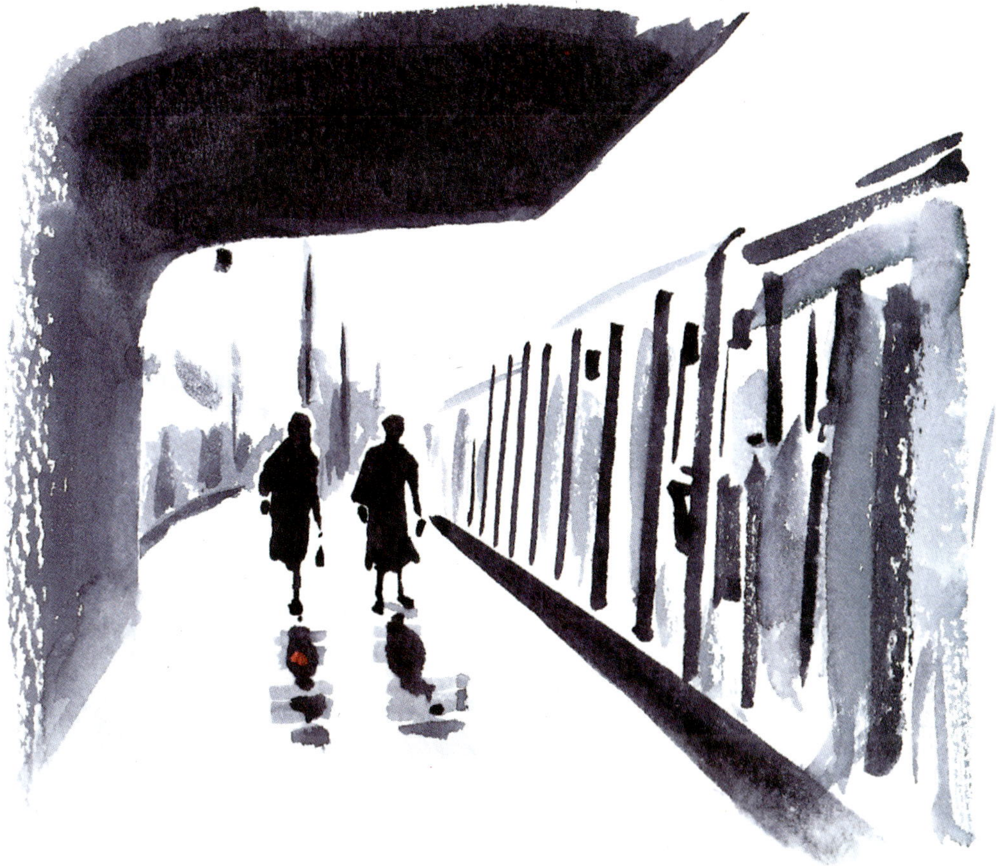

created by mixing two primaries; green is mixed from blue and yellow, violet from blue and red, and orange from red and yellow.

Tone
The lightness or darkness of an object or area in any painting, regardless of its colour or medium. In relation to objects, it also refers to the amount of light being reflected by a surface.

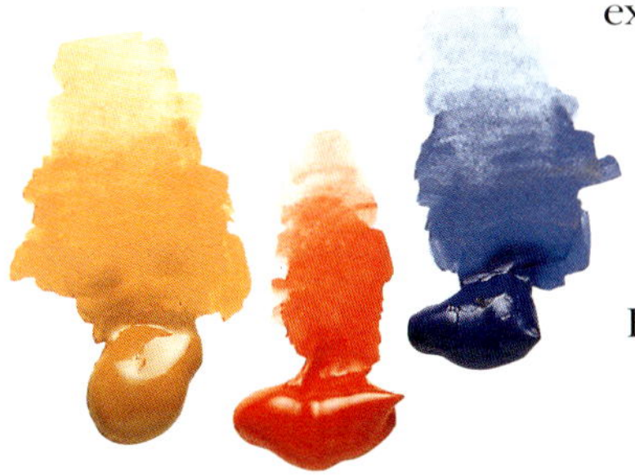

Translucency
Watercolour paint is translucent. This means that, when the paint is laid on to paper, any underlying colour will show through it. Watercolourists exploit this quality by building up their paintings with many thin layers of colour.

Warm and cool colours
Each colour has a 'temperature': when two colours are compared, one will appear 'warmer' or 'cooler' to the eye than the other. The distinctions can be made by ascertaining what leaning each colour has – if it leans towards blue it will be cooler than if it leans towards orange.

Watercolour wash
A wash is a layer of transparent paint. You can produce different types of wash with watercolour; flat washes are even and contain only one paint colour; gradated washes develop evenly from dark to light or from one colour to another; and variegated washes combine different colours and variable tones in random combinations.

Wax resist
Because watercolour is water-based, it reacts to areas of paper that have oil or wax on their surface. To create special effects, you can use wax crayons, candles or other oil-based painting media to block areas of paper before applying watercolour paint over the top. This is known as wax resist.

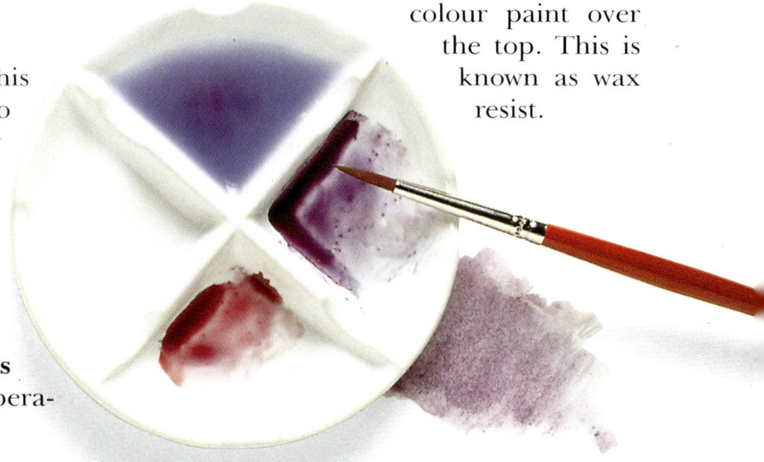

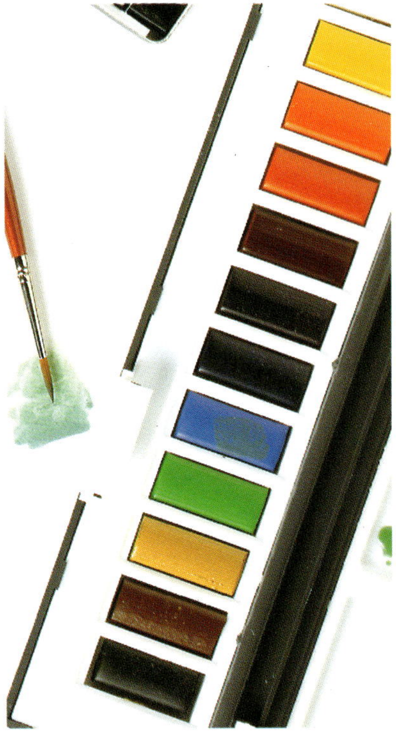
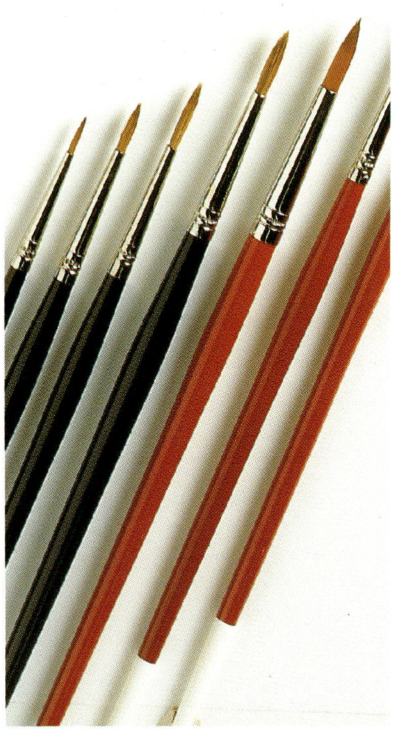
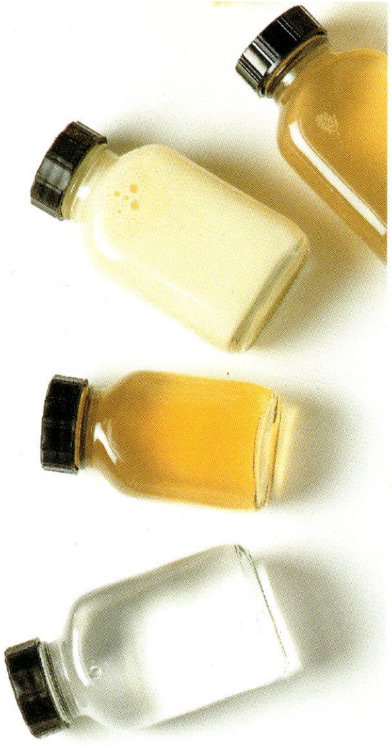
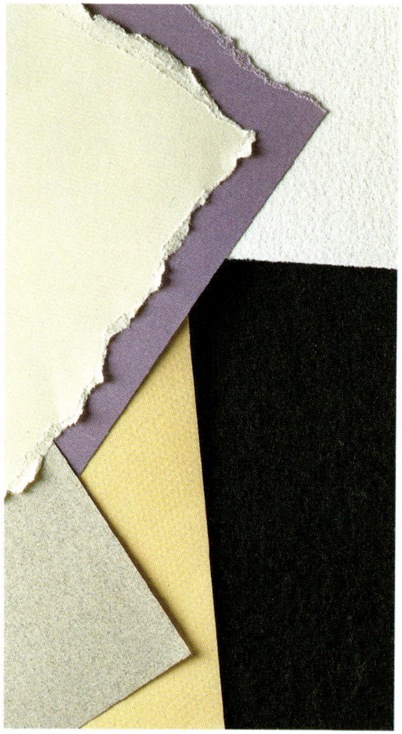

Tools and Materials

Before you set to work, you need to purchase some art materials. There are plenty of paints and watercolour tools to discover at the art shop. On the following pages, the whole range of watercolour materials is described, from which you can choose those best suited to you.

Watercolour Materials

There are many watercolour materials to choose between – here is a selection that you might discover awaiting you on your first visit to the art shop.

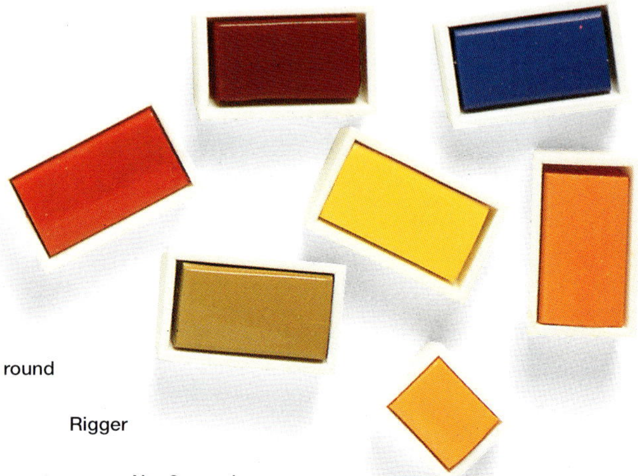

Whole and half pans of dry watercolour paint. Buy these for colours you use most frequently.

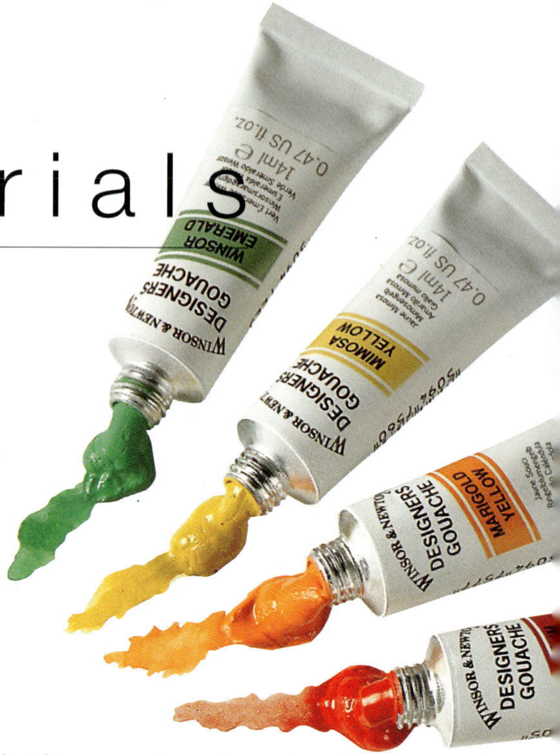

Body colour or gouache can be purchased in tube form. When mixed with watercolours, it renders the paint opaque.

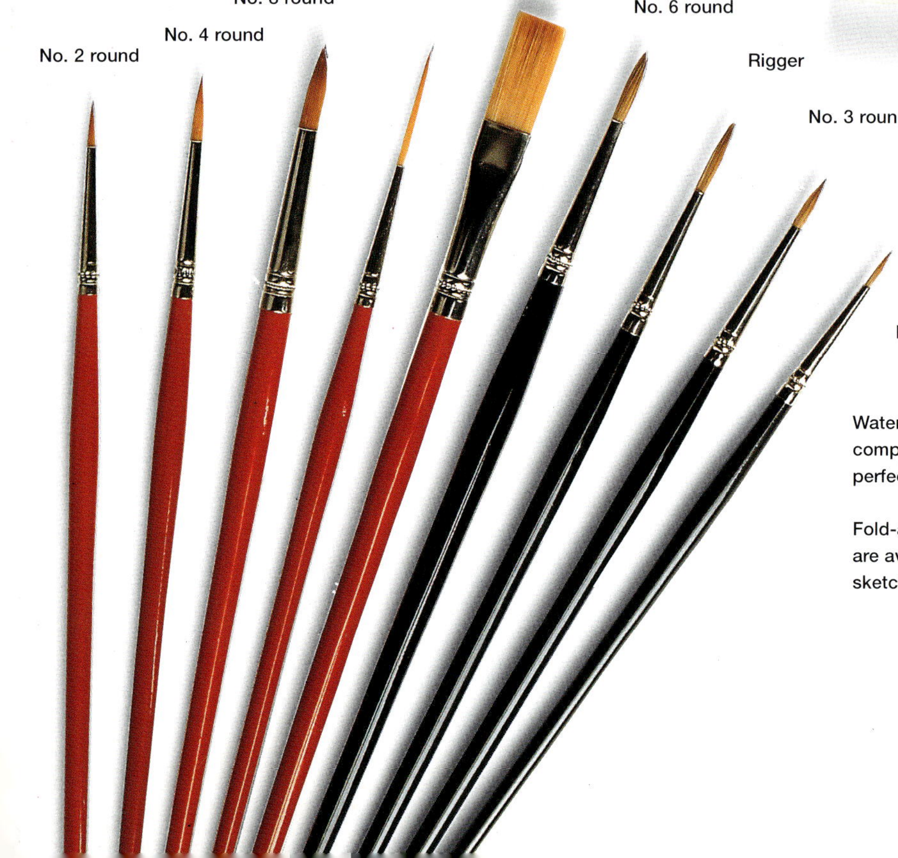

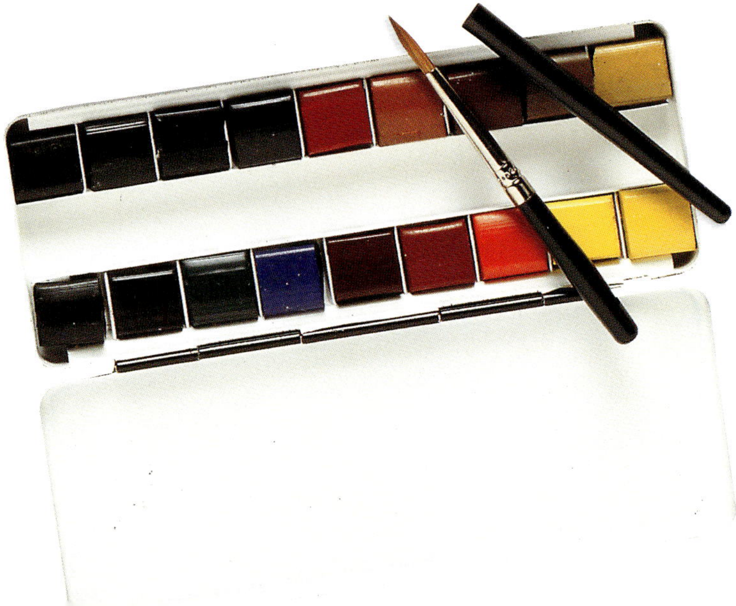

Watercolour palette with compartments to carry half pans, perfect for painting expeditions.

Fold-away watercolour paint brushes are available that fit into watercolour sketching boxes.

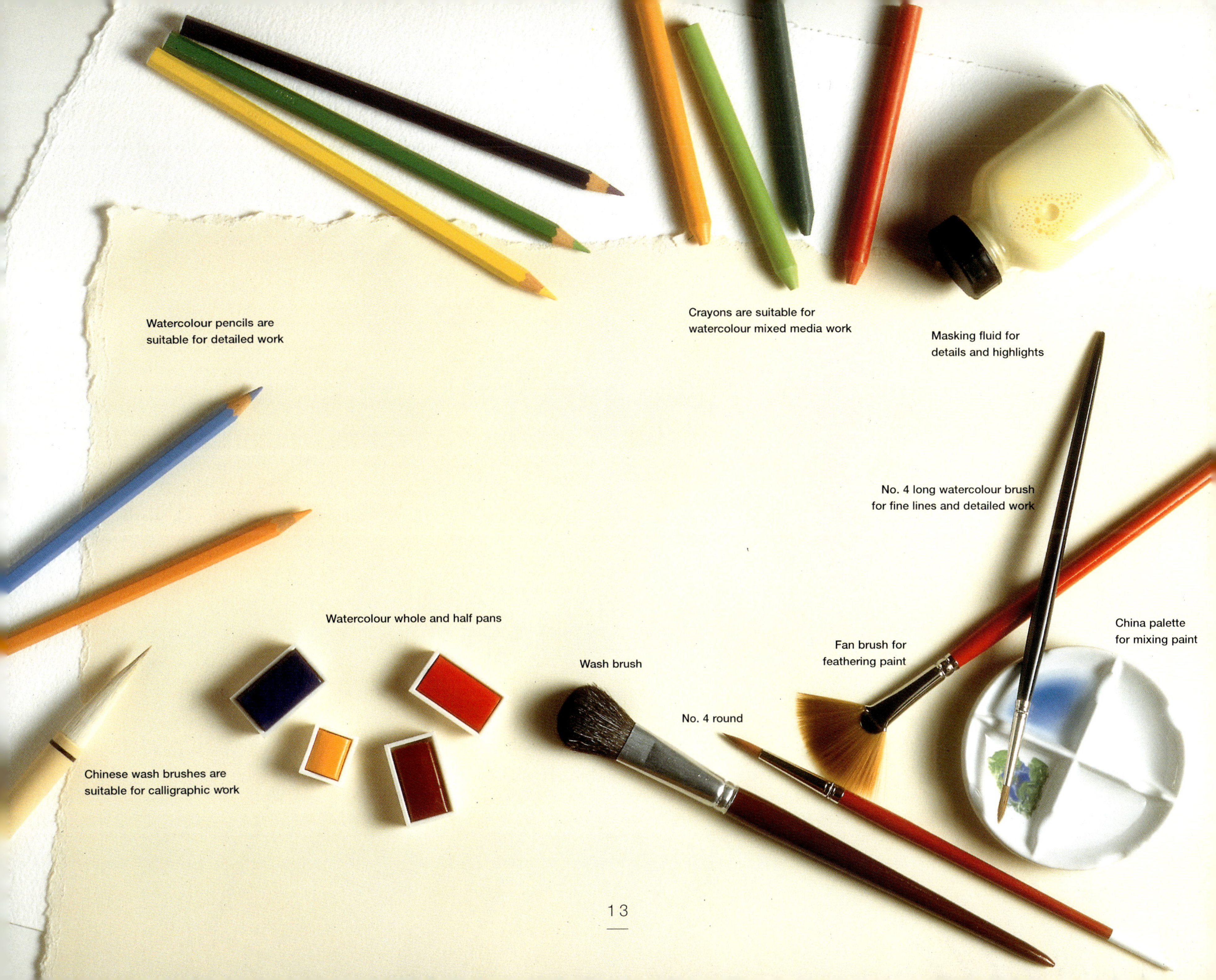
Watercolour pencils are suitable for detailed work
Crayons are suitable for watercolour mixed media work
Masking fluid for details and highlights
No. 4 long watercolour brush for fine lines and detailed work
Watercolour whole and half pans
China palette for mixing paint
Fan brush for feathering paint
Wash brush
No. 4 round
Chinese wash brushes are suitable for calligraphic work

Watercolour Paints and Pencils

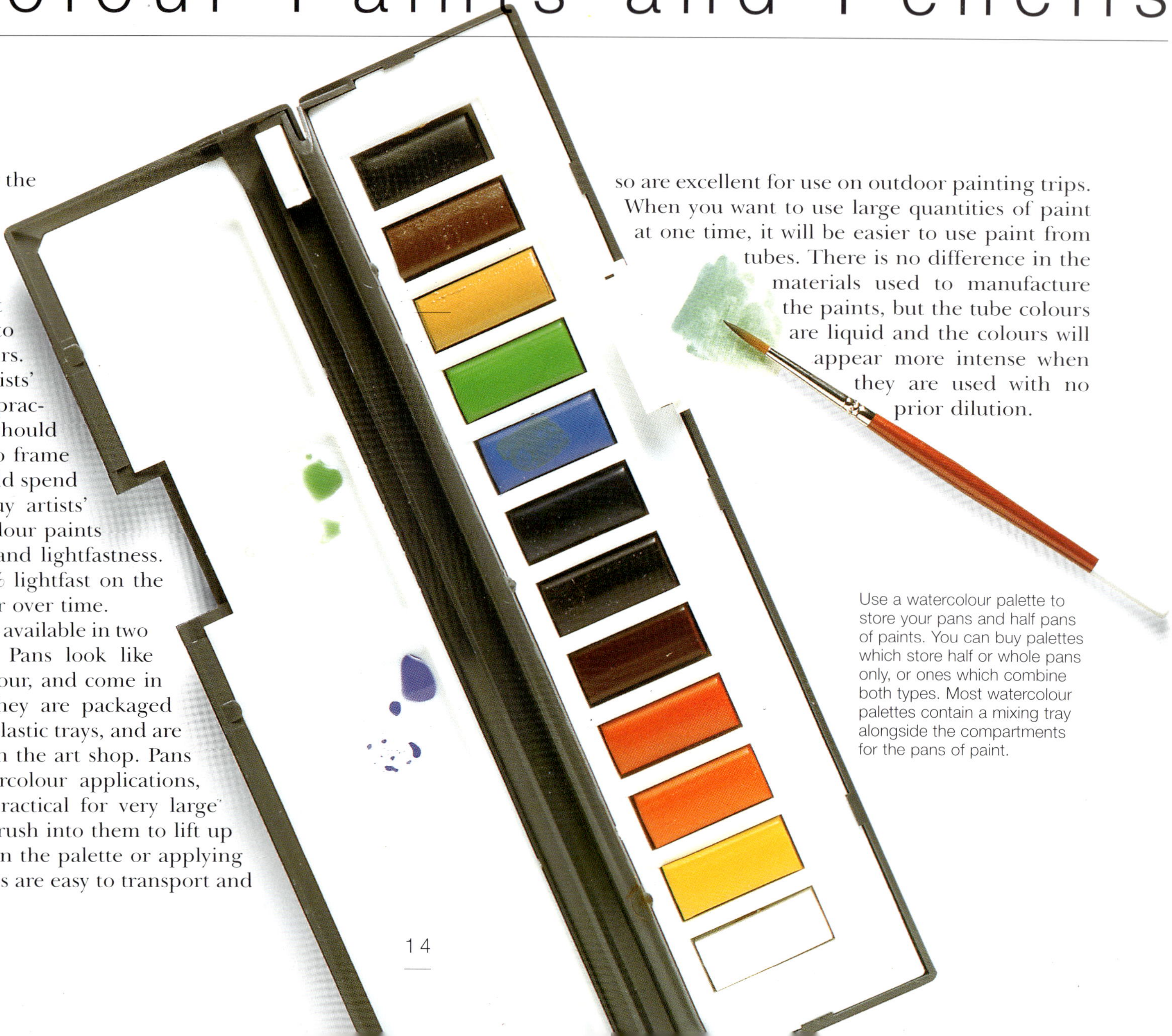

Don't be daunted by the large selection of watercolour paints available in art shops. Once you know a few facts about watercolour it shouldn't be too difficult to select some suitable colours. Most ranges come in artists' or students' quality. For practice, students' quality should suffice, but if you want to frame and hang work, you should spend the extra money and buy artists' quality. Different watercolour paints vary in pigment quality and lightfastness. Those described as 100% lightfast on the label should not discolour over time.

Watercolour paints are available in two forms: pans and tubes. Pans look like small, hard tablets of colour, and come in whole and half sizes. They are packaged either in paper or small plastic trays, and are often stored in drawers in the art shop. Pans are suited to most watercolour applications, although they are not practical for very large paintings. Dab a damp brush into them to lift up colour before mixing it on the palette or applying it direct to wet paper. Pans are easy to transport and so are excellent for use on outdoor painting trips. When you want to use large quantities of paint at one time, it will be easier to use paint from tubes. There is no difference in the materials used to manufacture the paints, but the tube colours are liquid and the colours will appear more intense when they are used with no prior dilution.

Use a watercolour palette to store your pans and half pans of paints. You can buy palettes which store half or whole pans only, or ones which combine both types. Most watercolour palettes contain a mixing tray alongside the compartments for the pans of paint.

Watercolour pencils are the perfect partner for watercolour paint when you want to refine details or add texture to a painting. Watercolour pencils do not carry the same labelling as their paint equivalents, as there tends to be fewer colours. Match the colour of the wood-encasing with the colour of watercolour paint you wish to associate it with. Alternatively, you can buy watercolour pencils in solid crayon form.

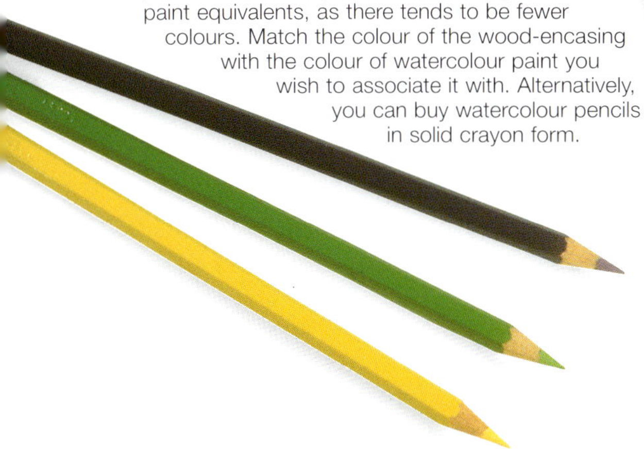

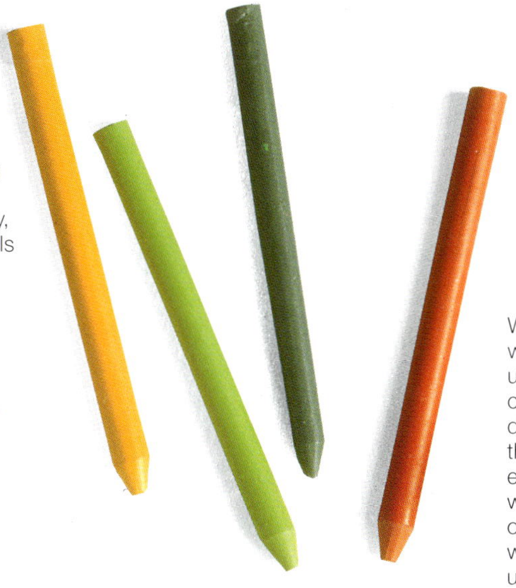

Water-soluble crayons are waxy in texture, and can be used like traditional crayons, or can be dissolved and blended on the paper to create an effect like a watercolour wash. They can be used on their own, combined with watercolour paint, and used for wax-resist effects.

If you do not have a watercolour paint box which contains mixing compartments, you can purchase china or plastic tiles or palettes in which to mix your colours before applying them to paper. China tiles will keep the paint wet for longer than plastic ones.

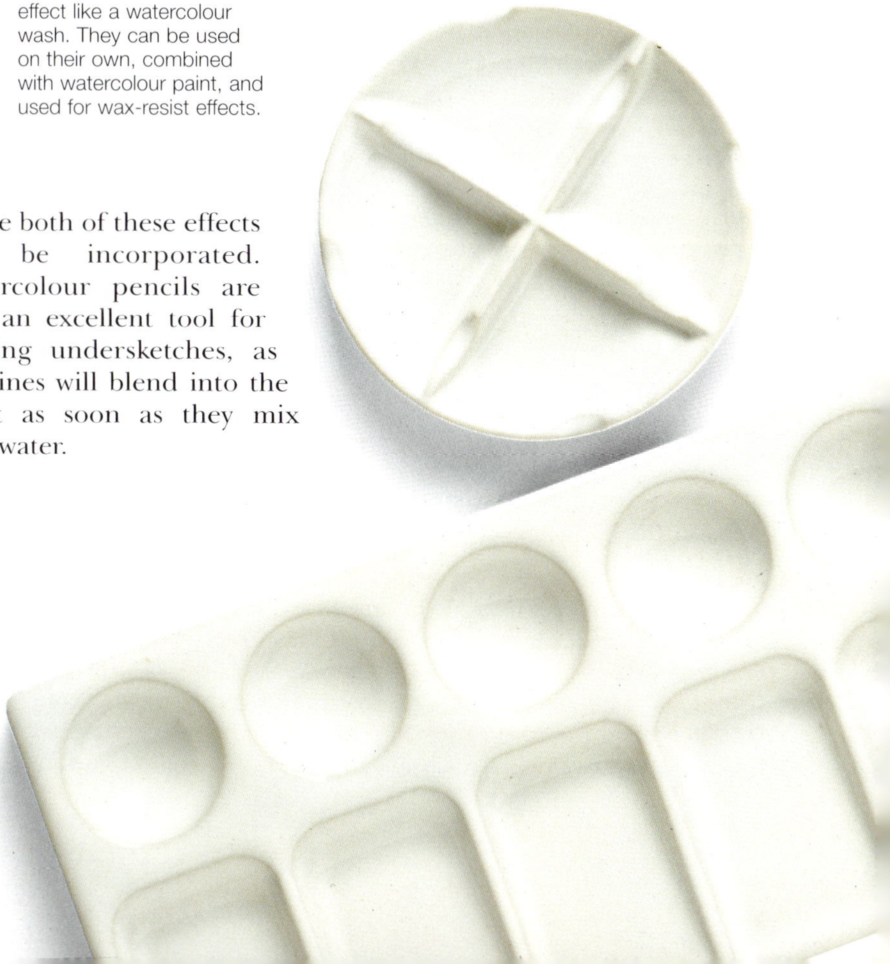

Watercolour pencils are made from the same materials as watercolour paints; in fact, they could be described as pans of watercolour encased in wood. They are very useful to have to hand – to use either on their own or in combination with watercolour paint. They provide the option of making very fine, dry lines and details without the risk of flooding or dispersion, which are natural by-products of working with paint.

You can buy watercolour pencils individually, but it is more economical to buy them in a set. Twelve colours should be adequate to begin with. Watercolour pencils do not carry the same names as their paint counterparts, and the range of colours is smaller. Light and dark versions of most colours are available, with a few mid tones thrown in for the more frequently used colours, such as yellow, blue and green.

Watercolour pencils can be applied to the paper dry, and then blended with a damp brush so that they appear much like a watercolour wash. Alternatively, they can be left as a defining element in the painting. They are best used in conjunction with wet watercolour, where both of these effects can be incorporated. Watercolour pencils are also an excellent tool for making undersketches, as the lines will blend into the paint as soon as they mix with water.

Watercolour Paper

Watercolours need to be applied to an absorbent surface, so they are usually painted onto paper. Specially manufactured watercolour papers are available. They come in varying degrees of absorbency and surface texture, and are suitable for a wide range of applications. There are three surface textures to choose between – rough, semi-rough (also known as 'not'), and smooth. Each is made in a different way, rough and semi-rough papers being cold-pressed, and smooth papers being hot-pressed. All papers are sized – that is,

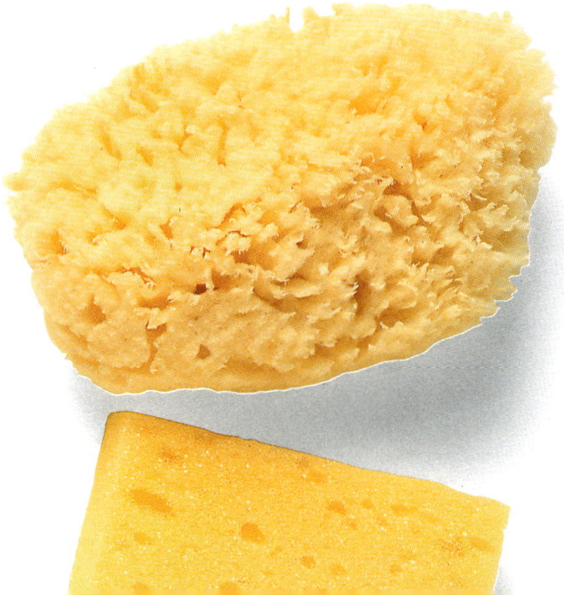

one or both sides of the paper are treated with a fluid to make them hardy to repeated applications of watercolour. Use rough paper when you want to make interesting textures, but otherwise stick to a medium-weight (300 gsm/140 lb) not paper for the exercises in this book.

Smooth or hot-pressed paper is untextured and absorbs watercolour paint very slowly. The paint can therefore be manipulated on the surface for longer than with cold-pressed papers. This makes the paint more difficult to manage on smooth papers, and you would be better off saving it until you feel confident with the medium. Here, it is recommended for the final project.

Stretching watercolour paper

Lightweight watercolour paper, that is, any paper that weighs less than 300 gsm (140 lb), will need to be stretched or it will buckle when it is wet. This is done by drenching the paper in a tub or bath of warm water, or running water from a tap over it until it is saturated. Then lay the paper on a board and use a sponge to smooth it flat. Tape down the edges of the paper with dampened gumstrip, and then leave it to dry in a horizontal position. The paper should dry flat and tight as a drum, and will not then buckle when you paint on to it. If you don't want to stretch your own paper, ready-stretched blocks of watercolour paper are available.

You can use watercolour paper in many different ways. Once you have stretched it, you should leave it to dry out completely before adding new applications of paint or water. For some watercolour techniques, such as wash work, you will probably want to redampen the surface of the paper before you brush paint across it. For other applications, such as dry brush or stipple, you are more likely to prefer to leave the paper dry, and add the paint direct to it.

Helpful Tips

● Always have a clean sponge to hand when dampening watercolour paper – it is a handy prop for wetting the paper, as well as mopping up any residual water you don't want.

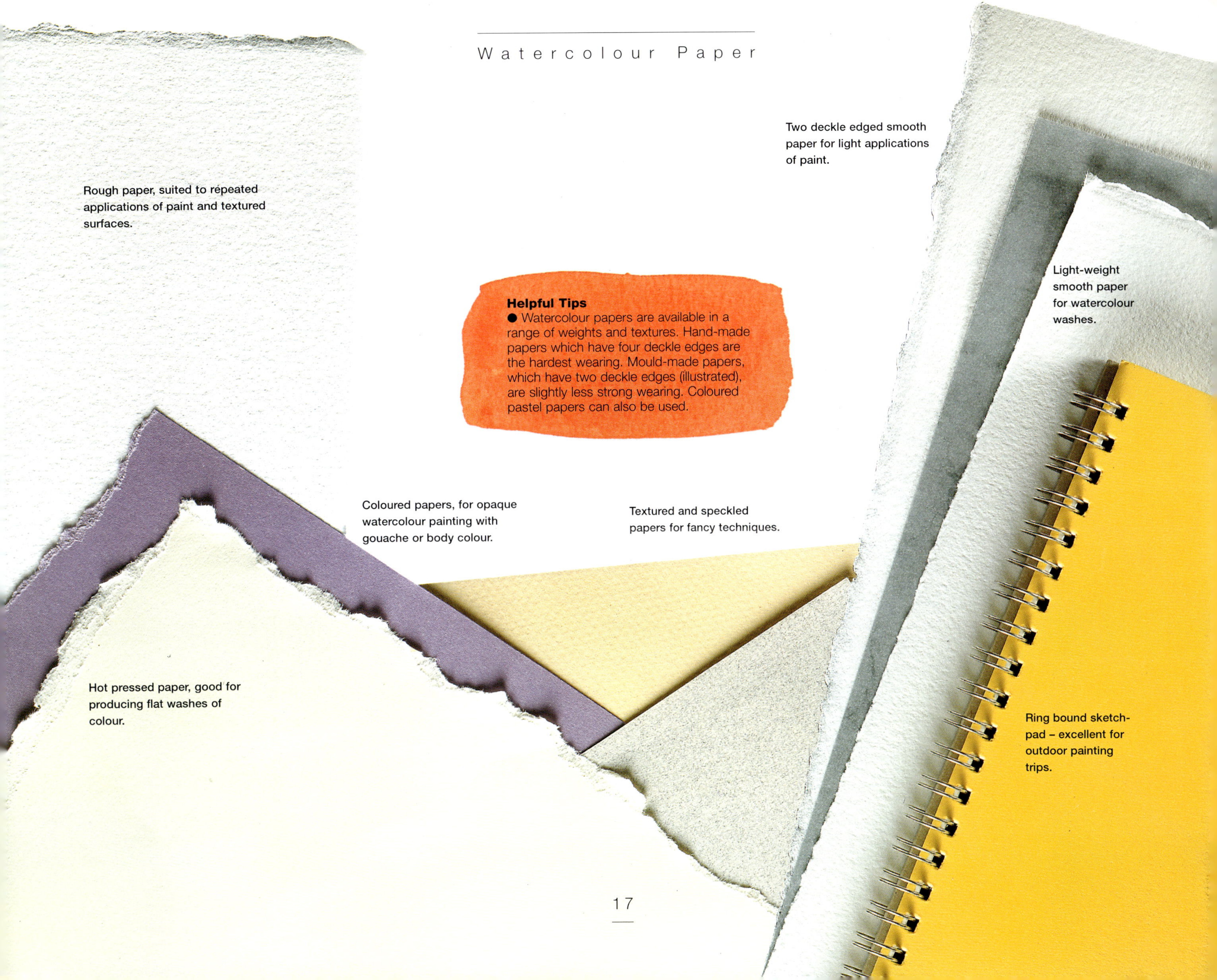

Rough paper, suited to repeated applications of paint and textured surfaces.

Two deckle edged smooth paper for light applications of paint.

Helpful Tips

● Watercolour papers are available in a range of weights and textures. Hand-made papers which have four deckle edges are the hardest wearing. Mould-made papers, which have two deckle edges (illustrated), are slightly less strong wearing. Coloured pastel papers can also be used.

Light-weight smooth paper for watercolour washes.

Coloured papers, for opaque watercolour painting with gouache or body colour.

Textured and speckled papers for fancy techniques.

Hot pressed paper, good for producing flat washes of colour.

Ring bound sketch-pad – excellent for outdoor painting trips.

Brushes

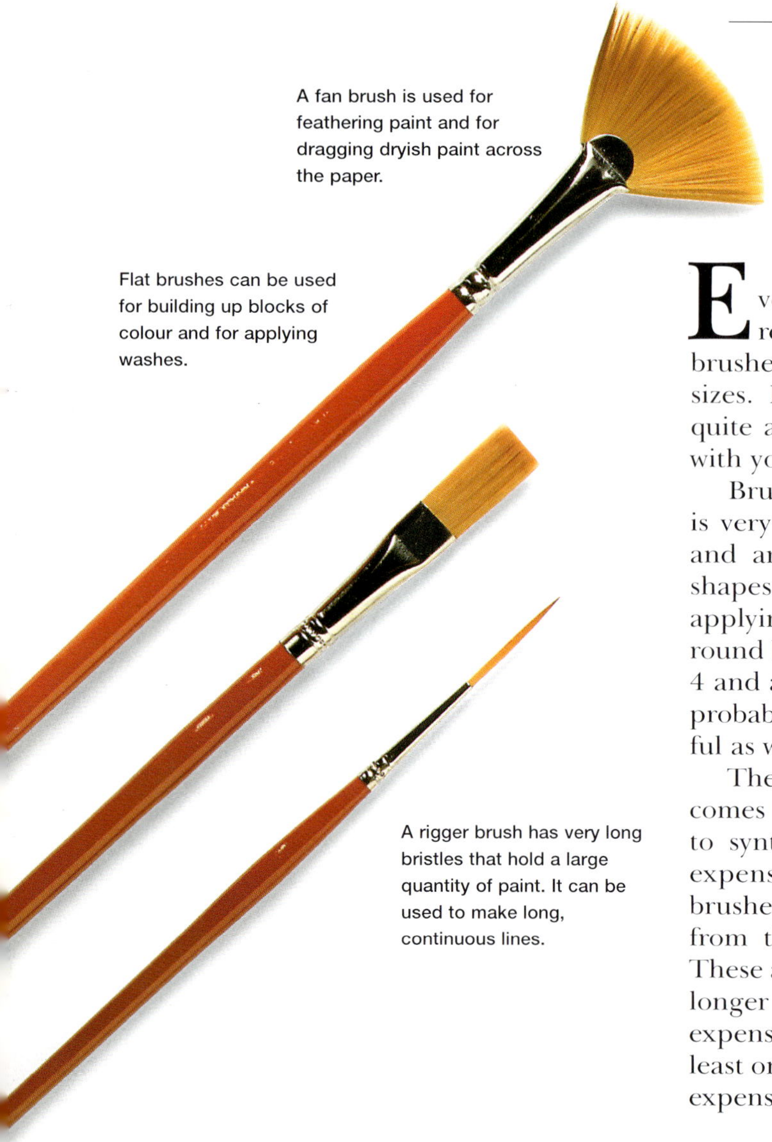

A fan brush is used for feathering paint and for dragging dryish paint across the paper.

Flat brushes can be used for building up blocks of colour and for applying washes.

A rigger brush has very long bristles that hold a large quantity of paint. It can be used to make long, continuous lines.

Even a short browse in an art shop will reveal a treasure-trove of watercolour brushes in a large variety of shapes and sizes. In time you will probably build up quite a collection of favourites, but to start with you only need to acquire three or four.

Brush sizes begin at a modest 000, which is very fine, and go up to about a size 12, and are available in both round and flat shapes. Larger brushes are available for applying large areas of wash. Try a few round brushes – say, two between sizes 2 and 4 and a no. 8, and one wash brush. You will probably find a 2.5 cm (1 in) flat brush useful as well.

The hair from which brushes are made comes from a range of sources, from natural to synthetic, some of which are far more expensive than others. The best-quality brushes are made from sable, which comes from the tail hairs of the Siberian mink. These are springier and hold their shape for longer than other types of brush. They are expensive, but most watercolourists prize at least one or two among their collection. Less expensive but still very good natural hair brushes include squirrel, pony and ox. Some cheaper brushes are made from a combination of natural and synthetic hair.

Although sable brushes are the best quality, they are also the most expensive. If you become a serious watercolourist, however, you are sure to want one sable brush in your collection. If you can only afford one, you would be wise to purchase a no. 8. The quality of the hairs will ensure that you can use this brush for both fine line work and wide sweeps of wash.

Helpful Tips

- Chinese brushes are extremely versatile – used on their side you can produce wide brush marks. Held at their tips you will be able to make fine calligraphic marks.
- The larger the brush head, the greater amount of paint it will hold, so ensure that you use a large brush for expansive work.
- To keep your watercolour brushes in the best condition, always wash them gently with warm water and a very pure toilet soap after use, and rinse them well.

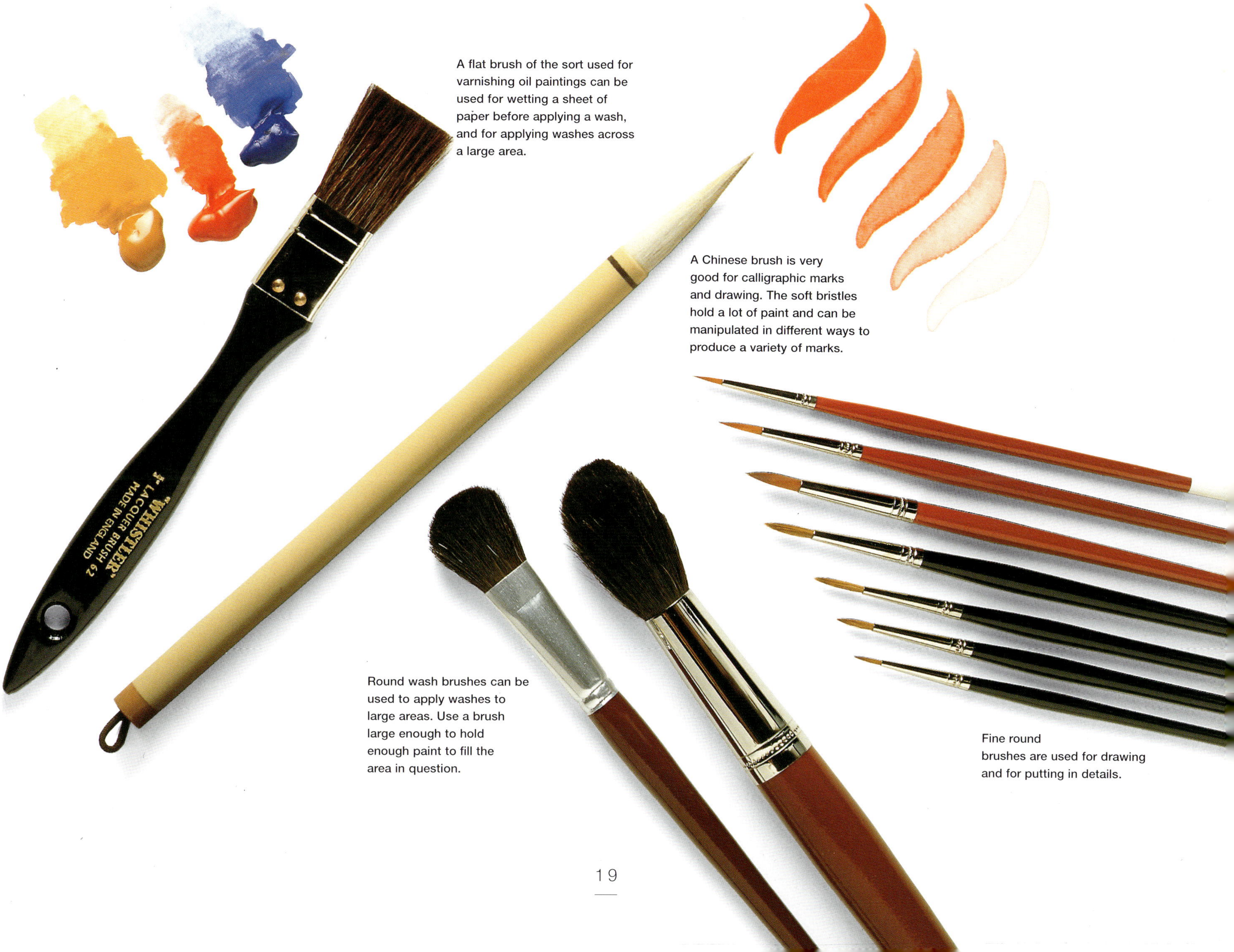

A flat brush of the sort used for varnishing oil paintings can be used for wetting a sheet of paper before applying a wash, and for applying washes across a large area.

A Chinese brush is very good for calligraphic marks and drawing. The soft bristles hold a lot of paint and can be manipulated in different ways to produce a variety of marks.

Round wash brushes can be used to apply washes to large areas. Use a brush large enough to hold enough paint to fill the area in question.

Fine round brushes are used for drawing and for putting in details.

Watercolour Props

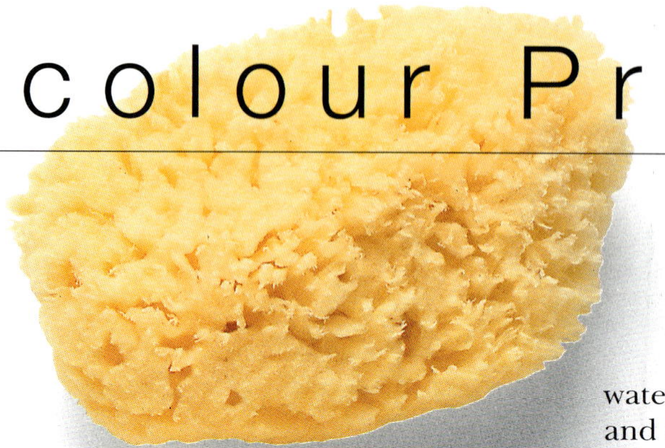

Sponges can be used to apply or lift off paint to create textural effects.

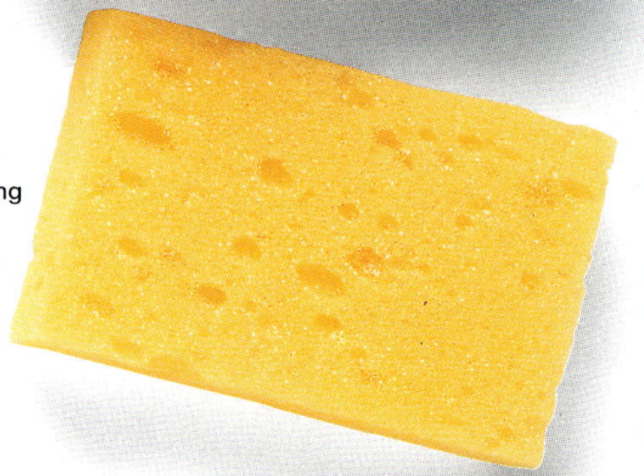

A damp sponge is also useful for removing excess water from the brush before applying paint.

Although most watercolour effects can be produced with watercolour brushes, there are some additional tricks that will enhance your work, and these will require alternative props – most of which can be found around the home. A plastic palette knife will enable lines to be scored into the surface of wet paint to produce textures and highlights. To spatter paint, save an old toothbrush that has seen better days. To lift paint off the paper, or to blend small areas, a cotton bud is best. Other blotting materials include a damp or dry kitchen cloth, a sponge or blotting paper. Kitchen paper can also be useful.

A palette will be needed to mix paint in. There are a number to choose from, and price will probably affect your choice. Round ceramic paint-mixing dishes with lids are useful for keeping paint wet, although you will need quite a few if you use nothing else. A more cost-effective alternative, and possibly the best choice for watercolour painting, is the sectioned tile, which contains small indentations or dimples at the bottom for holding water. This type of mixing dish enables you to add water to the paint without returning time and again to the water jar.

One essential watercolour prop is a masking medium – either tape or fluid. If you can only afford one type, go for the fluid as it is the most useful watercolour prop you could hope for. This medium is used for blocking out areas of the paper to keep them free of paint, in order to create really crisp highlights.

Watercolour props can mean anything at all that makes your working practice simpler. Different artists will find that different props suit their needs best. Most household items will double up as watercolour props, so you should have no problems in finding tools to support your work. The most crucial props are those you use for mopping up paint and water – watercolour can be a messy job!

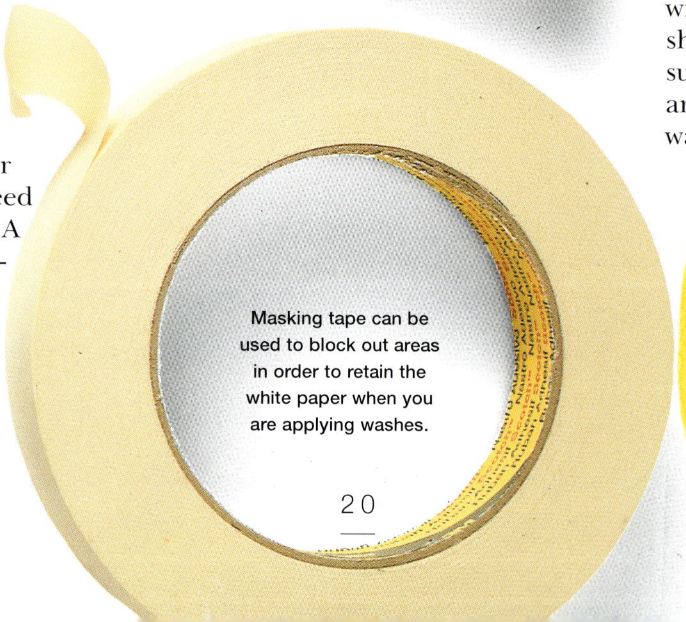

Masking tape can be used to block out areas in order to retain the white paper when you are applying washes.

Helpful Tips

- Removing masking fluid can be a tricky task – you can easily rip the paper, or find that you have left tiny particles of the fluid stuck to it. To avoid this, use a small putty eraser to remove the fluid – a most useful prop.

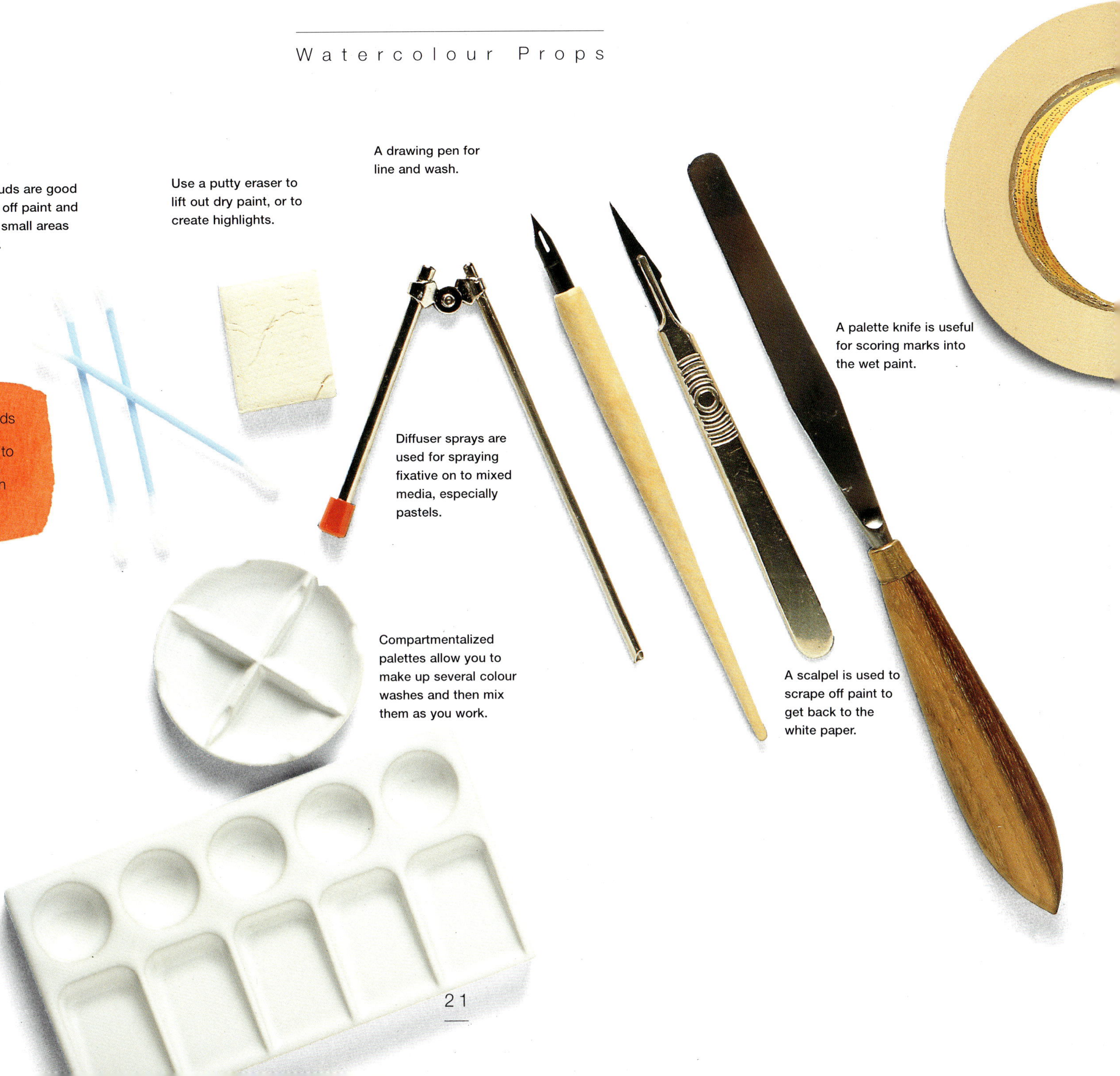

Cotton buds are good for lifting off paint and blending small areas of colour.

Use a putty eraser to lift out dry paint, or to create highlights.

A drawing pen for line and wash.

A palette knife is useful for scoring marks into the wet paint.

Helpful Tips

● Use cotton buds to blend small areas of paint or to add highlights to your pictures with body colour.

Diffuser sprays are used for spraying fixative on to mixed media, especially pastels.

Compartmentalized palettes allow you to make up several colour washes and then mix them as you work.

A scalpel is used to scrape off paint to get back to the white paper.

Extenders and Retarders

Seasalt granules will make interesting textured effects when spattered over watercolour paint.

Using finer granules of salt, you will produce more refined texture effects than the larger seasalt granules.

Although wonderful pictures can be painted with just a few pans or tubes of paint, there are several materials that can extend your options and technical range. These media are called retarders and extenders, and are usually on display alongside watercolour paints and brushes in the art shop. Bottles marked ox gall, glycerin, gum arabic or masking fluid will mean nothing if you haven't used watercolour before. Discover a few tricks of the watercolourist's trade, however, and you will soon be queuing to purchase them!

Because watercolour paints are water-based, their drying rate is influenced by the paper and the humidity levels in the place where they are being used. Sometimes you may wish to slow down this drying time. Add a few drops of glycerin to the watercolour water, then mix it with the paint as usual, and you will soon notice a great difference. Not only does glycerin slow down the drying time of the paint, but it also makes it thicker and more malleable. Gum arabic or honey mixed with water will also slow down watercolour's drying time, but they will make the surface of the paint more shiny, too. Used without due care, they may dehydrate the paint and cause it to crack up on the paper, once dry. As a result, mix only a small amount of any extender or retarder to your wet paint, and only add more as you become accustomed to the effects that these additions will produce.

There may be occasions when you want to speed up, rather than slow down, the paint's drying time. Turner added a drop of alcohol to his paints when he wanted to retard the drying rate. These days, such exotic habits have been replaced by the use of specially manufactured media such as ox gall.

To make watercolour paint thicker and more opaque, Chinese white body colour can be added, as can process white, a medium generally used by photographers to touch up black-and-white images. Both will change the paint from translucent to opaque, blocking out any underlying colour once it has been laid down.

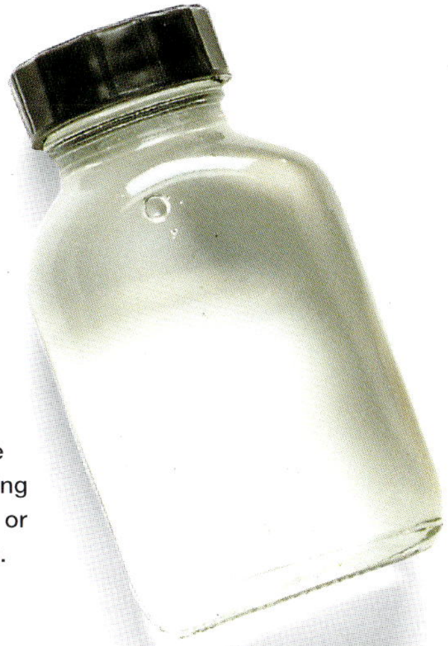

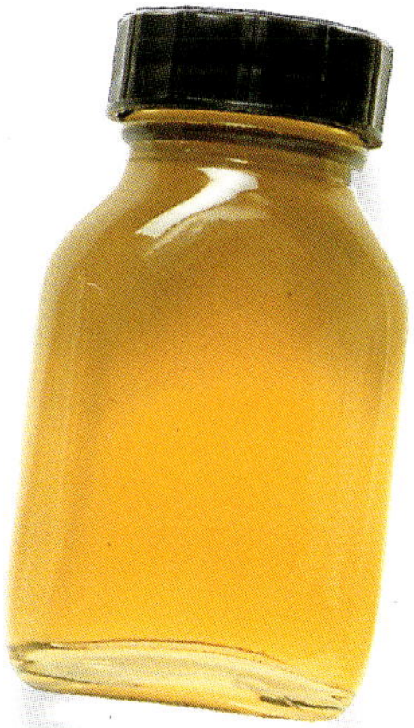

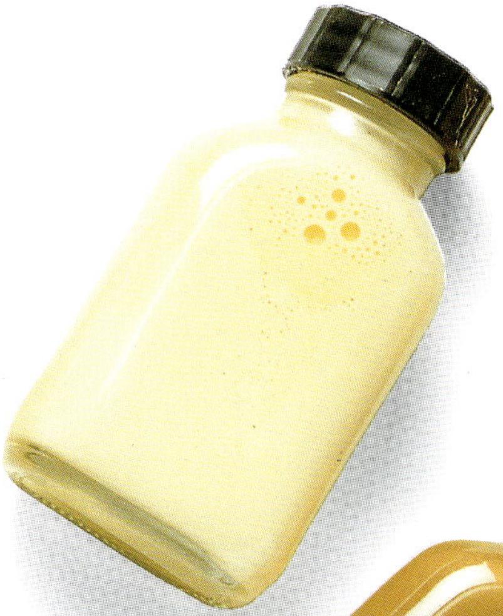

Masking fluid is painted on to areas where highlights are wanted in order to retain the whiteness of the paper.

Glycerin slows down the drying time of paint, giving you more time to add in or blend additional colours.

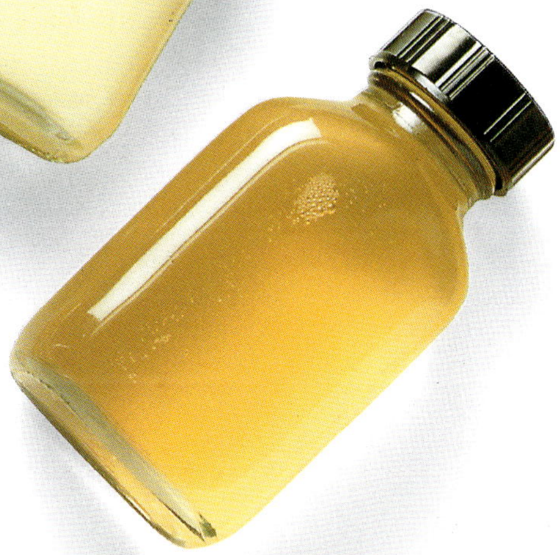

Gum arabic gives the paint lustre and increased transparency, and slows down the drying time. Use it sparingly as it can make the paint layer unstable.

Ox gall speeds up the drying time of the paint so that you can superimpose layers of colour sooner.

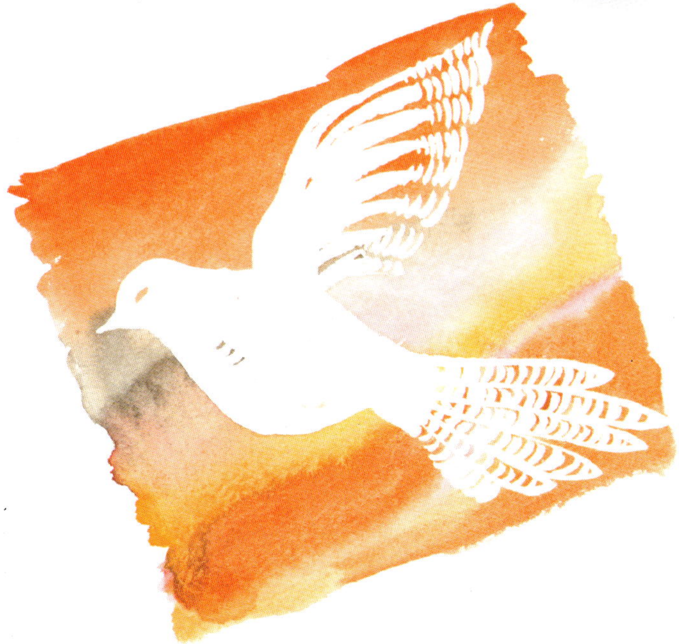

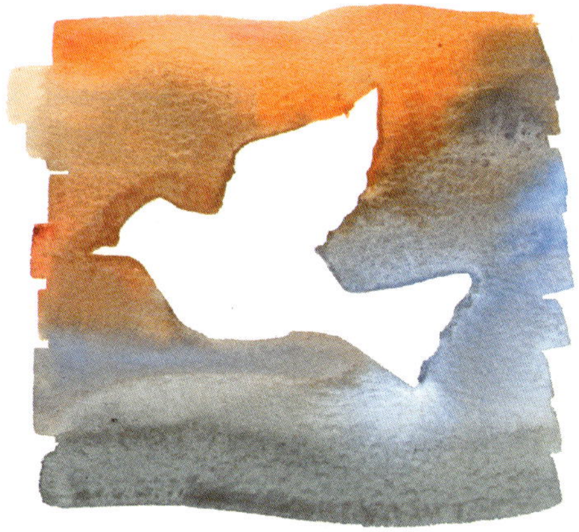

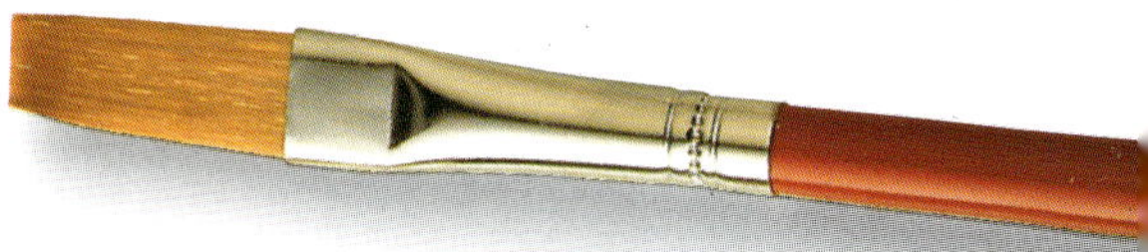

Mixed Media

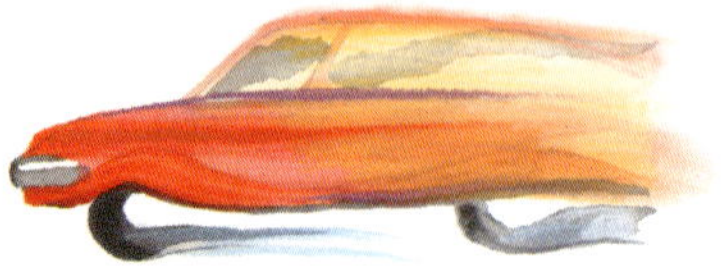

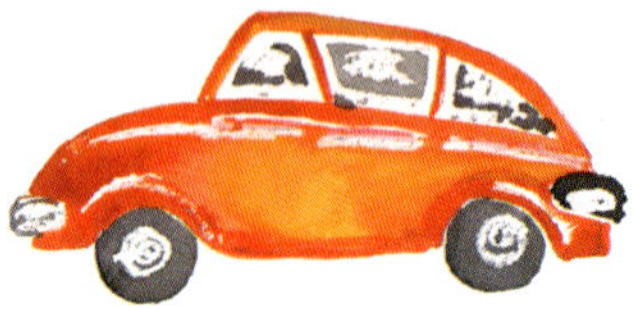

Once you have become familiar with watercolour paints and the materials that can be added into them, you could try out some other effects. There are a number of alternative paint media that combine well with watercolours producing interesting and unusual textures and colours. There are no rules that set down what is 'allowed', so feel free to experiment with mixed-media techniques. Some materials will work better in combination with watercolours than others. Watercolour is a subtle and fragile medium, and won't take too kindly to a more conspicuous medium sharing its space. Treat the paint with sensitivity, making sure the additional media enhance and don't overwhelm it.

Some common choices for watercolour mixed-media paintings include gouache, soft and oil pastels, wax crayons, acrylic and pen and ink. Try using any of these in combination with watercolour to see what results can be achieved.

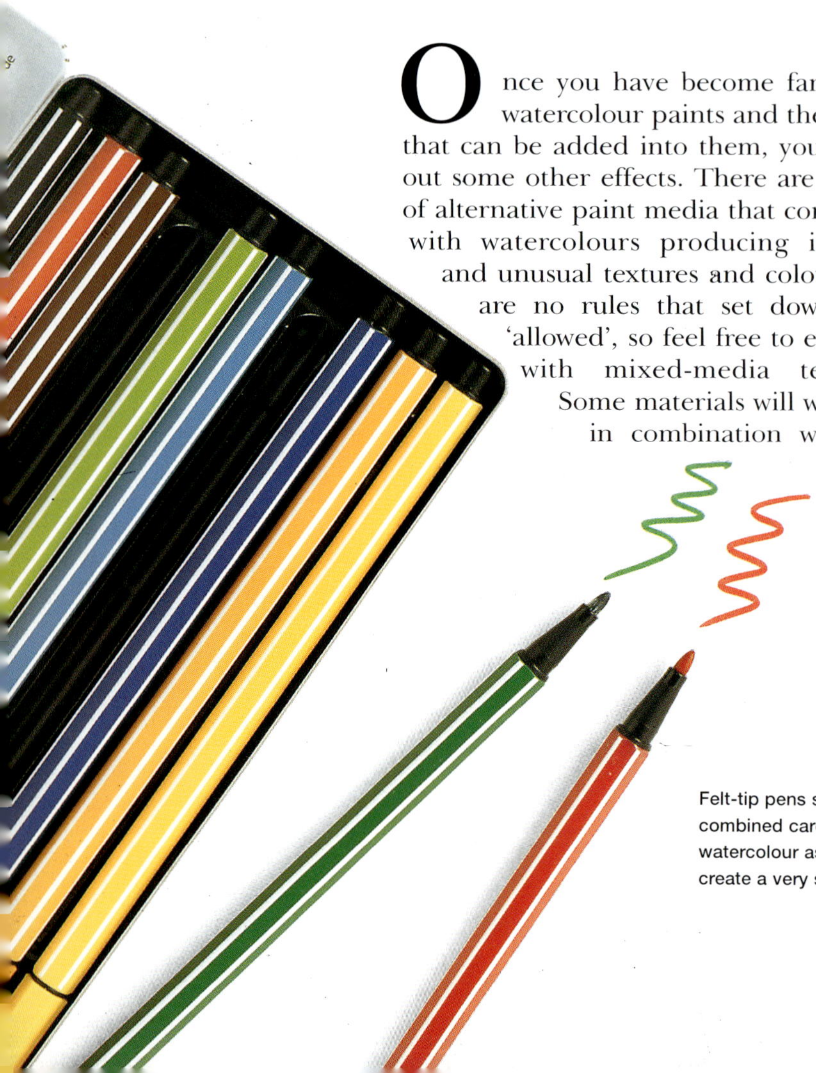

Felt-tip pens should be combined carefully with watercolour as they can create a very strong contrast.

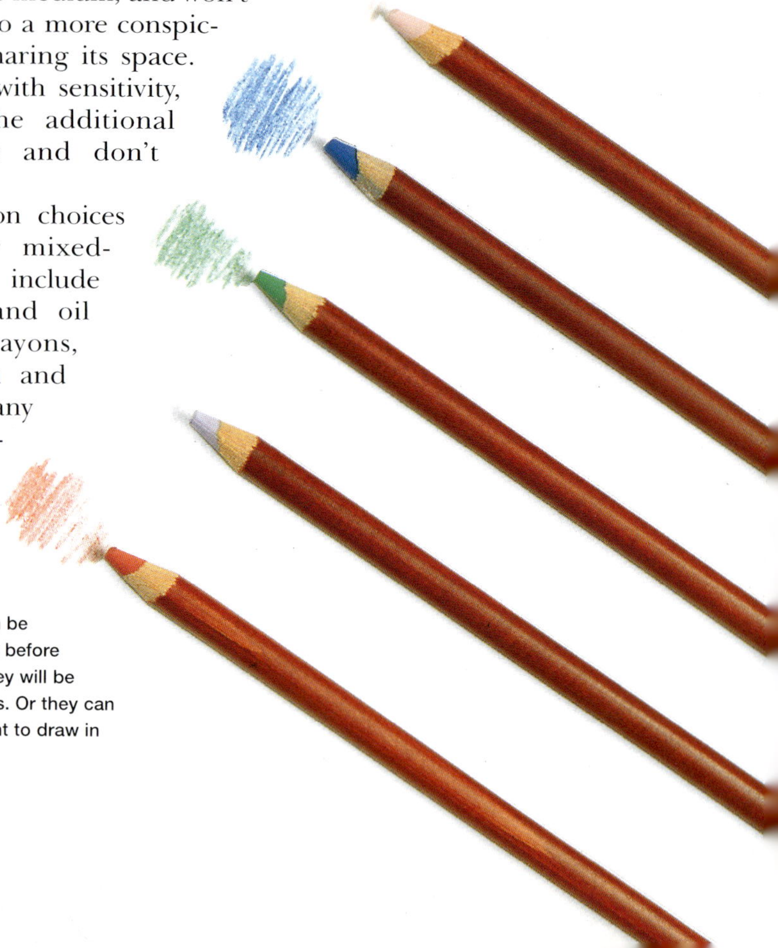

Watercolour pencils can be used to draw guidelines before applying paint, when they will be dissolved by the washes. Or they can be applied over dry paint to draw in details, or add texture.

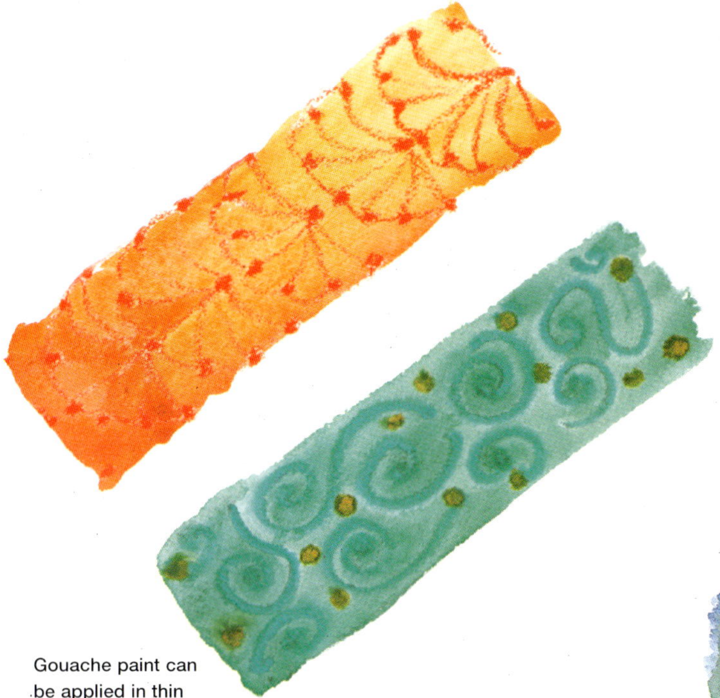

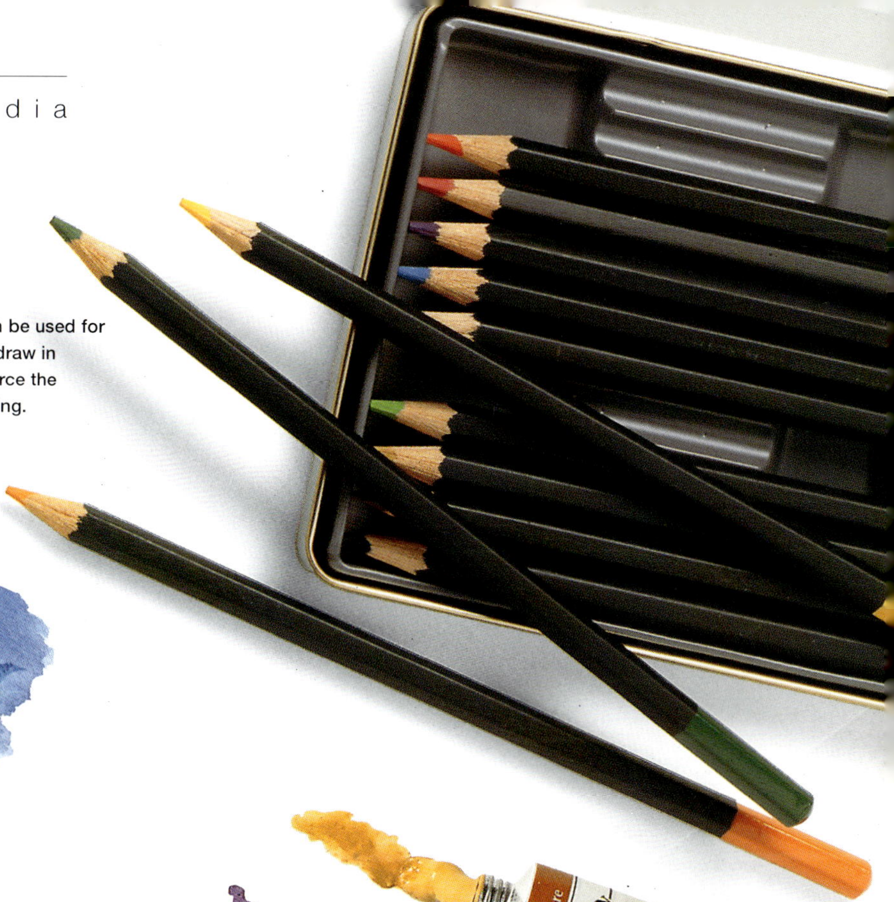

Colour pencils can be used for line and wash, to draw in details or to reinforce the drawing in a painting.

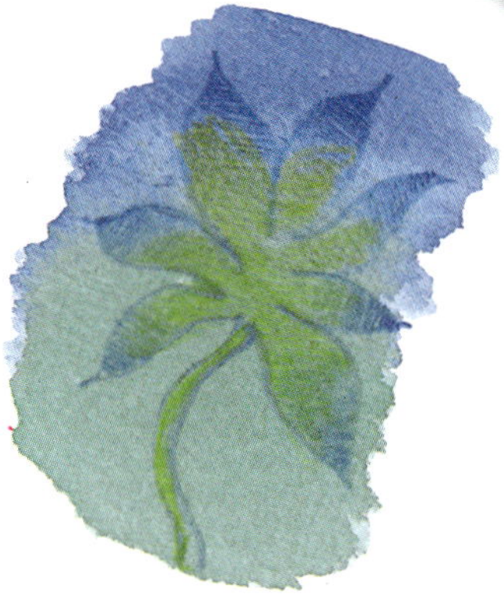

Gouache paint can be applied in thin semi-opaque layers to cover mistakes or add highlights.

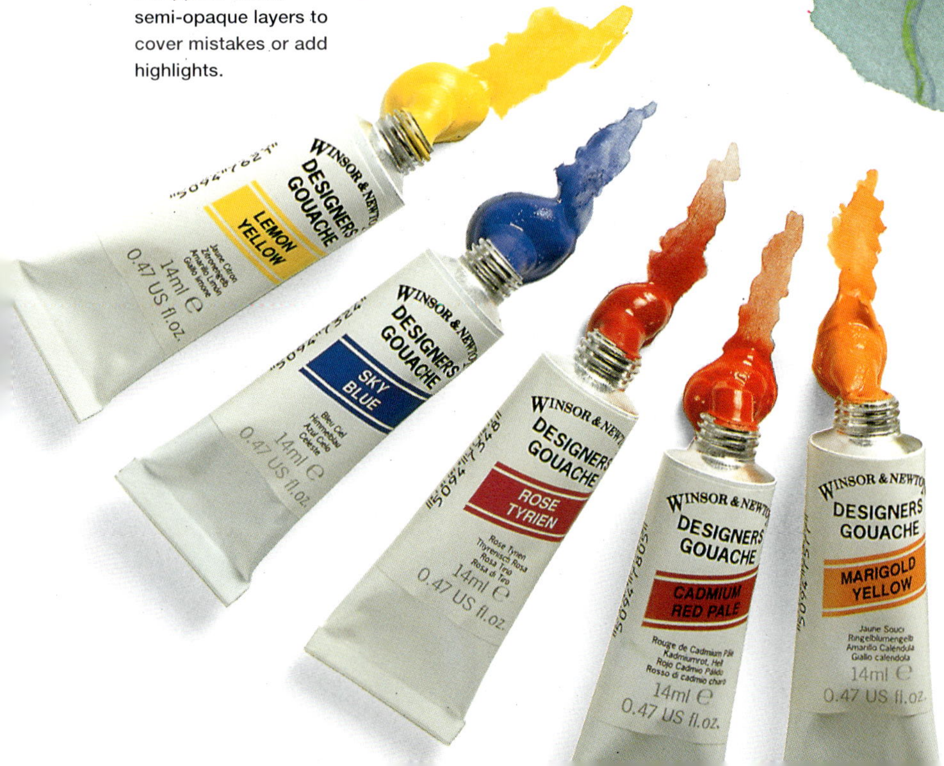

Acrylic paint is water-based and can be used to apply thick, opaque layers of colours over watercolour paint.

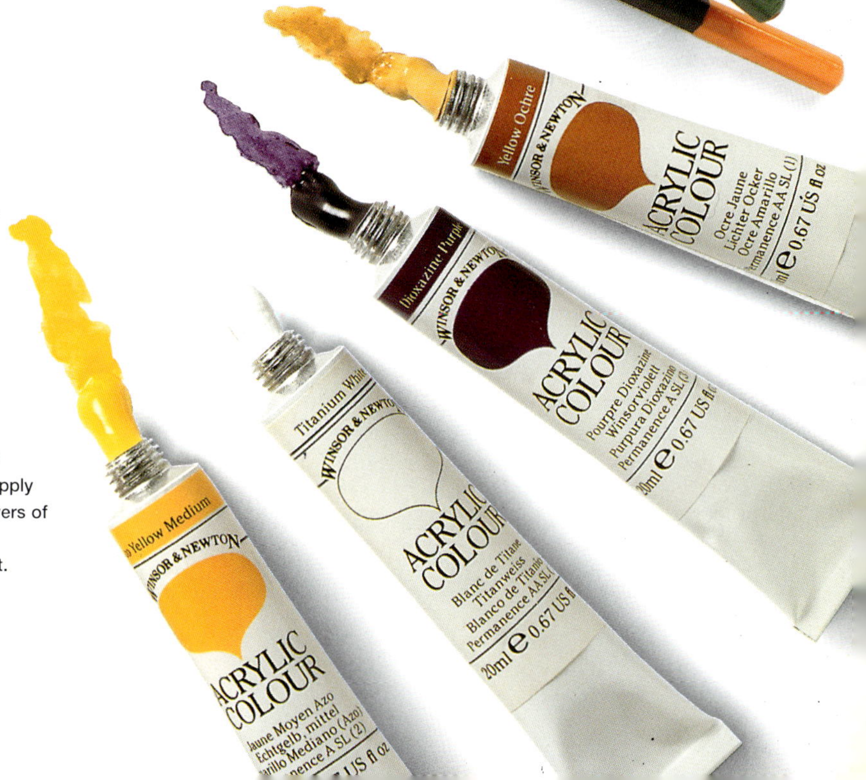

Mounts and Frames

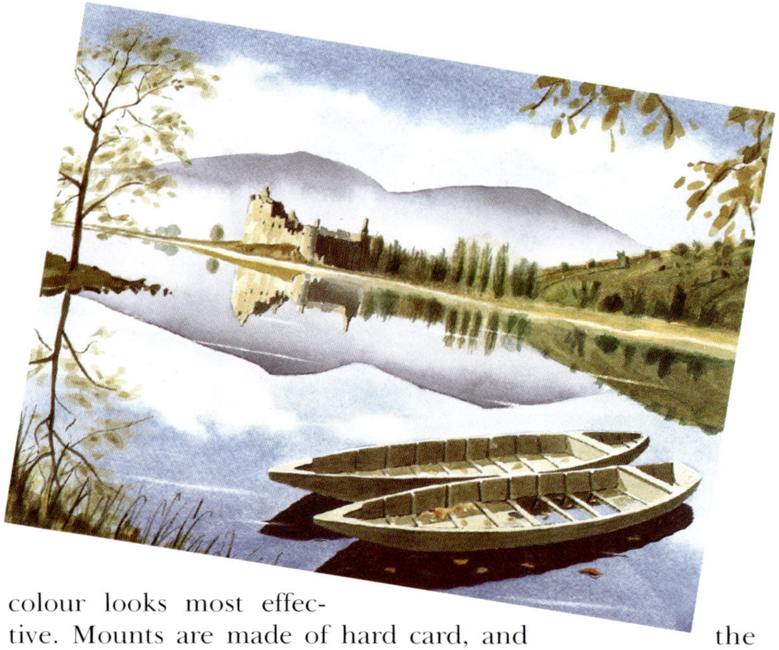

To make your paintings complete, you will need to decide how to frame them. Although your own taste should play a part in your choice of frame and mount, the style and size of the frame should be dictated by the painting, not the wall space it is going to fill.

You can buy the tools and materials to build your own framing system, but it is a costly way to start out, and not to be recommended for the complete beginner. It is more sensible to visit a local framer and ask their advice. If you'd don't know where to start, your local art shop ought to be able to give you a recommendation. A good framer is an invaluable asset.

Always remember to take your pictures with you to get advice on the perfect frame for a piece of work. You really won't be able to choose a frame or mount without the picture in front of you, so don't even attempt to. If you choose a mount that is tonally incompatible, or a frame that is too dominant for the painting inside, you will mar the quality of your work. You should be able to hold different mounts next to your work to see which colour looks most effective. Mounts are made of hard card, and are dyed to different colours and finishes. Always choose an acid-free card to frame your work, as one which is not pH-balanced will discolour the watercolour paper over time.

Choosing the best frame is difficult, as there are so many styles to choose between. Although your choice must be personal, there are certain principles you can follow to make selection process easier. Think of the nature of your painting before you choose the frame. Watercolours are usually fragile, delicate works of art, and will not be enhanced by thick, ornate, grandiose frames. They are far more sensitively contained within finer frames. They also need to be protected from everyday stress, so should be framed behind glass.

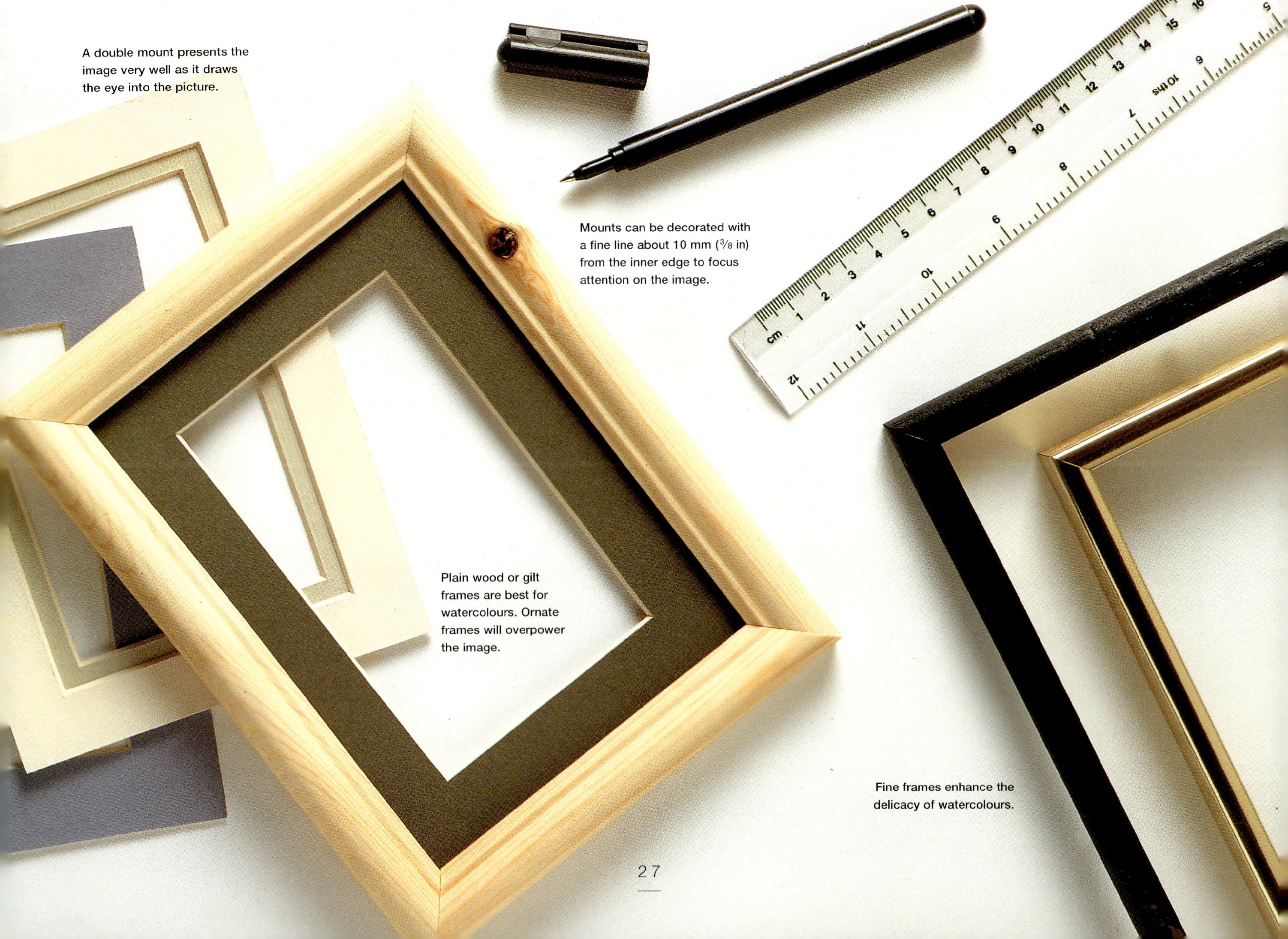

A double mount presents the image very well as it draws the eye into the picture.

Mounts can be decorated with a fine line about 10 mm (3/8 in) from the inner edge to focus attention on the image.

Plain wood or gilt frames are best for watercolours. Ornate frames will overpower the image.

Fine frames enhance the delicacy of watercolours.

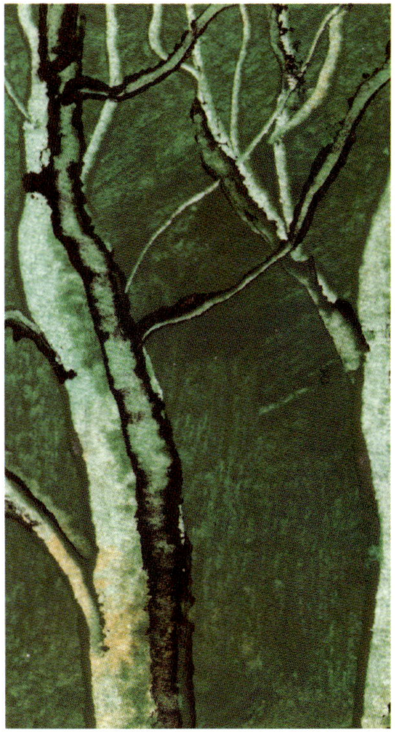
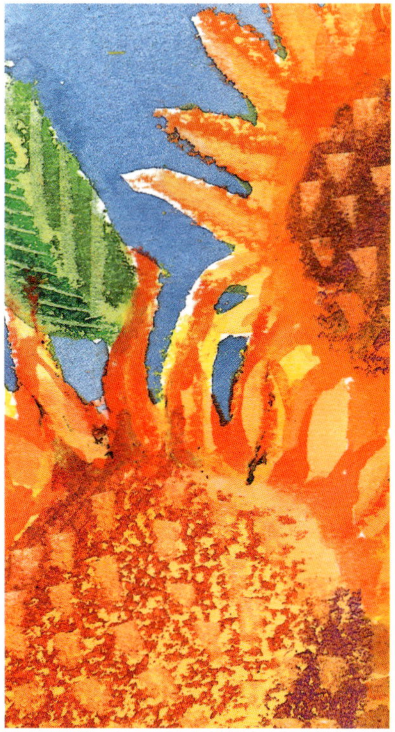
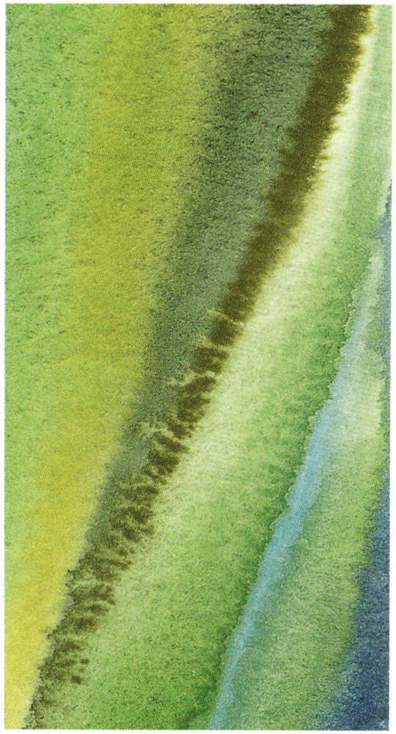
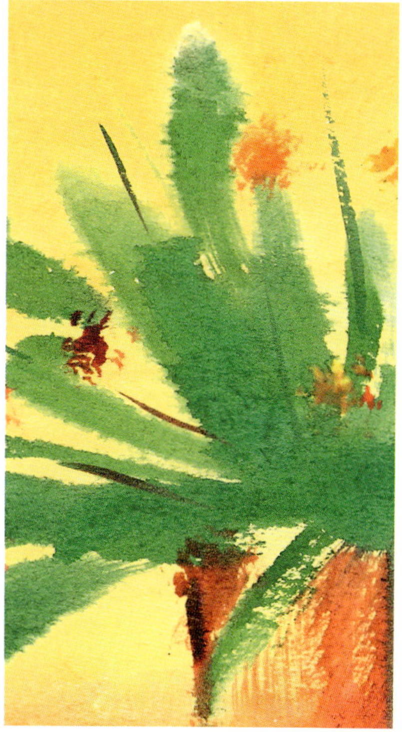

Techniques

It is worth spending some time experimenting with fundamental watercolour techniques before launching into a painting project. A good technical grounding will provide the skills and confidence to gain full enjoyment from putting watercolour into practice. This section will show you how to master a variety of watercolour techniques, ranging from the theory of using colour and creating an attractive composition, to the ways in which the paint can be applied to produce the precise effects you want to achieve.

Warming Up

It is important to feel completely at ease with watercolour paints and brushes when you set to work on a painting. Before approaching the projects in this book, therefore, it is a good idea to warm up.

Warming up for a painting session should be both a physical and a mental activity. First of all, prepare your work area. Make sure that you will be comfortable. All the materials that will be needed should be laid out close to hand so that you don't have to reach far for them. Any paper that needs stretching should be prepared in advance. If you stand to work, test out the height of your work surface in relation to your brush hand – will you have to lean at an uncomfortable angle? If so, you need to alter the height of your work surface. If you sit to paint, ensure that you have a comfortable, upright chair, and that there is enough room on either side for elbow movements. Then make a note of where the light is entering the room. If you are working in daylight, position yourself so that the light falling on the paper will be as even as possible. Consider the time of day as well. Will the light change as you work? If you are working direct from the subject, mark the direction of the light in relation to the subject in one corner of the paper so that you have a reference for keeping highlight and shadow areas consistent.

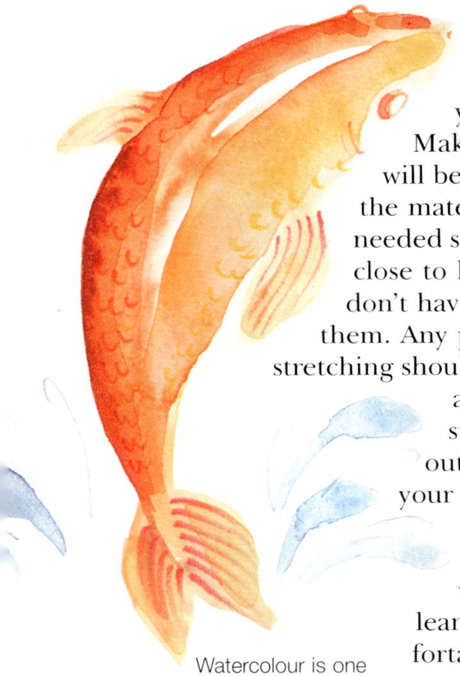

Watercolour is one of the most subtle and delicate of the painting media. Just a few simple strokes can produce the most poetic of images.

Next, consider your own mental state. Are you in the mood to paint? Sometimes it is difficult to switch into painting mode. If you are feeling a little out of practice, a few warm-up exercises should soon have you concentrating on the job in hand. Take each brush in turn and, using any colour, make some swift doodles on a large sheet of paper. Experiment with each of your brushes, holding them at different angles and in different places along their handles. The closer your fingers are to the bristles, the more control you will have. Hold the brush handle at the end furthest from the bristles and your marks will become much more gestural. Use your whole arm, feeling each brushstroke through the movements that you make. In this way you will become more involved in the process of painting.

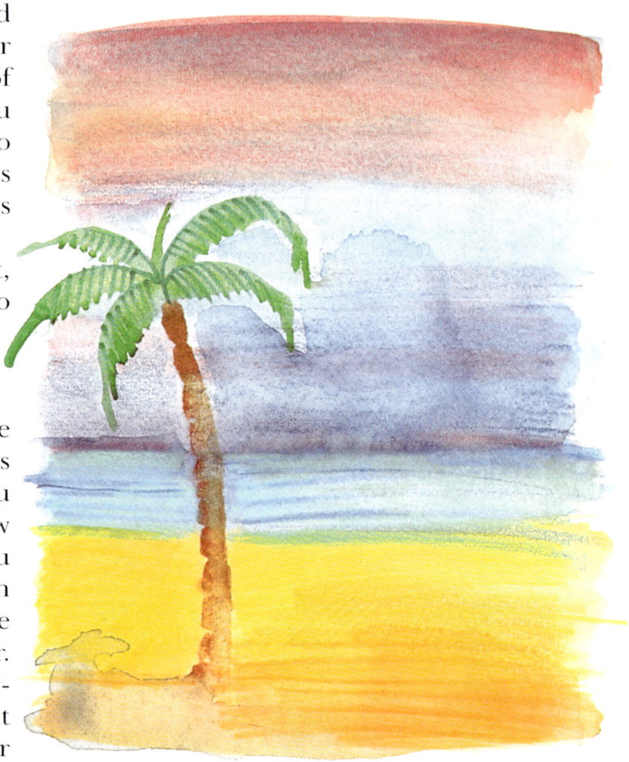

Practise making watercolour washes by laying thin layers of wet paint on to the paper and allowing them to melt into one another. Once they have dried, add a few lines to produce a simple but decorative illustration.

Practise dry-brush painting – that is, allowing one mark to dry before adding another one, using dryish paint, over the top, to produce a gestural yet controlled painting. This technique allows you to experiment with different overlays of colour. Vary the tones and wetness of the paint to create subtle variations in the appearance of the paint marks, as shown here.

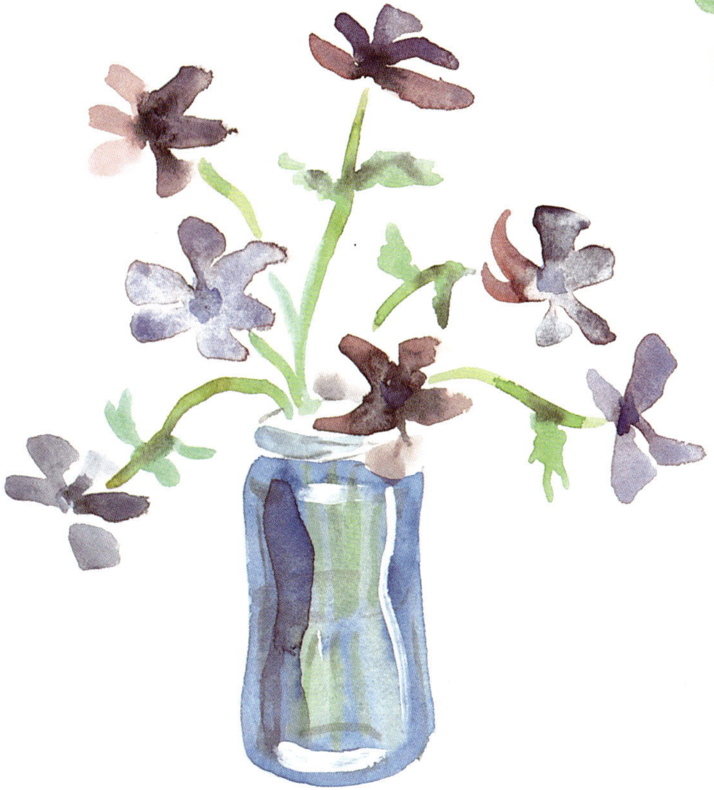

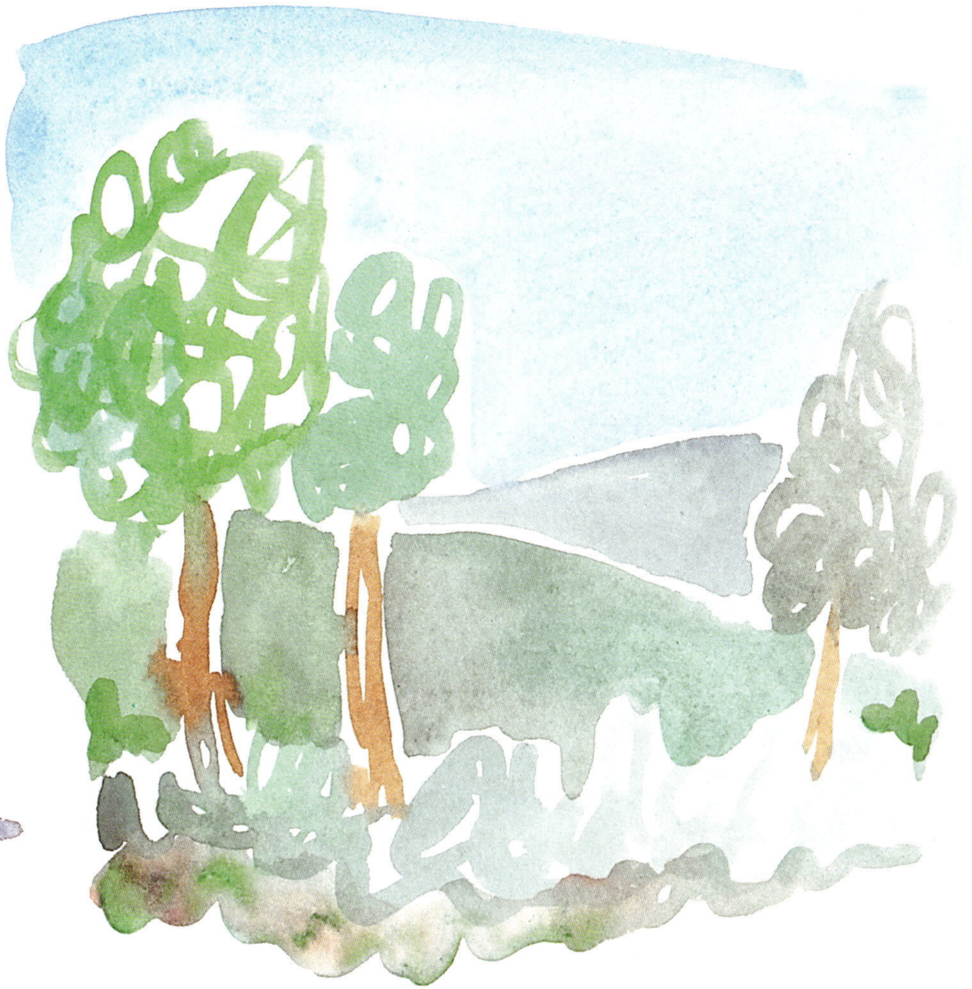

The landscape lends itself particularly well to watercolour painting, and a few simple marks can soon be turned into a panoramic vista. Here, a range of brushstrokes has created an atmospheric landscape scene, using just a few fresh colours, in a simple sketch to warm up before beginning to paint.

A Basic Palette

Watercolour is one of the most versatile of all the painting media – one colour can produce a wide range of tints and shades and quite a limited palette can produce colourful and varied paintings. In fact, the three primaries – red, yellow and blue – are enough to start with. These colours are called primaries because they cannot be created by mixing other colours together.

Experiments with the three primaries will reveal how far they can be extended. Different dilutions of any one colour will make at least six shades. This makes watercolour painting extremely versatile, as well as very cost effective. And as you discover how to control the strength of a colour through the amount of water that is added to it, and how to mix colours, it will become obvious that even a limited number of colours hold far greater potential than at first appears.

Although paintings can be made using only the three primaries, the range of colours can be extended considerably by mixing the primaries to produce secondaries. There are several versions of red, yellow and blue. There are warm yellows, such as cadmium, and cooler ones, such as lemon. There are warm reds, such as cadmium, and cool ones, such as scarlet lake. The same applies to blue; a cerulean gives a far cooler tone than a rich, warm French ultramarine. With one warm and one cool version of each primary it is possible to build a versatile palette. You don't need a green, or even a white or black. Dark and light tones can be mixed from the primary colours, and the paper can be left free of paint for white areas.

If you don't feel confident about mixing colours, the experiments described here illustrate how to create an extended palette. This will provide you with a good selection of pre-mixed colours, as well as an excellent basis for colour mixing experiments, once you have mastered the skill.

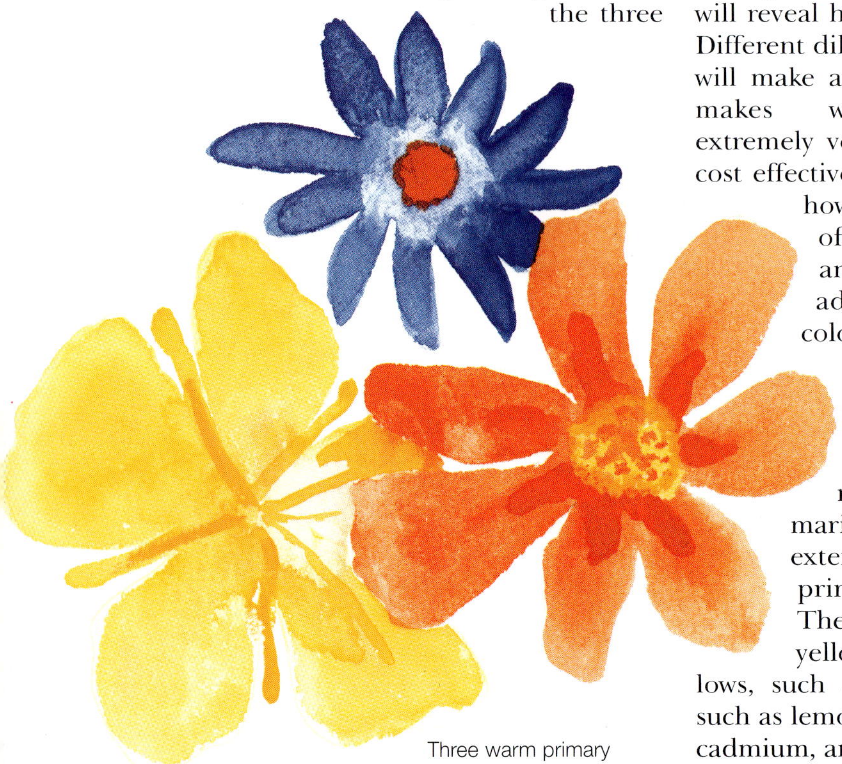

Three warm primary colours – cadmium red, cadmium yellow and Prussian blue – can be mixed to create a range of warm hues.

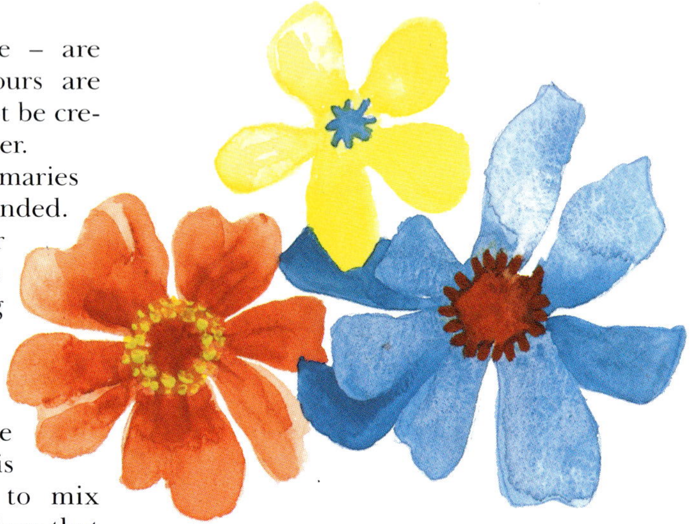

Three cool primary colours – scarlet lake, lemon yellow and cerulean blue – can be mixed to produce a range of cool hues.

Developing a tonal range with one colour

LEFT and BELOW Varying amounts of water are added to a single colour to produce a range of tones that vary from a deep colour, when the paint is only slightly diluted, to a pale tint when it has been mixed with plenty of water. A painting could be made using just one colour in this way.

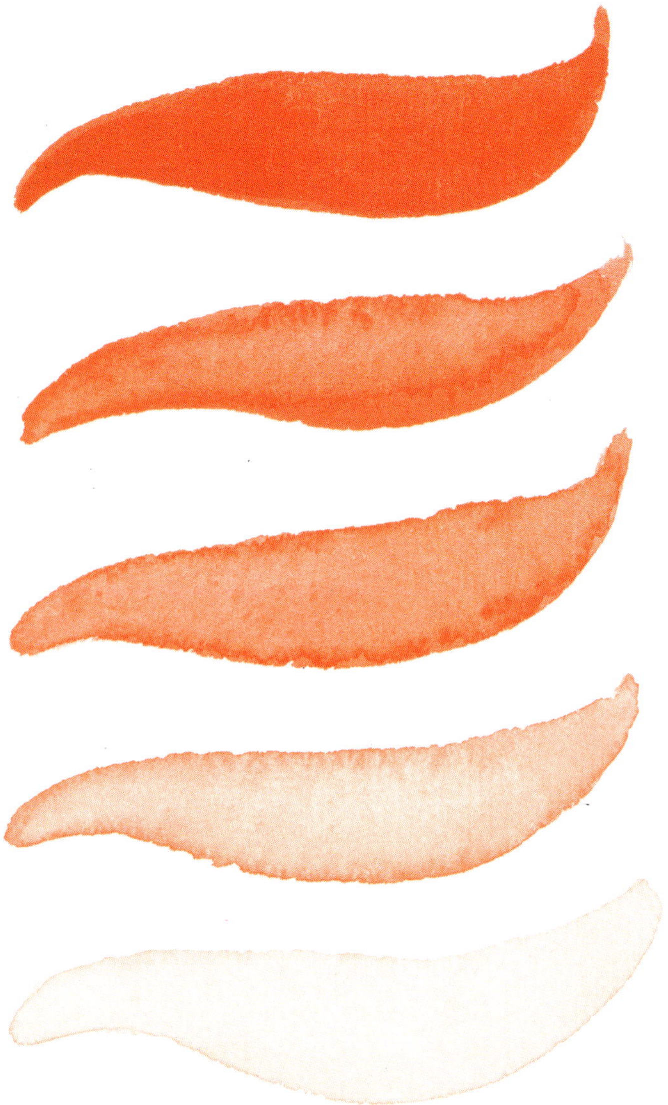

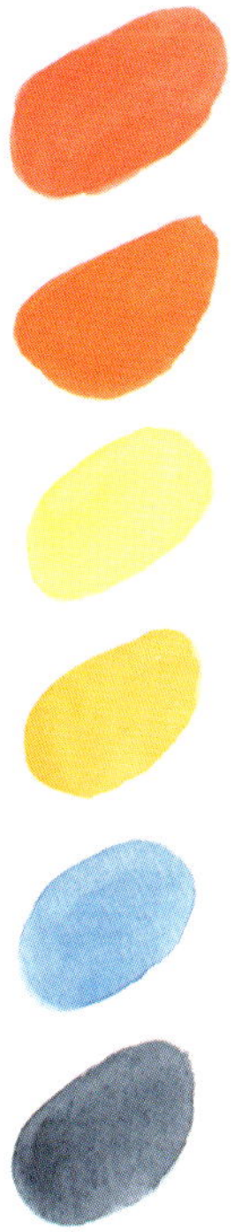

ABOVE A suitable limited palette: scarlet lake, cadmium red, lemon yellow, cadmium yellow, cerulean blue, Prussian blue.

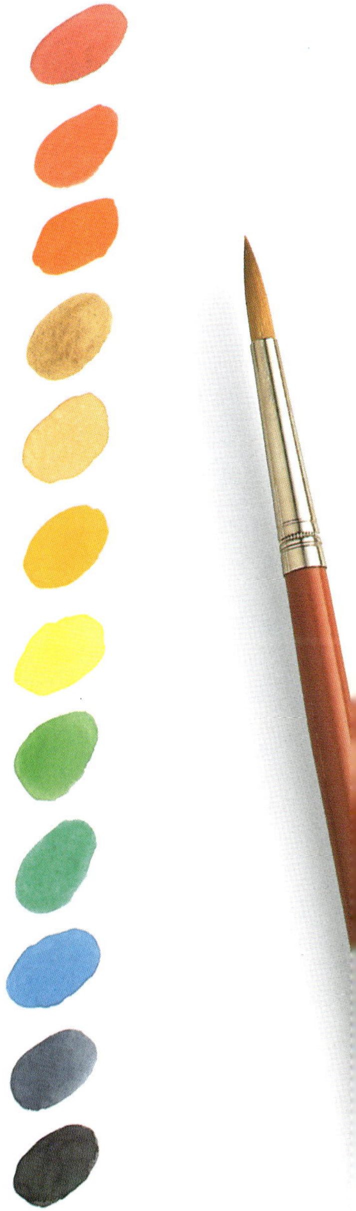

RIGHT For a more extended range, try: scarlet lake, cadmium red, lemon yellow, cadmium yellow, cerulean blue, Prussian blue, plus: alizarin crimson, yellow ochre, burnt sienna, Hooker's green, viridian and Payne's grey.

Colour Theory

An understanding of the scientific nature of colour will enhance your use of it when painting. To begin with, consider the way that colours are formally arranged. They form a kind of hierarchy, with primary colours at the top, and secondary and tertiary hues forming the second and third levels of colour. The method you choose to mix these primary, secondary and tertiary hues, (hue = pure colour) will effect the resulting colours that you achieve.

To improve your understanding of colour theory, first make a colour wheel, using the three basic primary colours, red, yellow and blue, arranged in a circle. The primaries cannot be mixed from other colours (they are the most pure colours in your palette), although you will find that you have a number of reds, yellows and blues to choose between. Some primary colours are cool in tone, while others are warm. While the paint on your colour wheel is still wet, blend any two primaries together, and you will produce a secondary hue. You will discover that red and yellow make orange, yellow and blue make green, and red and blue make violet.

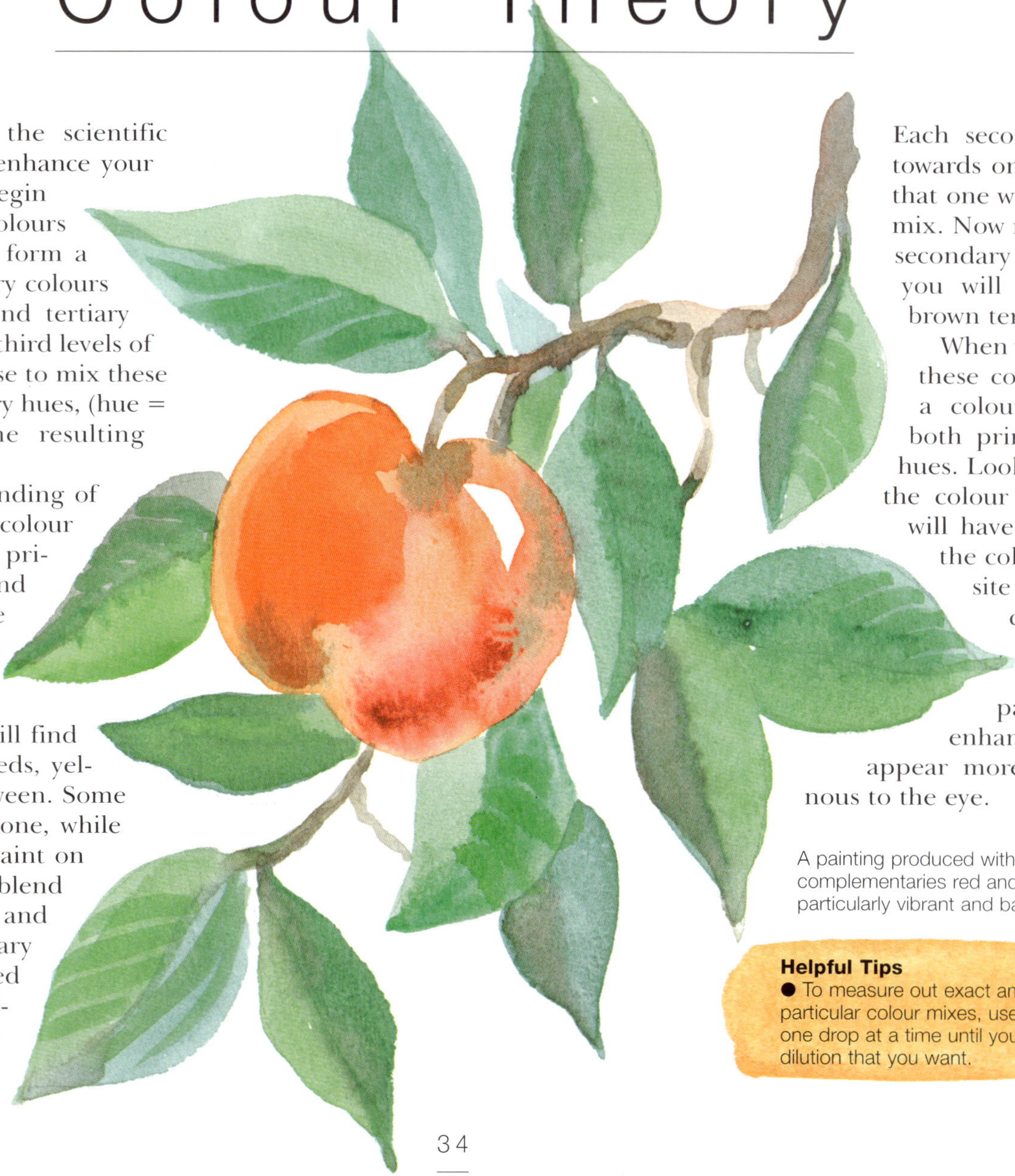

Each secondary hue will lean towards one of the primaries – that one which is greater in the mix. Now mix any primary and secondary colour together, and you will produce a grey or brown tertiary mix.

When you have tried out all these colour mixes, produce a colour wheel comprising both primary and secondary hues. Look at their position on the colour wheel. Each colour will have a complementary – the colour which sits opposite it on the wheel. Use complementary colours next to one another on a painting and each will enhance the other, so they appear more intense and luminous to the eye.

A painting produced with the complementaries red and green creates a particularly vibrant and balanced image.

Helpful Tips

- To measure out exact amounts of water for particular colour mixes, use a pipette to add one drop at a time until you have the colour dilution that you want.

The colour wheel
Mixing two of the three primary colours (yellow, red and blue) will produce the three secondary colours (orange, purple and green); mixing a secondary with a neighbouring primary will produce one of the six tertiary colours.

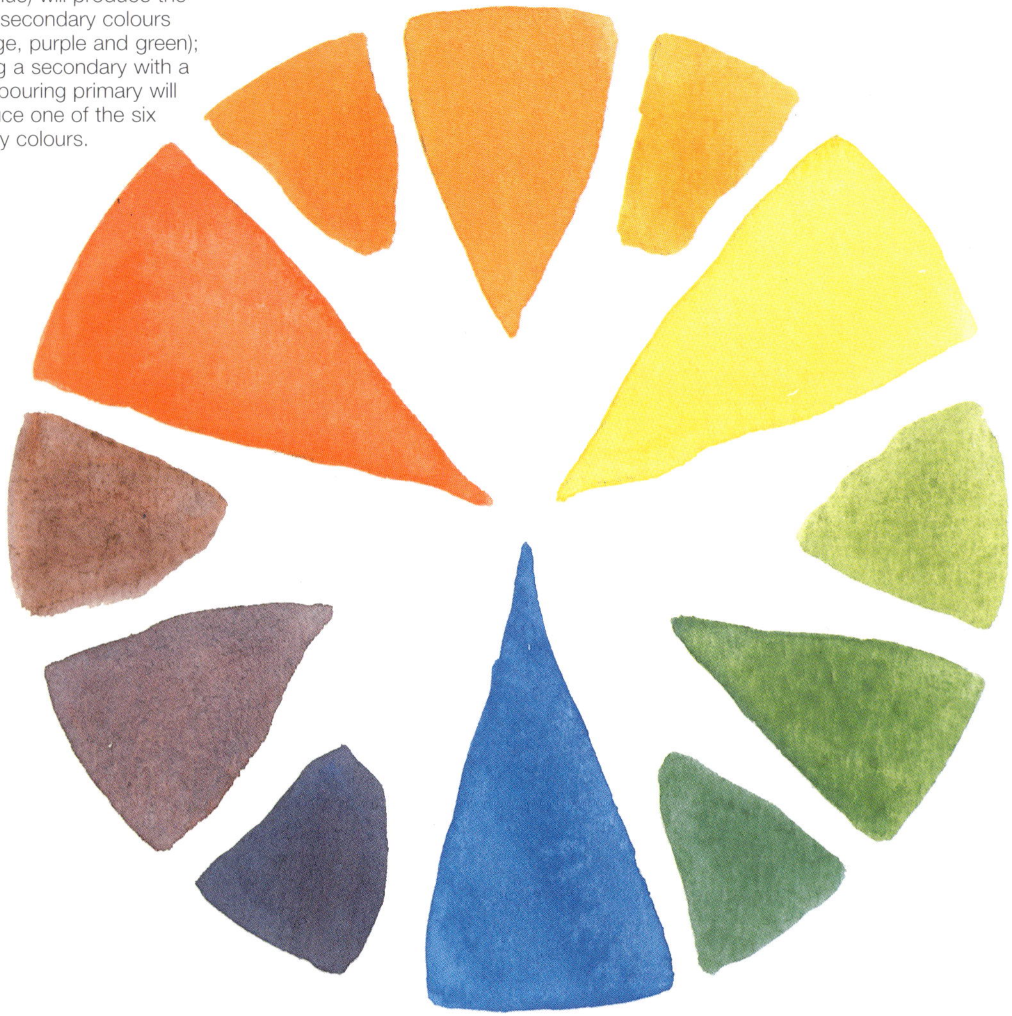

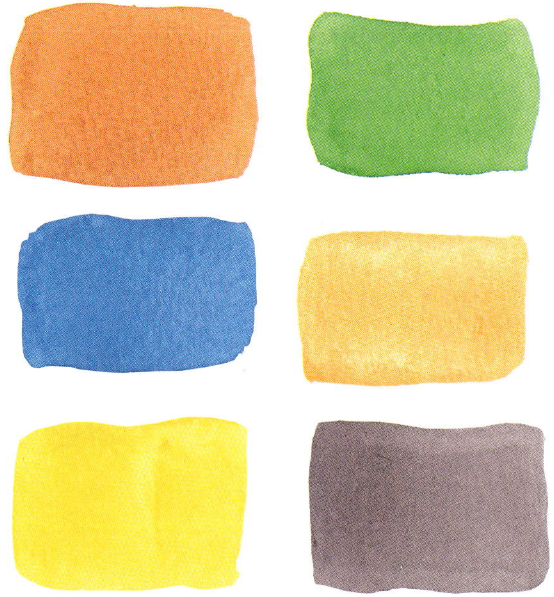

Complementary colours
Complementary colours are those that sit opposite each other in the colour wheel. So red and green are complementary, blue and orange, and yellow and purple.

Mixing the three warm primaries together produces warm secondary and tertiary hues.

If the cool primaries are mixed, the secondary and tertiary colours produced will also be cool hues.

Colour Mixing

It is much better to mix the colours that you want than to rely on tube colours. Once you have selected a colour range, perhaps from those suggested on the previous pages, you can start experimenting with the different methods of mixing. Watercolour paint can be mixed in a number of ways, and those colours that you mix yourself will contain a richness and vibrancy difficult to find in any colour out of a tube.

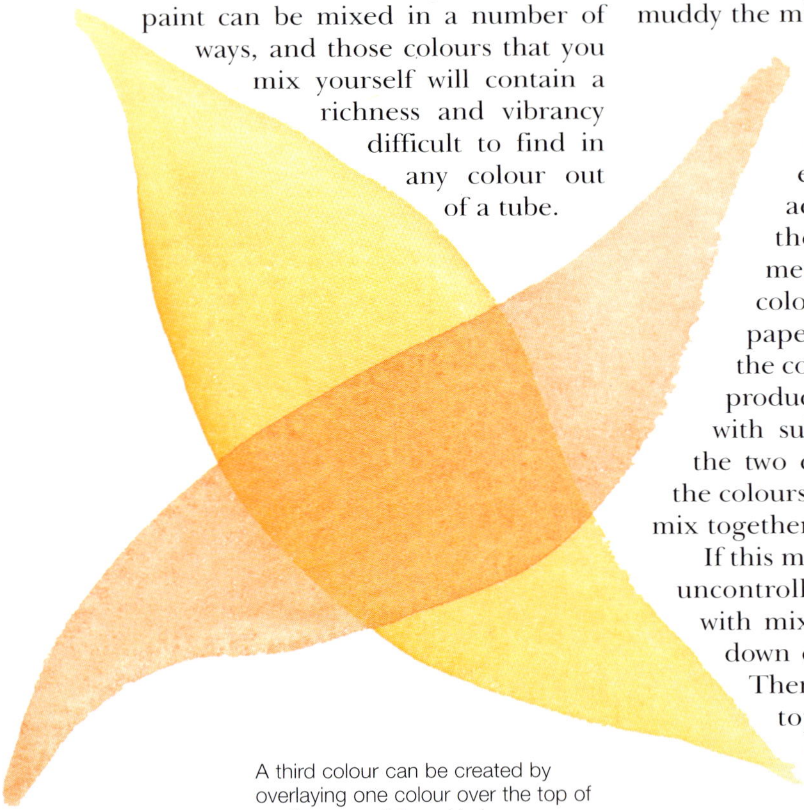

A third colour can be created by overlaying one colour over the top of another once it has dried.

One way to mix watercolour paint is on the palette, which produces a consistent blend. Always rinse the brush with clean water before picking up a new colour in order to ensure that traces of previous colours do not muddy the mixes.

Colours mixed in this way should be well blended. This might not always be the effect you want to achieve, however, and there are alternative methods, such as mixing colours wet into wet on the paper. With this technique the colours will melt together, producing more varied mixes with subtle but not complete blends of the two colours laid down. The wetter the colours, the more completely they will mix together.

If this method appears too random and uncontrollable, you could experiment with mixing colours wet over dry. Lay down one colour and allow it to dry. Then add a second colour over the top. The two layered colours combine to produce translucent mixes. Always lay the paler colour down first and add the darker one over the top, as paler colours laid over the top of darker ones will disappear into them. More than two colours can be layered with this technique, but remember to start with the lighter hues and add progressively darker ones over them. Watercolour painting is at its most subtle and poetic when you apply the paint in layers in this way.

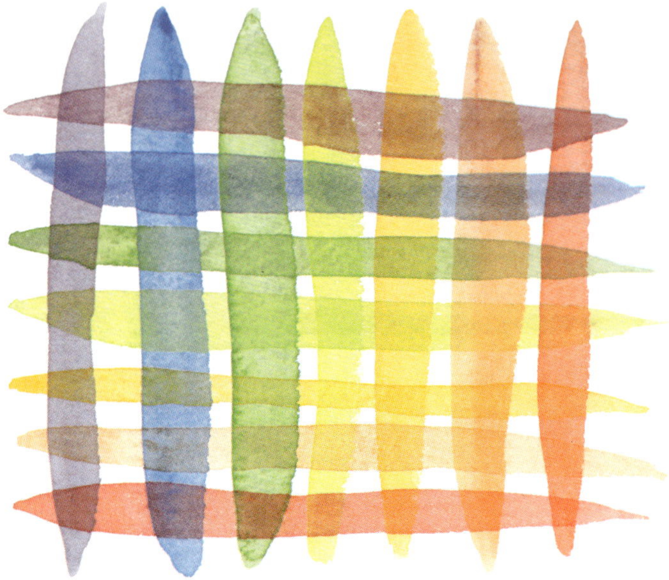

A whole range of secondary and tertiary colours can be produced by putting down colours wet over dry instead of pre-mixing them on the palette.

ABOVE Mix two colours together on the palette to produce a rich, tonally consistent third hue. Here (*top*) cadmium red and cadmium yellow have been mixed to create cadmium orange. Paint the red over the yellow to produce a slightly less consistent orange (*centre*). Mix the same two colours wet into wet on the paper and compare the results.

RIGHT By overlaying three colours wet over dry you can achieve a wide range of subtly graded hues. The colours will not have the density of premixed paint, and the translucent nature of the watercolour medium will be more obvious.

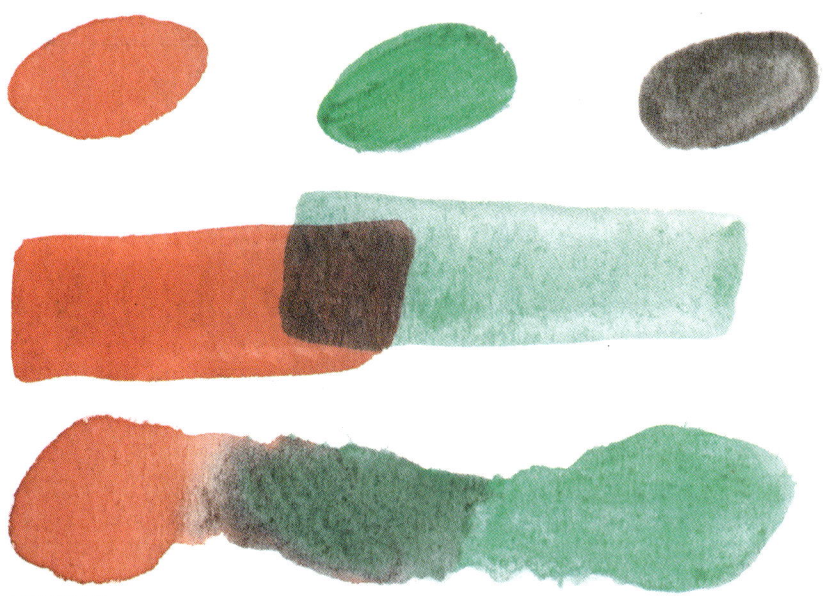

ABOVE When mixing two colours wet on dry, always paint the darker tone second, as paler hues are absorbed by a darker colour underneath. In these examples, viridian and alizarin crimson are combined in different ways to produce interesting results, to show just how versatile watercolour paint can be.

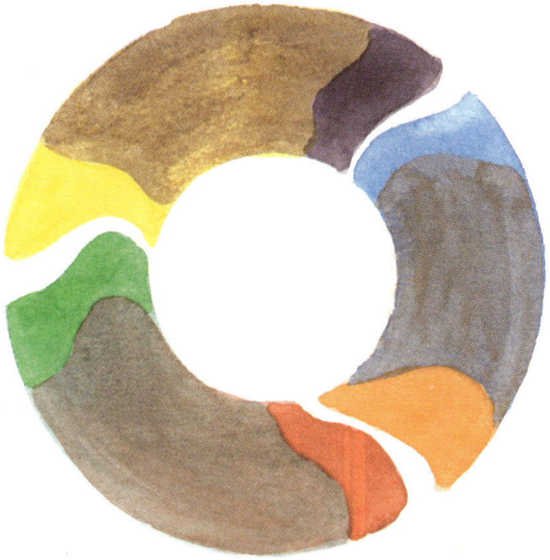

RIGHT Neutrals are produced by mixing two complementary colours. This produces far richer and less muddy greys and browns than equivalent neutrals achieved by adding black to the base colour. Neutrals mixed in this way will also tone better with the colours in the rest of the painting.

Monochrome Painting

To develop a wide tonal range with watercolour, you don't need to use a wide range of colours. In fact, using one colour, you can produce a sophisticated monochrome painting, in which the devices common to any more colourful watercolour work will still come into play. You can exploit any one watercolour to produce a whole painting.

Payne's grey is a particularly versatile colour, and is a good choice for monochrome watercolour work, as it can appear as anything from a rich dark blue to a purple to a very pale grey. As a result, you can use it to create the impression of distance, by diluting the paint more as the view recedes into the middle distance and background. This technique is known as aerial perspective. You can also use the colour very strong, in contrast to areas which you leave completely free of paint, to produce intense tonal contrasts, useful for building the impression of three-dimensional form, or enhancing areas in bright light or deep shadow.

When painting in monochrome, your use of these devices will become more important than when the tonal values of different colours create the impression of depth and form for you. Remember, too, that working in monochrome will enable you to produce highly atmospheric paintings – of dusk or dawn, for example, when the light becomes muted and tones appear to merge. Try experimenting with colours not obviously related to your subject too, perhaps using alizarin crimson to produce a tonal landscape, or Prussian blue to paint an interior scene.

BELOW Three-dimensional forms are developed using different strengths of colour for the different planes, leaving the brightest lights free of paint. Cylinders, spheres and cones, as well as subjects such as the delicate folds in a piece of fabric, can be modelled in this way to give the illusion of depth.

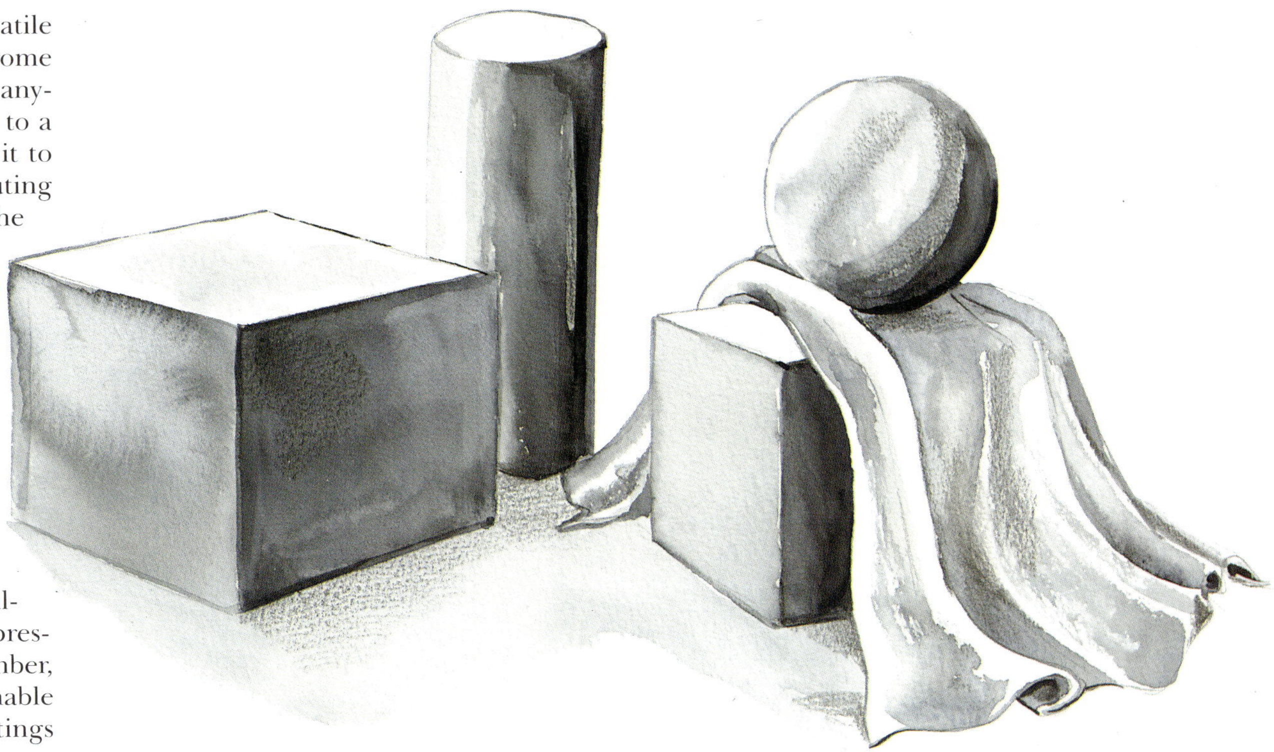

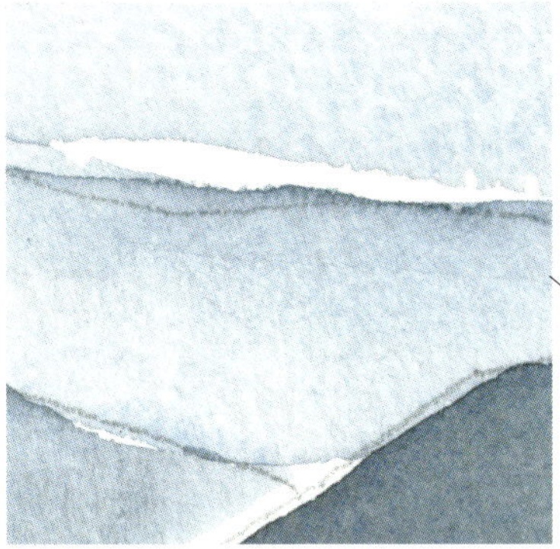

On the horizon line, the tonal contrasts are far less clear and the colour has paled, suggesting distance.

Controlling space through tone

Lovely, fresh landscape paintings that include a sense of detail and recession can be produced using just one colour. In this instance, Payne's grey has been diluted to varying strengths and used darker and thicker in the foreground, and paler towards the horizon line, to produce the impression of distance.

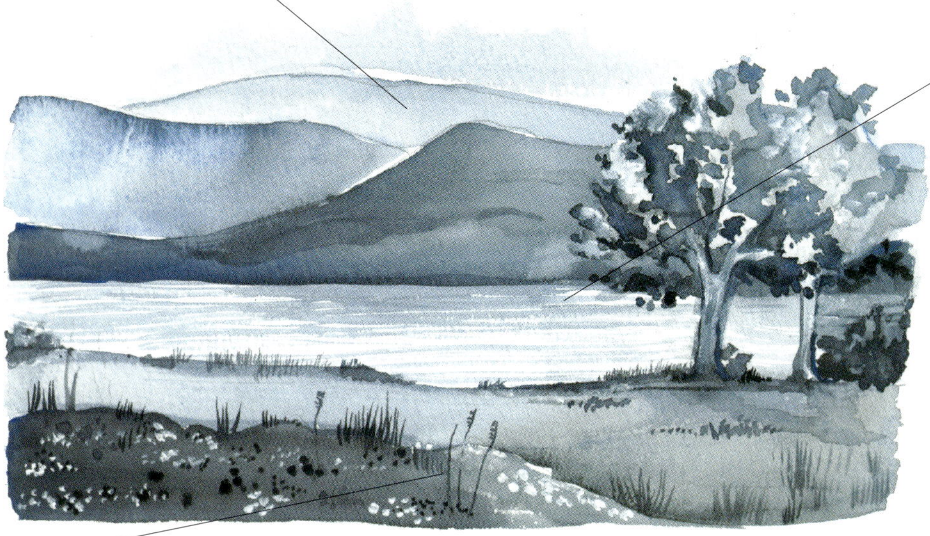

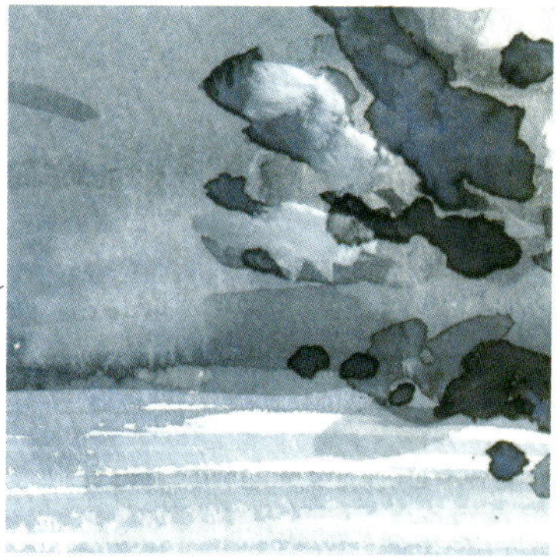

The tones are beginning to lose their contrast in the middle ground.

The foreground detail is well defined because the artist has used strong tonal contrasts.

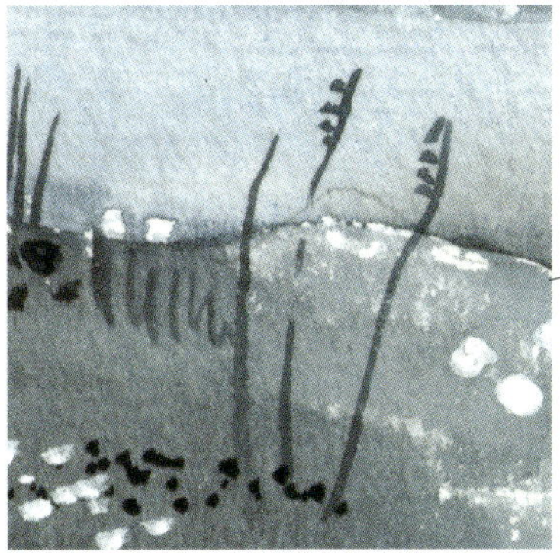

Helpful Tips

● Practise painting different tones with one paint mix before you start producing a picture.

Composition and Position

Composition describes the way in which elements are organized on the picture surface; every element will affect a picture's balance, and so its overall impact. It is crucial, therefore, that you arrange your subject matter with care as a bad composition will ruin a picture, however skilful your handling of the paint might be. A good way to learn about composition is to analyse the work of other artists. Try to identify the focal point (the most important element) in their pictures – how does your eye travel towards it? Perhaps you are led along a pathway, or through a series of developing colours, before your eye rests on a particular feature?

Before starting on a picture, take a long look at your subject. What viewpoint are you going to take? A high viewpoint will provide a completely different composition to a low one. You also need to decide whether to paint a small area from close in or to take a broad overview. Whatever you decide, lines, shapes and colours are crucial players in the composition stakes. If you create harmony between these elements, your pictures will be a resounding success!

The centre of interest does not need to be placed in the centre of the picture; in fact, such exact symmetry may make the work look dull. Balance needs to be created between the different elements, however, to encourage the viewer's eye to explore the whole picture surface. You could try creating tension by placing the centre of interest towards one of the edges of the paper, which will also suggest that the action continues outside the viewer's range. The centre of interest can be emphasized by placing more intense colours around it, or by a contrast in scale, or by employing extra-fine detail to describe it.

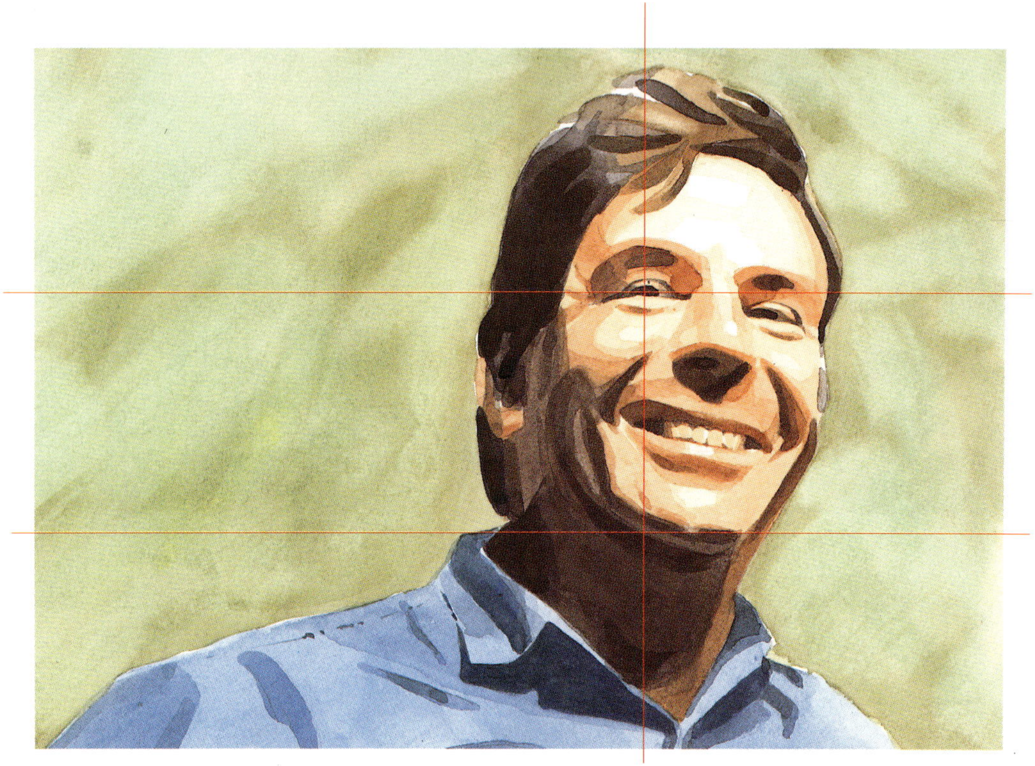

Rule of thirds
One simple way of making sure that your picture looks more attractive but not static is to use the rule of thirds. This involves placing your subjects roughly a third of the way in from the edge of the picture. Important parts, such as this man's eye, can be positioned where the lines cross.

Helpful Tips
- Space and tone are important in composition, and empty spaces can be as evocative as areas of intense activity. Have the confidence to leave white space.

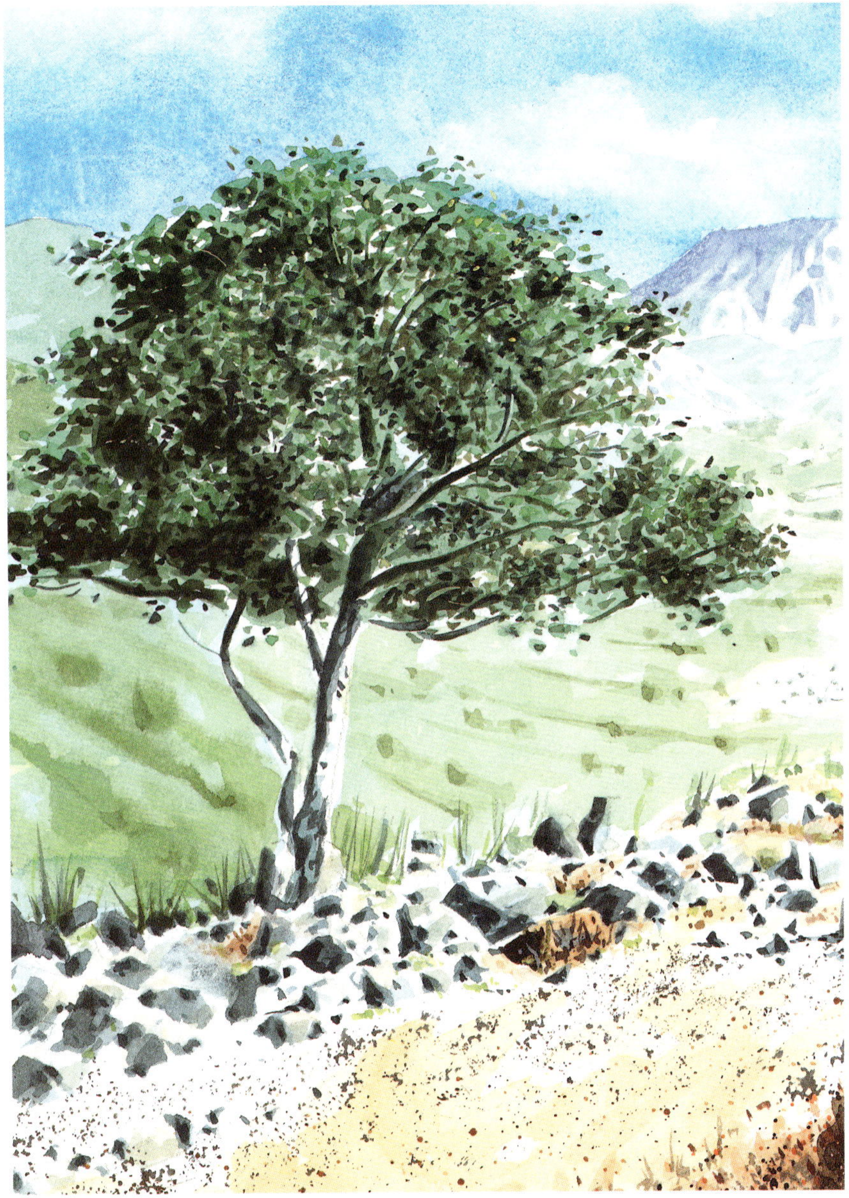

Choice of format
What you see can often be composed or framed in a variety of ways. For example, it is natural to paint a landscape in a wide, landscape shape. But you may find that you want to focus on certain things – such as the tree, or the distant rocks – rather than the whole scene. You can vary the shape of your picture to suit your subject.

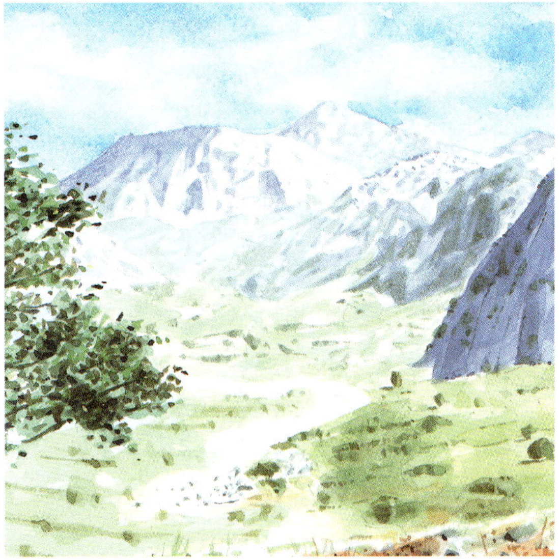

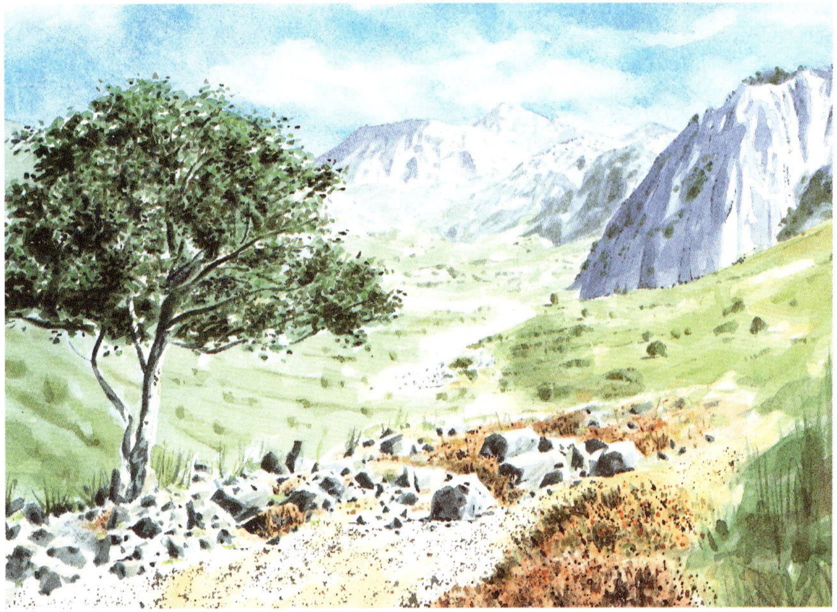

Composition and Shape

Harmonious paintings don't have to be lifeless, and the introduction of changes of pace within a picture will help to retain the viewer's interest for longer than a few seconds. You can create interest by using some unexpected colour contrasts, variations in the thickness of lines, different shapes, and changes in the nature of the brushwork. Nevertheless, you must always make sure that the composition is balanced and harmonious, regardless of the specific elements it contains.

Your choice of composition will affect the sense of harmony in a work, and it is worth being aware of the options available. One element that it is all too easy to forget when you are painting is the eye of the viewer. Try to direct the viewer's attention around the painting. Space objects carefully, or arrange them in an interesting manner, to produce paintings that the viewer will want to spend time exploring.

Symmetry is one way to balance a composition, although what might at first glance appear balanced and pleasing may not hold the viewer's attention for long, whereas by shifting the centre of interest off-balance a painting can be made more interesting. Compositions do not have to rely on symmetry and asymmetry, however. Alternatives include curvilinear compositions, which encourage the viewer's eye to move around and into the centre of the picture, and triangular compositions, which draw the eye up the central axis of the picture.

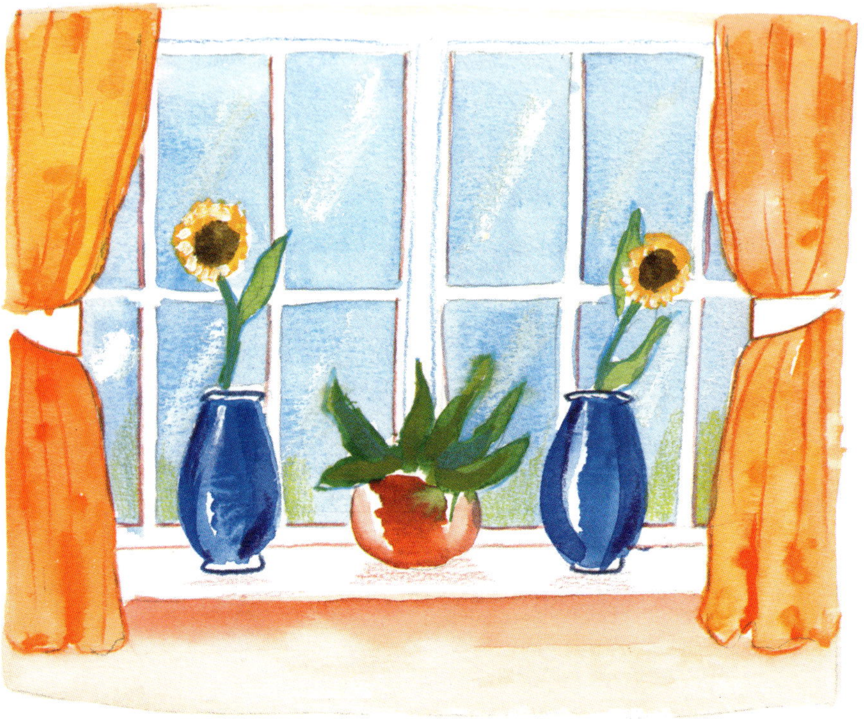

A symmetrical composition may appear interesting and harmonious at first glance, but for how long does it hold your attention?

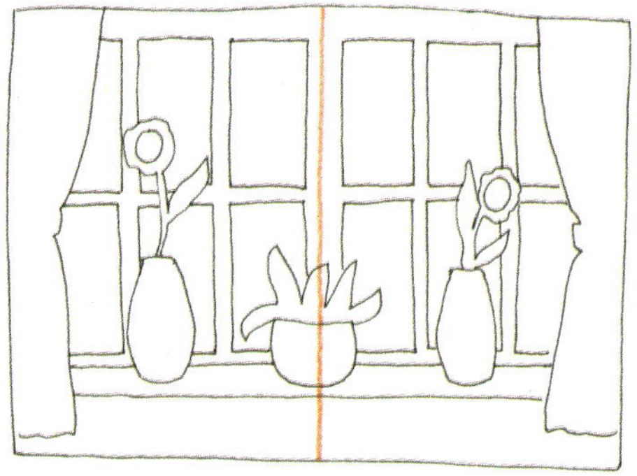

Experiment with different compositions, using a pencil and a rough piece of paper before applying your ideas to a full painting project. In this way you will be sure to choose the most suitable option for your requirements. Just a few rough lines will give you a clear impression of your composition.

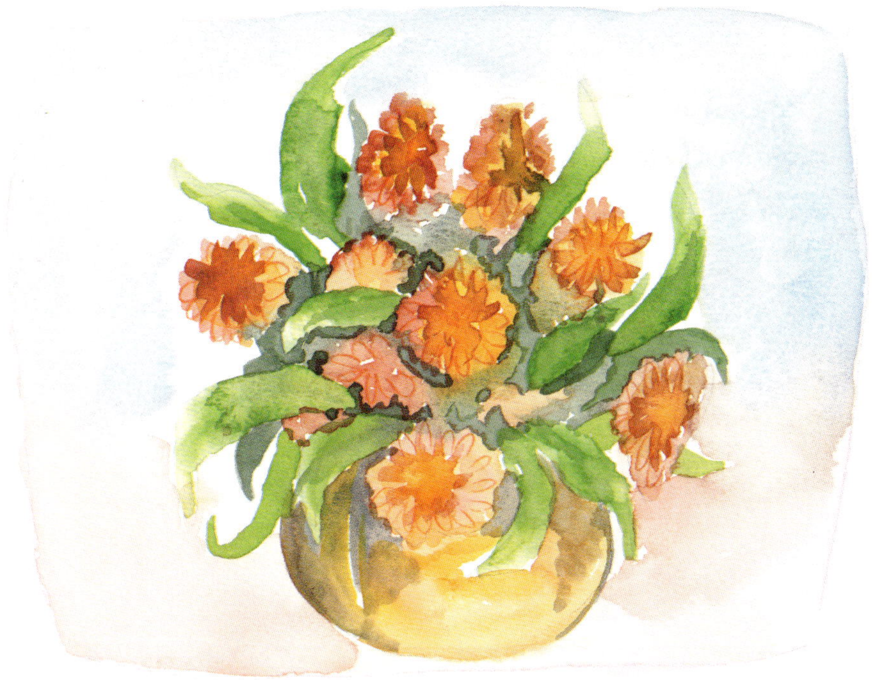

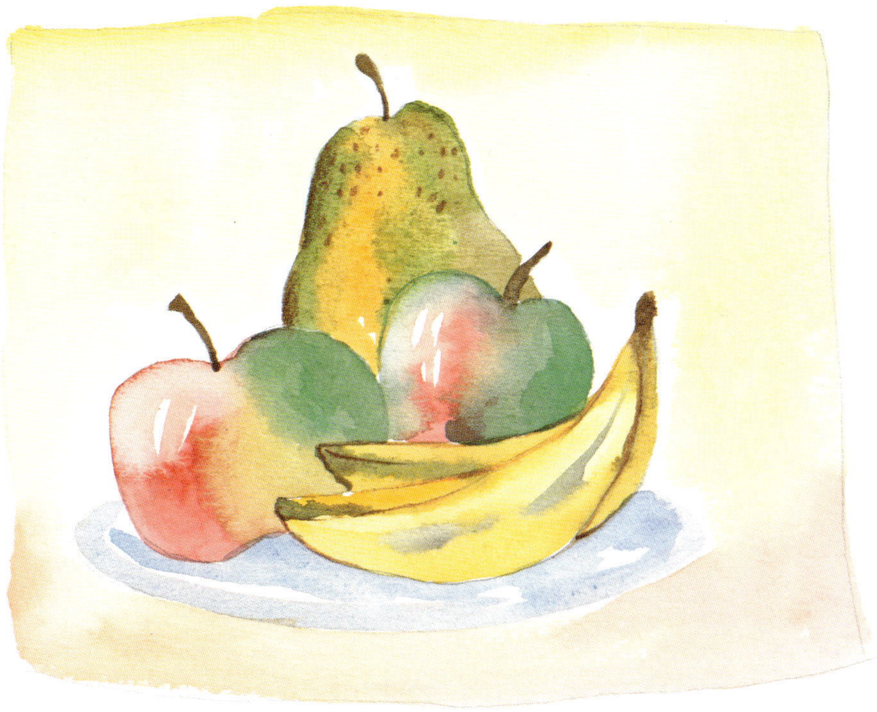

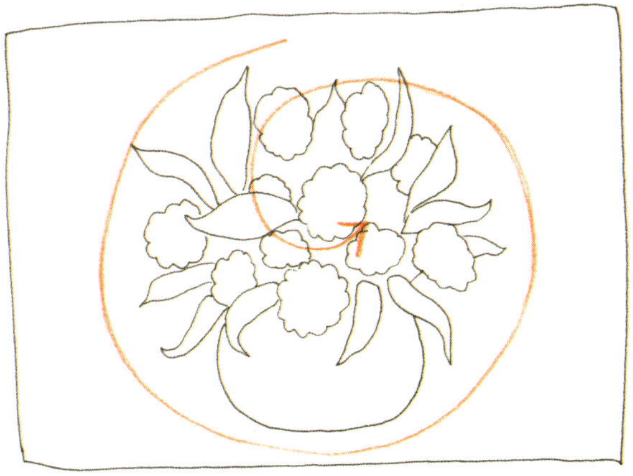

A curvilinear composition draws the eye around and into the centre of the painting. This shape will hold the viewer's attention for longer than a very symmetrical arrangement.

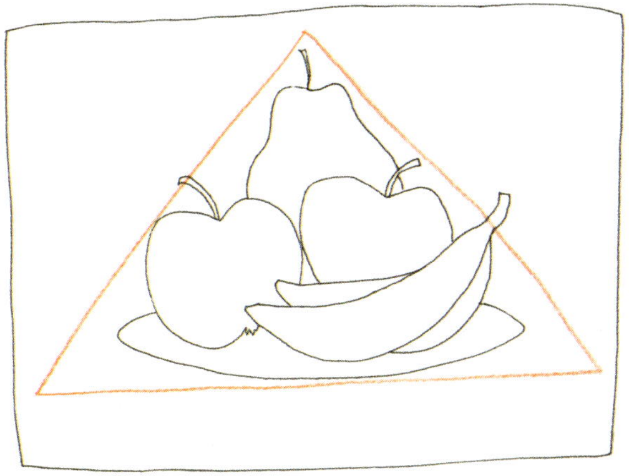

A triangular composition leads the eye from the base of the picture up to the top, ensuring the whole composition is read.

Perspective

Perspective provides a means of showing the illusion of three dimensions on the two-dimensional picture plane. Paintings in which depth, distance and solid forms are portrayed without an understanding of perspective are likely to look unconvincing. Perspective is based on a set of fundamental rules that will bring about the same results every time they are used. Once these principles have been mastered, they can be used in any paintings. There are three types of perspective: linear, overlapping and tonal or aerial.

The horizon line is the point at which the sky and land meet in a landscape, and it coincides with your eye level. The horizon line is an essential factor when using linear perspective because parallel lines extending away from you converge towards each other, and meet on the horizon line. The point at which they meet is called the vanishing point. All the elements in a scene become smaller as they approach the horizon line, and converging parallel lines provide a guide to their relative sizes. When overlapping perspective is used, the elements in the foreground take precedence over any that lie further away. The elements in the foreground will also appear larger than those they overlap. By painting a series of overlapped objects, which decrease in size toward the horizon line, you will produce an effective impression of depth.

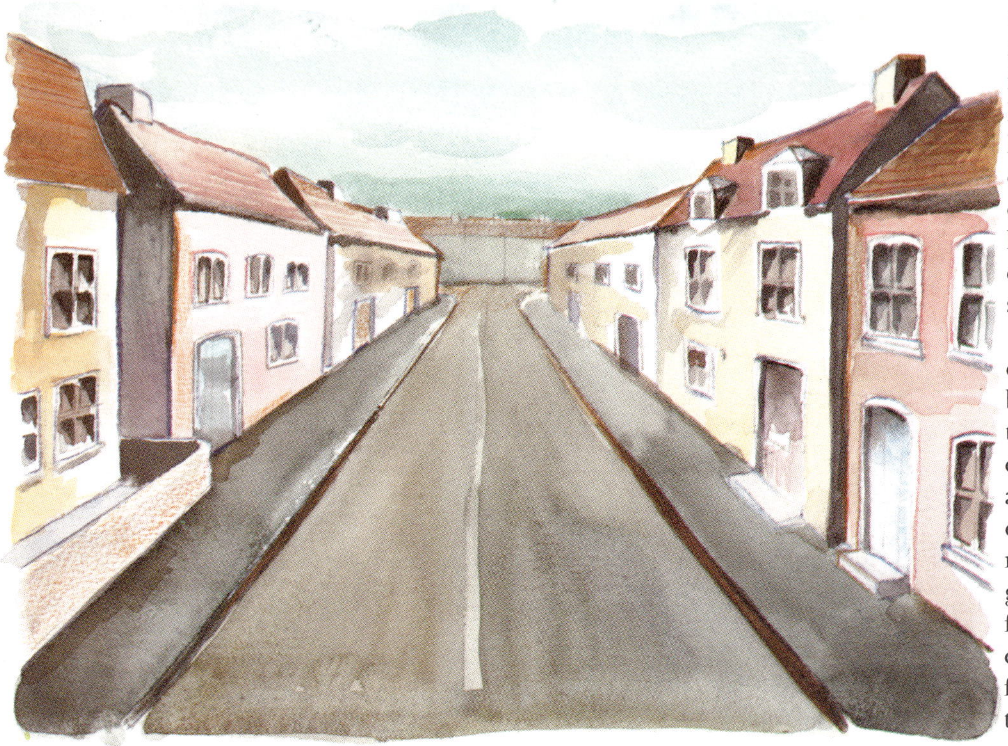

Linear perspective
Distance is achieved in this street scene through perspective lines that converge at the vanishing point in the middle distance. The composition is evenly balanced and the eye is drawn through it, down the street.

Tonal perspective depends on reduction, too, but this time in intensity of tone. Use strong, bold colours in the foreground, and lighten them in tone by diluting them more as they recede into the middle ground. Some colours are far more recessive than others – those cool primaries, for example. Blue is a particularly recessive colour, and is often used to link the horizon line in a landscape with the sky above it. The colours close to the horizon line should be the most cool and pale in the painting if you want to create depth. When painting a sky, allow the colours to become more intense towards the top of the paper, as this will make the sky appear to exist overhead as well as in the distance.

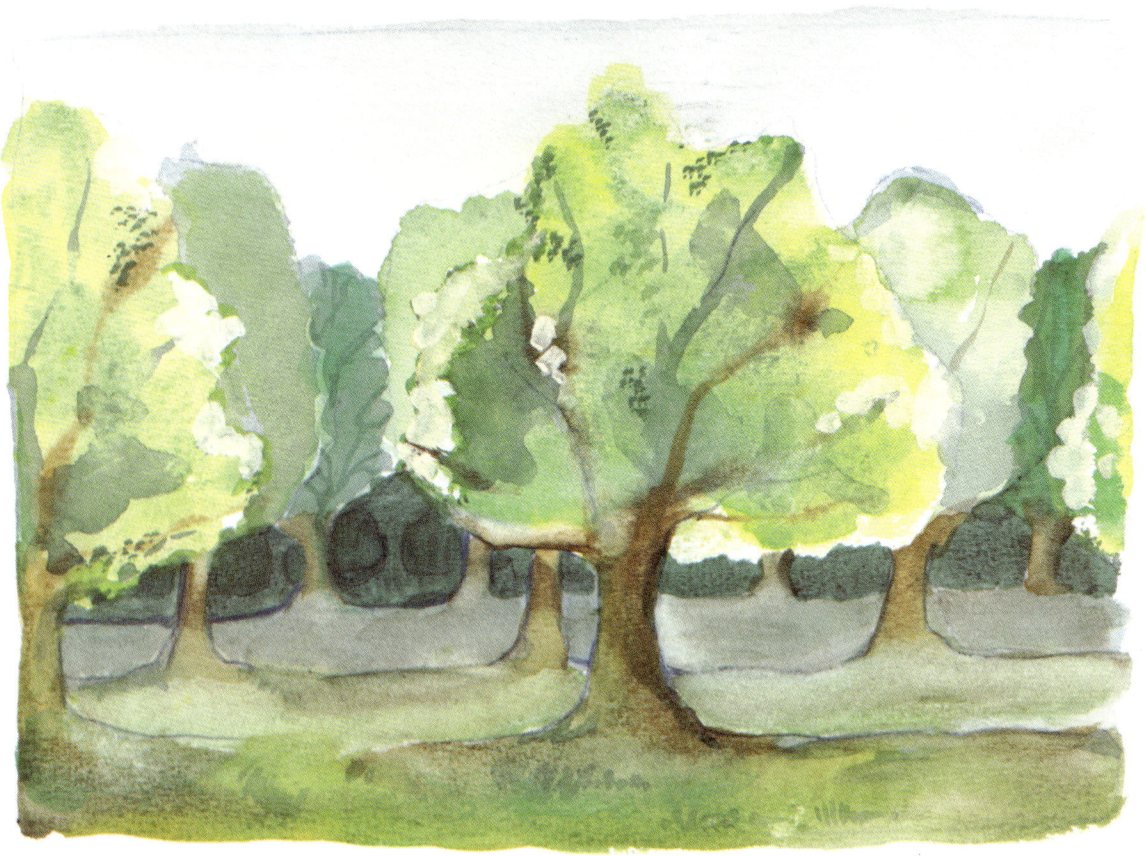

Overlapping perspective
The trees in the orchard overlap, with those in the foreground appearing far larger than those behind, successfully producing an impression of depth and distance.

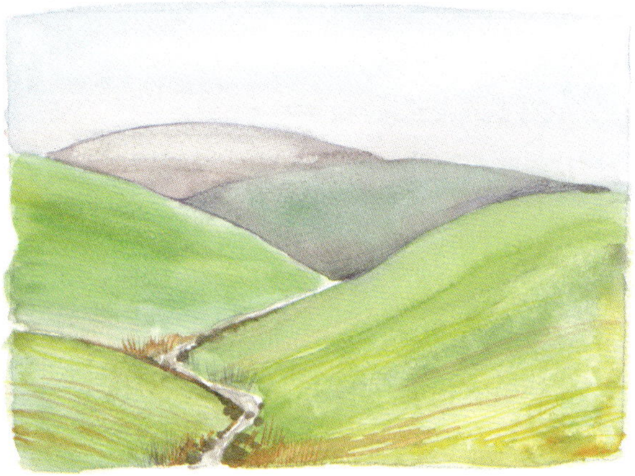

Tonal perspective
The stream leads the eye from the intensely coloured undergrowth in the foreground through to the distance, where the colours become pale and more delicate.

Helpful Tips

● Try standing up straight and considering a scene. Make a thumbnail sketch of what you see. Now drop down to your knees and examine the scene again. See how greatly the perspective has altered your view.

Flat Washes

Wash work is synonymous with watercolour painting. Whatever other skills you may or may not perfect, the wash is a fundamental and essential one to master. Watercolours are used by diluting paint to various intensities of colour. A wash may cover the entire drawing, or just a small area. It may be made from one colour or a combination of two or three. It can be flat and unchanging, or show some variation in the strength of colours, produced by varying the ratio of water to paint. You may choose to add fine details with other watercolour techniques, but you will always need to apply washes. Because of this, it should be the first technique that you tackle.

The flat wash contains only one colour, applied evenly so that the paint dries without variation in its tone or texture. To achieve an even finish, the flat wash must be applied very quickly. If you hesitate while working, or repeat a stroke, the paint will not dry completely flat.

To achieve evenness, dampen the paper before applying any paint. This will help the paint to spread evenly over the paper, and reduces the likelihood of hard edges developing between each stroke of paint. Use a large, flat wash brush to achieve the most even finish. To make more textured washes, work on dry or only slightly damp paper.

Laying a flat wash
Mix up a large quantity of colour. Using a large, flat or wash brush, paint a line of colour across the top of the paper, from left to right (*top*). On reaching the other side, do not lift the brush off the paper. Instead, turn it around and continue the line from right to left, picking up the bottom edge of the first line of paint as you go (*middle*). On reaching the first side, lift the brush cleanly off the paper, recharge it with paint, and continue in the same vein, back and forth until you reach the bottom edge of the paper (*bottom*).

Helpful Tips

- Mix up a large quantity of colour before starting, because it is essential to keep going until you have finished applying the wash.
- If the paper is too wet, it will buckle and the paint will run in streaks. Mop up any water with a rag or sponge before you start painting the wash.
- Tip or hold the board at a 45° angle to help the paint spread evenly down the paper.
- If the wash does not appear to be flat as you work, don't worry! As it dries, the particles of pigment should disperse evenly to produce a flat colour.

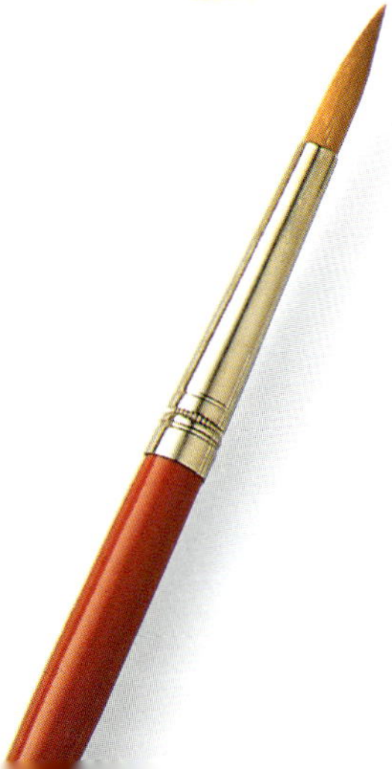

Creating shapes with flat washes

A flat wash can be used in a small area of a painting, or to produce a coloured ground to work on. In this instance, the latter option has been taken.

The yellow wash looks very flat.

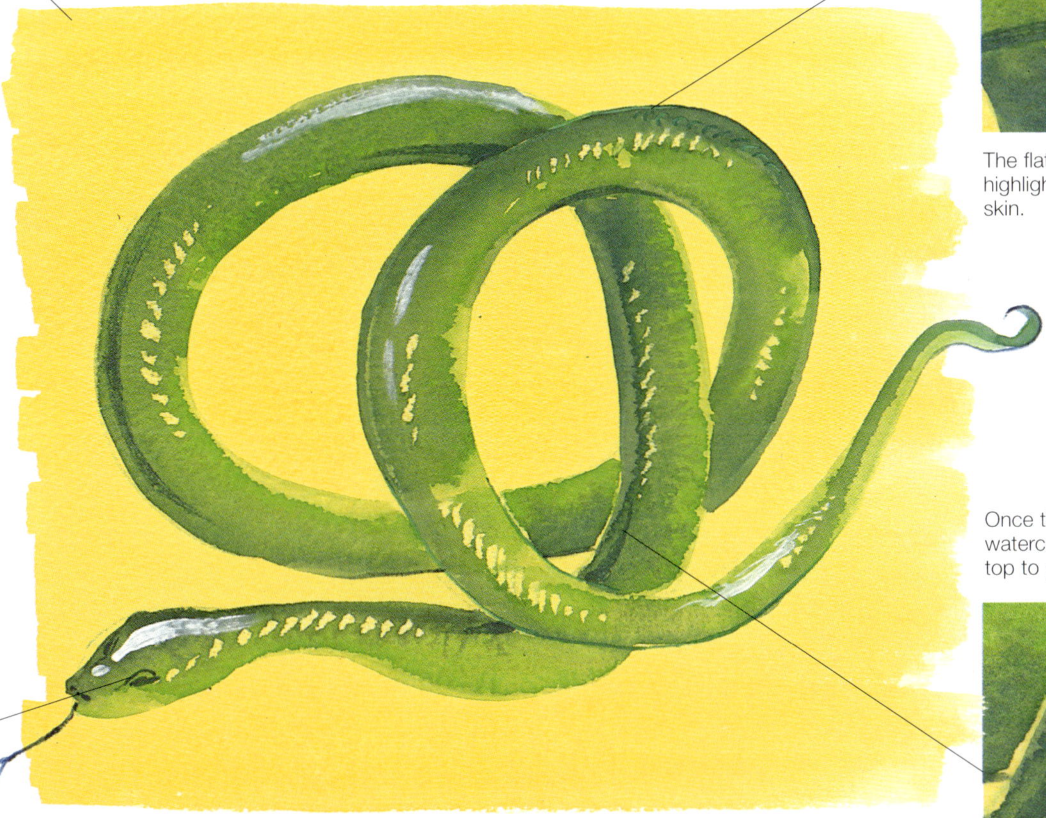

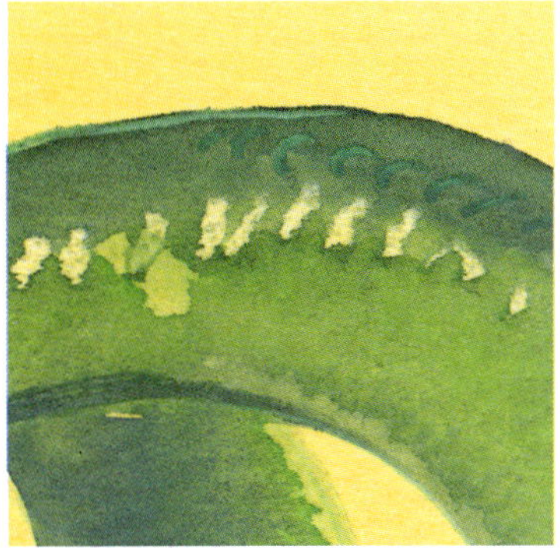

The flat wash colour is used to highlight the pattern in the snake's skin.

Fine details are added once the picture is completely dry.

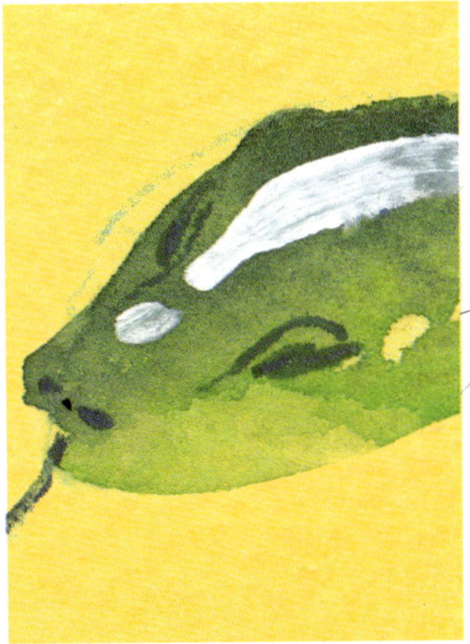

Once the wash is dry, layers of green watercolour paint are added over the top to produce the snake motif.

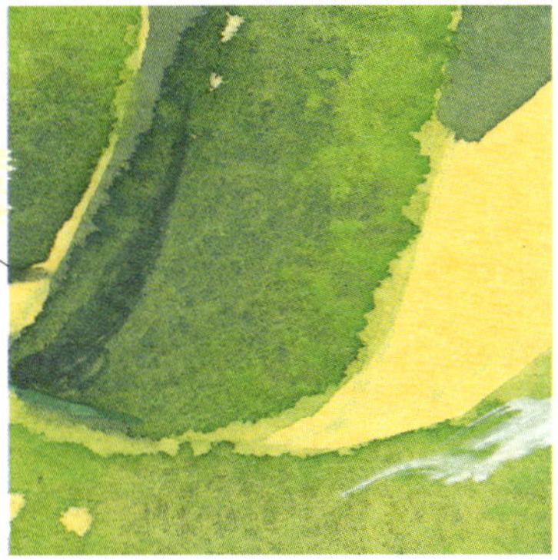

Gradated Washes

A gradated wash is produced in a similar way to a flat wash: by working a loaded brush steadily down the watercolour paper, applying paint back and forth in horizontal lines. However, instead of reloading the brush with paint of the same colour intensity, apply increasingly dilute colour so that the wash pales as it develops. The difficulty lies in creating a smooth transition from dark to light without letting the wash develop in a series of stripes. Work on dry paper so that the different tones don't blend together completely and flatten out, but make each brushstroke very wet so that they blend a little along the edges.

The gradated wash is useful for painting any subject that requires a subtle, yet progressive change in colour from light to dark: clear skies and open expanses of water are good examples. For a wash that is lighter at the top than at the bottom, apply the wash and when it is dry turn the paper upside down and continue with the painting.

Once you have mastered the basic technique, try some variations. For example, grade a sky wash from dark to light towards the horizon line, and then begin a second colour wash that grades from light to dark for the landscape in the foreground. You could also try grading from a dark colour into a different, paler colour to achieve the illusion of depth or range of field.

Laying a gradated wash
Place your board at a slight angle and begin the wash by painting a line of watercolour from left to right across the top edge of the paper. Do not lift off the brush when you get to the end of the first line. Instead, turn the handle around and work back across the paper. Work backwards and forwards across and down the paper, picking up on the lower edge of the previous line of paint as you allow the wash to descend. Rather than refilling the brush with paint at the end of each third line, however, load it with paint and water so that the colour becomes more dilute. At the bottom of the paper, the wash should be transparent. Do not rework the wash while it is still wet. As it dries, the particles in the pigment will settle into the surface of the watercolour paper.

Helpful Tips
- Practise painting washes on rough pieces of paper before using good-quality watercolour paper, as you will not perfect the technique on your first try.

Landscape and washes
A simple, atmospheric landscape can be captured using just two gradated washes. The paint melts and furs into the paper, giving the picture a misty appearance suggestive of an autumn dawn. Specks of white paper reflect through the paint, emphasizing its translucent qualities.

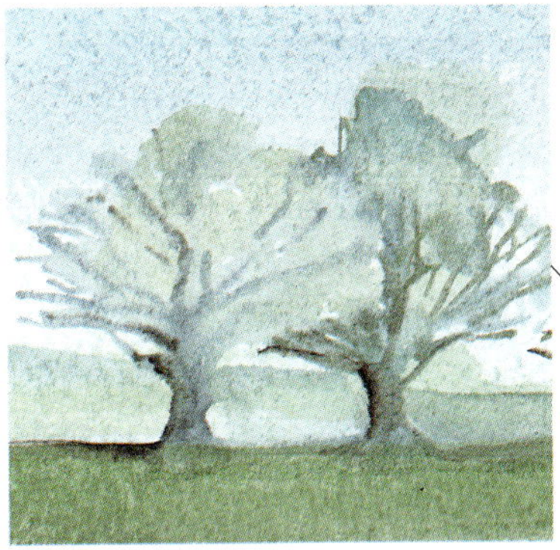

While the two gradated washes are still damp, use a no. 4 brush to 'tickle' in the simple shapes of the trees. The paint will fur into and soften the surrounding washes.

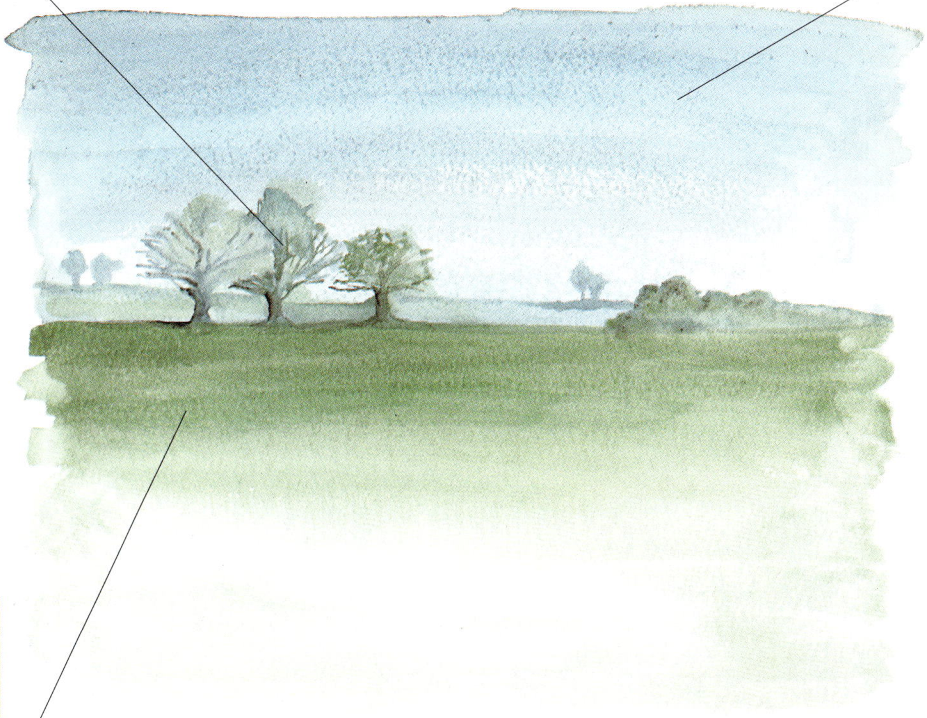

In some areas, the paper shows through the paint, creating a lively and sparkling surface. This will occur most noticeably when the brush and paint are quite dry.

Grade the wash from the very dark to the paler by adding more water to the paint as you develop the wash down the paper.

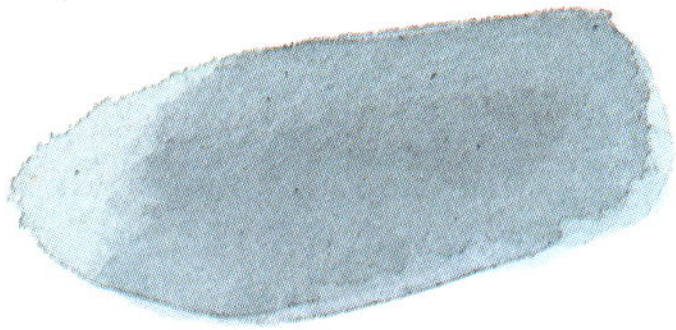

Helpful Tips
- A 2.5 cm (1 in) brush is the most effective wash brush. Smaller brushes can be used, but the wash will not look so smooth. Use whichever two colours suit the subject, but to create a subtle gradation choose tonally compatible hues.

Variegated Washes

There will be times when you won't want to create a flat or gradated wash of colour, but will still want to cover large areas of the paper with washes of paint to give a 'ground' or colour to your paper, before adding detail over the top. In situations where different tones blend together over a single area – for example in a wide open space such as an ocean or hayfield – you may wish to paint a more uneven wash. This is when the variegated wash comes into its own.

Unlike its more precise relatives – the flat and gradated washes – the variegated wash has more fluid boundaries. As it varies in tone or colour, it can be used in many contexts. The variegated wash can be made from one or more colours, and these can vary in strength and consistency. This does not make the technique random. It is possible to paint controlled variegated washes that dry smooth and blended. Alternatively, feel free to experiment with less controlled effects. Variegated washes don't conform to rules. Random mark-making can create the most effective results, especially as watercolours interact particularly well where they are allowed to bleed into one another on the paper. And additional colours can be dropped into a variegated wash to make even more interesting, if random, textures and colour mixes.

Laying a variegated wash
Variegated washes can appear in many forms – they do not have to run vertically in stripes across the paper.

This variegated wash is similar in technique and effect to a gradated wash. It simply incorporates a range of different colours as it works down the paper.

Here more colours are added to make a more variable wash.

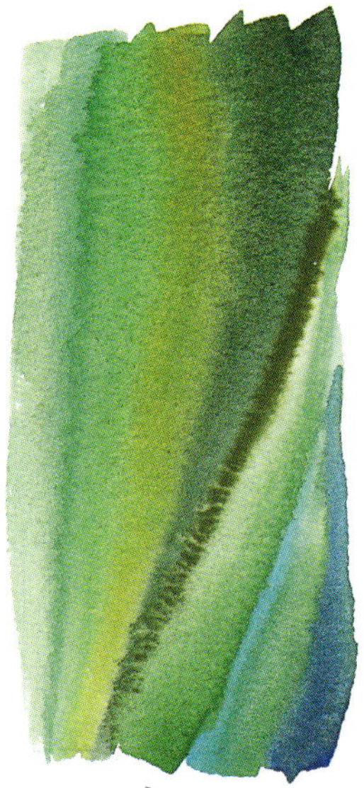

In this instance, the paint is washed across the paper in diagonal sweeps to produce a spiral effect.

Variegated washes can be made in just one colour, the intensity of which is varied throughout the application.

The degree of control that can be exercised over variegated washes will rely, to a degree, on the wetness of the paper. The damper the paper, the further and quicker the colour will spread and the more difficult the wash will be to control. To keep control, use slightly damp paper and respray the surface with a water diffuser as you work.

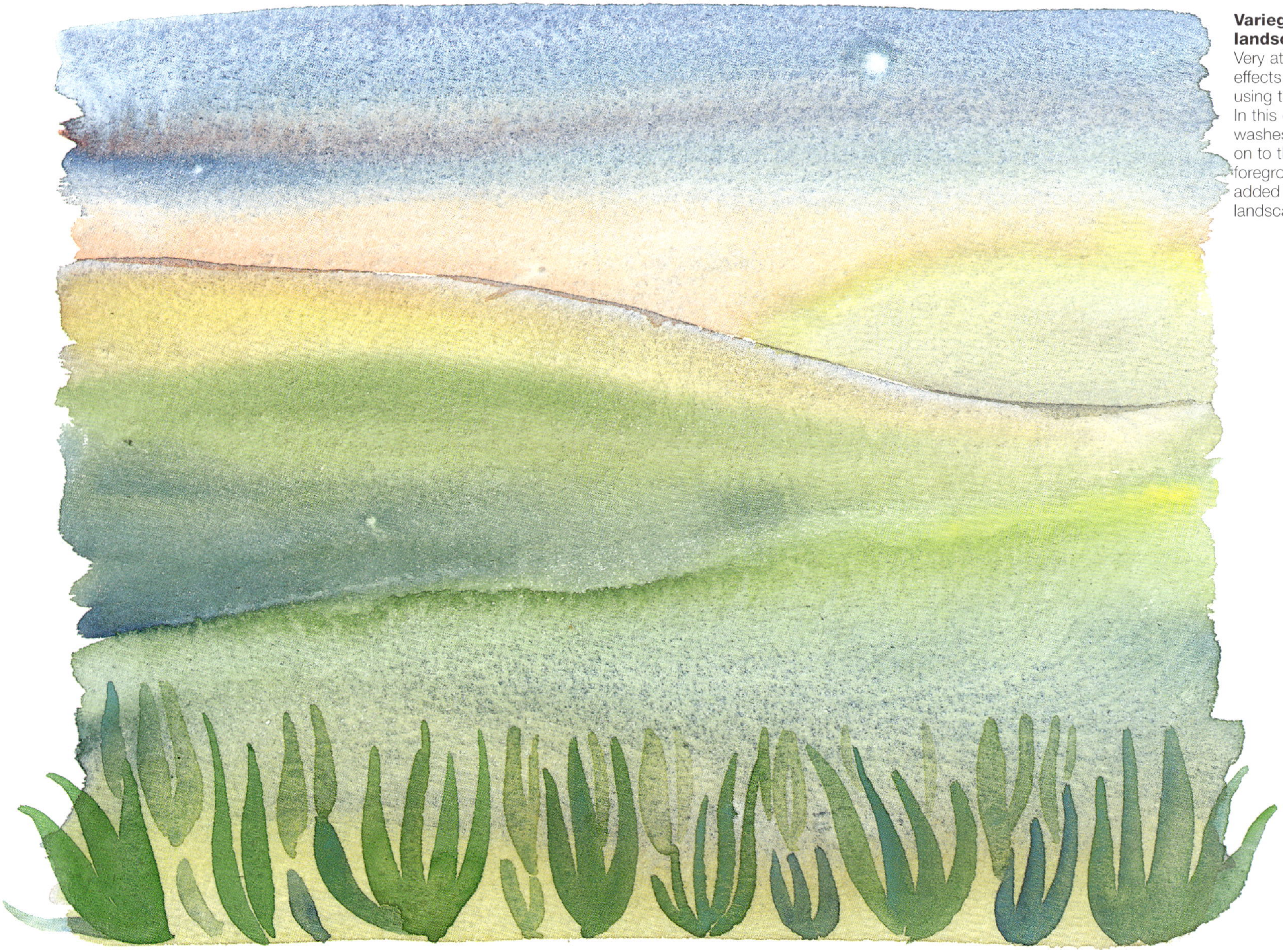

Variegated-wash landscape
Very atmospheric landscape effects can be produced by using the variegated wash. In this example, a series of washes have been overlaid on to the paper. Once dry, foreground details are added to substantiate the landscape scene.

Wet into Wet

Painting wet into wet shows the watercolour medium at its most tantalizing. The technique speaks for itself – new colours are laid down while the previous applications are still wet, and the wet colours melt into one another on the paper. Edges will always be soft around areas of colour that have been applied to wet paper; and the wetter the paper, the softer the edges will be.

Wet into wet is a semi-random technique because the direction that the paint will choose to take on wet paper can never be completely controlled, although if the paper is tilted up at an angle, then the direction in which the wash will run can be controlled to an extent by gravity. In addition, the drier the paint being applied, the less far it will spread. If the brush is dabbed on a slightly damp sponge or rag after the paint has been picked up in order to suck out excess water, the paint will only spread a little way on the paper, giving an area of intense colour that is slightly fuzzed around the edges.

When colour is dropped into a wash that is still wet, the two colours will not blend completely. The second colour will push the first out of its settled position, and the two will melt and fur together at their edges. Traces of the first colour may be absorbed into the second. These effects can be manipulated by tilting the board at different angles, or by blowing air over the paint with a straw, so forcing it to move around.

The most wonderful, marble-type effects can be produced by working wet into wet. Unfortunately, when dry, these impressions often lose their freshness and sparkle. To retain them, don't mix too many colours together, and try to keep wet-into-wet work fresh and spontaneous. Watercolour always dries paler than it appears when first laid down, so it is worth over-compensating for this in the initial stages of a painting by making the colours slightly more intense than you actually want them to appear.

Paintings can be produced using just the wet-into-wet technique – Turner often did this. The method is most effective for capturing such scenes as he depicted – misty mornings, storms at sea, the changing cloud formations in a sky. However, pure wet-into-wet can lack real form, and once you have achieved the desired effect, you may wish to overlay subsequent washes on dry areas to add structure and details.

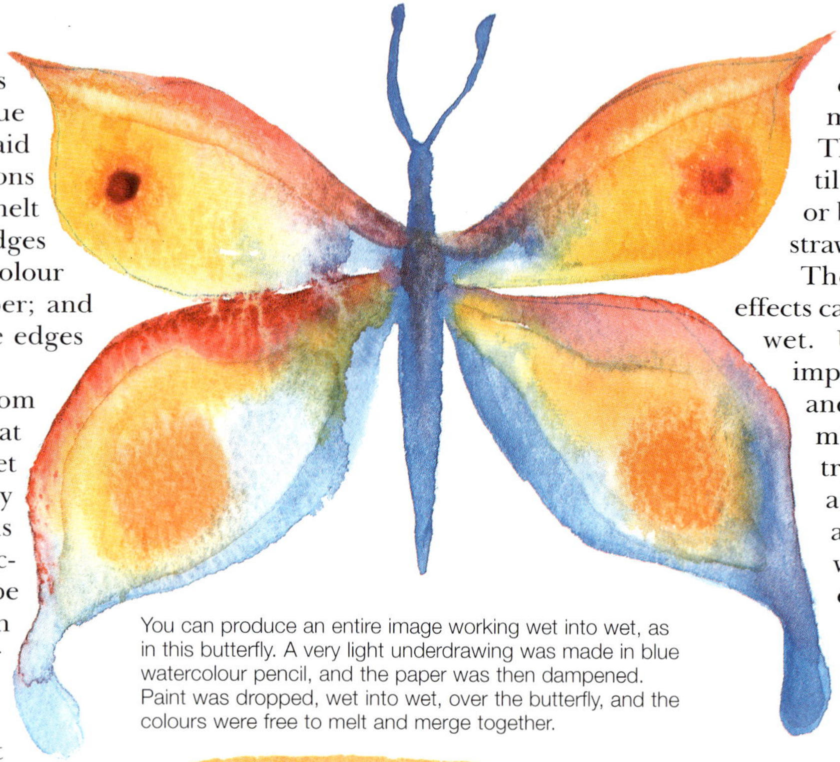

You can produce an entire image working wet into wet, as in this butterfly. A very light underdrawing was made in blue watercolour pencil, and the paper was then dampened. Paint was dropped, wet into wet, over the butterfly, and the colours were free to melt and merge together.

Helpful Tips

- Wet-into-wet effects can be used in local areas in a painting – it does not have to act as a 'ground' over the entire surface.
- Different degrees of wetness will produce varied effects – the wetter the paint, the less control you will have!
- If you want to continue working wet-into-wet after the paint has dried, use a spray diffuser or an old plant-spray filled with clean water to re-wet the surface.

LEFT Lay down a flat block of your first colour, then drop a second colour into the middle of it while the first block is still very wet. Watch as the second colour melts and furs into the first to produce a soft, fresh effect.

LEFT Dampen the watercolour paper. Using three colours, paint wet lines of watercolour adjacent to one another, and watch as they spread and melt into one another round the edges.

LEFT Again, dampen the watercolour paper. Now drop four colours on to the paper in a square, and watch how they merge and blend to produce additional colours where their edges melt together. There are no hard edges between the colours shown.

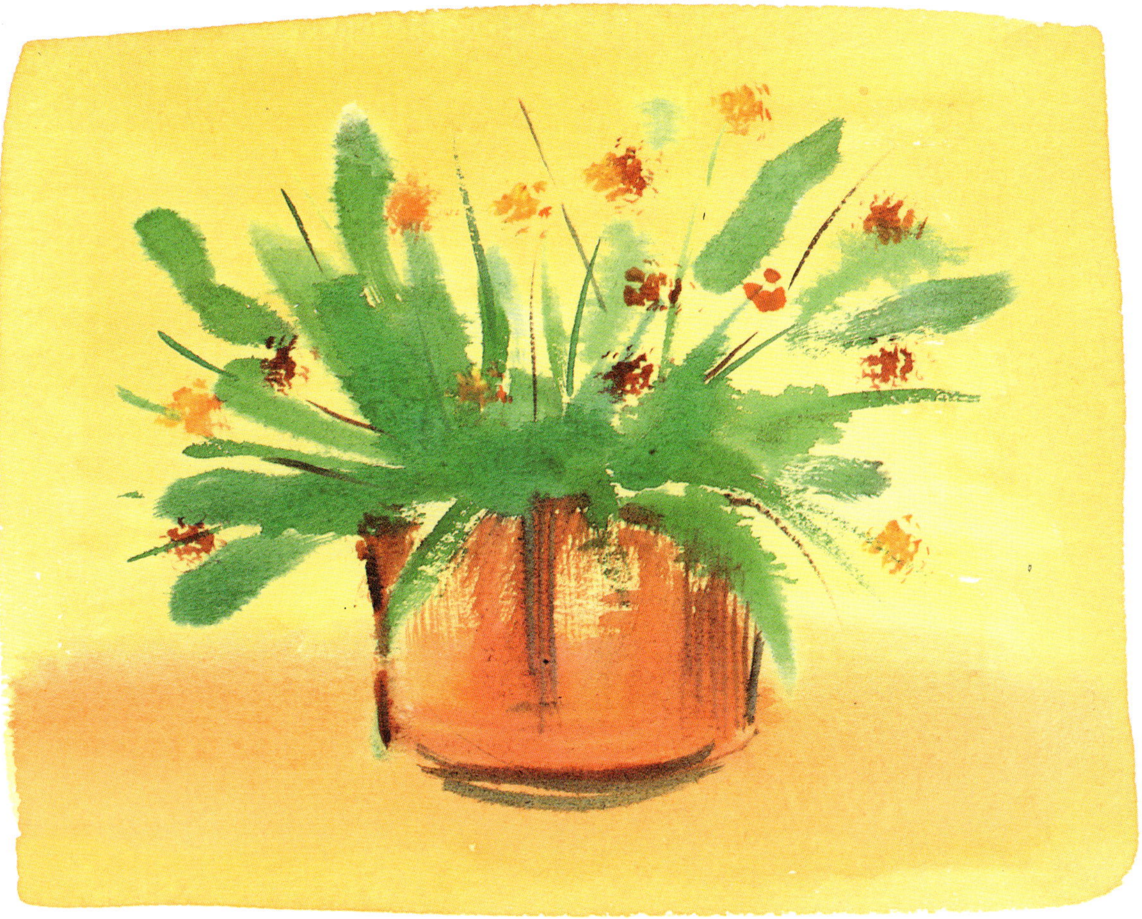

ABOVE Intense colour can be created by using a dry brush loaded with paint on a wet background wash. To do this, first lay a wash. While it is still wet – you have to work quickly! – dampen the brush, dry it quickly on a clean cloth or sponge, load it with colour, and paint your picture. The new colour will bleed into the background wash, creating this intense effect.

RIGHT Different degrees of wetness in the three versions of this landscape produce very different results. In the first, the tree has been painted straight away while the background is still wet. The background is semi-dry in the second, while in the third it has been left to dry completely before the tree is added.

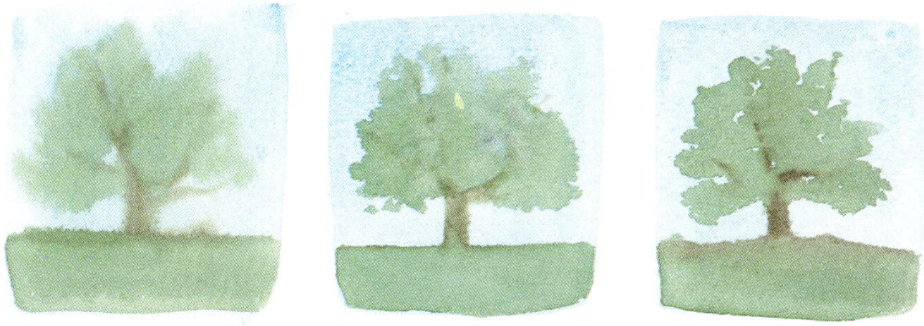

Wet on Dry

One colour laid over another once the first has dried produces very different effects to those obtained by working wet into wet. Unlike the previous method, with wet on dry painting the effects and appearance of the paint can be controlled with reasonable consistency because watercolour paints do not spread across dry paper but sit where they are put, and dry with hard edges.

Watercolour paint is transparent, or semi-transparent, when dry. Any dry colour on the paper will have an effect on the colour and tone of those laid over the top. Each layer of colour will darken the tone of that area of the painting. The colours achieved by laying a wet colour over a dry one will differ from those that are pre-mixed on the palette. Think of the effects that can be achieved with layers of different-coloured tissue papers, and you will begin to understand how watercolour works.

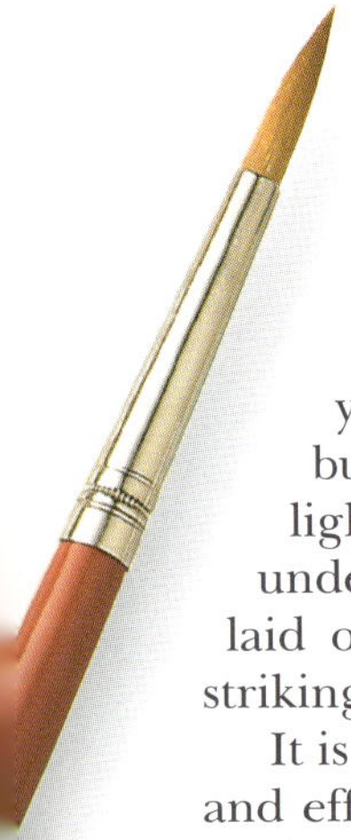

Because watercolour is translucent, you should work from light to dark, building up tones slowly and subtly. If light colours are laid over dark, the underlying colours will dominate those laid over them and the effect will be less striking.

It is worth experimenting with the colours and effects that can be achieved by building up layers of colour over dry paint. Ensure that any one colour is completely dry before you apply a second one over the top of it, or the two colours will fur together. It is not wise to use more than three or, in special cases, four overlays of colour as the medium will start to lose its spontaneity and freshness.

You can add interest to wet on dry watercolour work by varying the degrees of dryness or wetness on your painting. Sometimes furred effects will provide a new dimension to a painting.

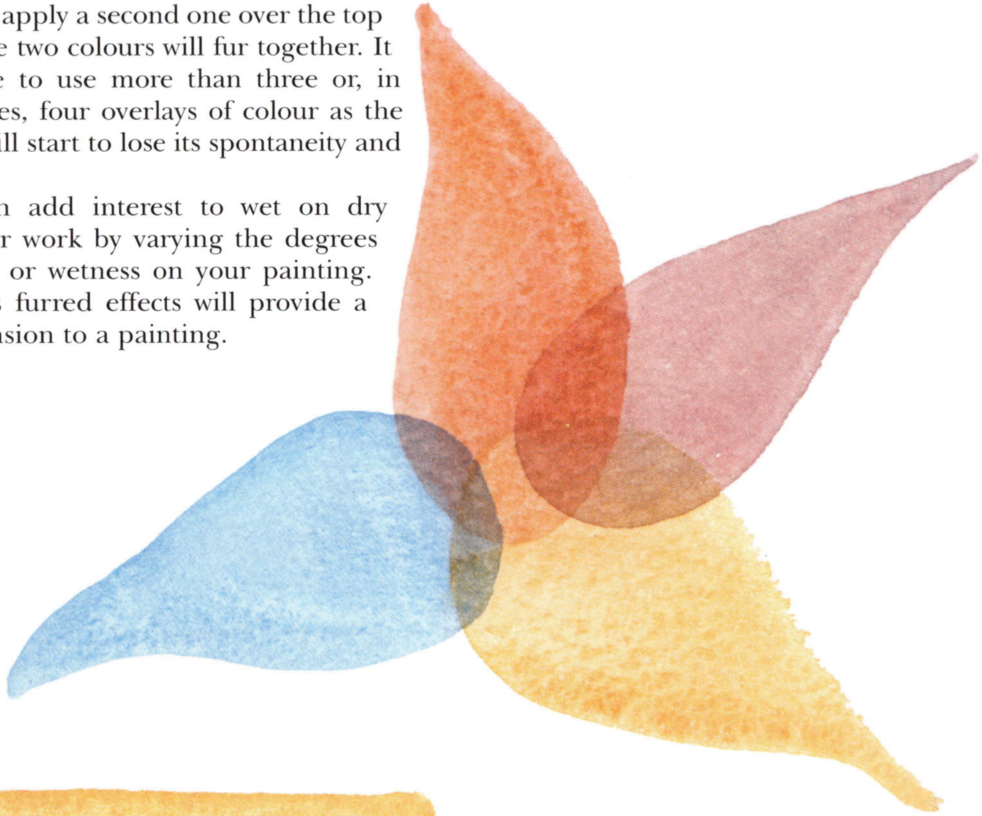

Helpful Tips

- Leave areas of the paper free of paint to allow the white of the paper to show through and read as highlights.
- Speed up the drying process by using a hairdryer to dry each layer of colour.

ABOVE The more colours you overlay wet on dry, the greater the tonal range you will achieve with the paints. Make sure each layer is completely dry before you add another to keep the results crisp and clean. Varying degrees of intensity can be achieved by layering colours.

First the background wash is laid wet into wet, then allowed to dry completely before details are added.

Layering washes

Working wet on dry allows you to maintain complete control over the watercolour paint. Wet-into-wet techniques are far less manageable when you are first starting out. Here the layers of colour remain visible through the sails and boat, yet do not detract from the overall impression.

Helpful Tips

- Test how dry your watercolour paint is by touching the paper with the back of your hand, which will detect any remaining dampness far more effectively than your fingertips.

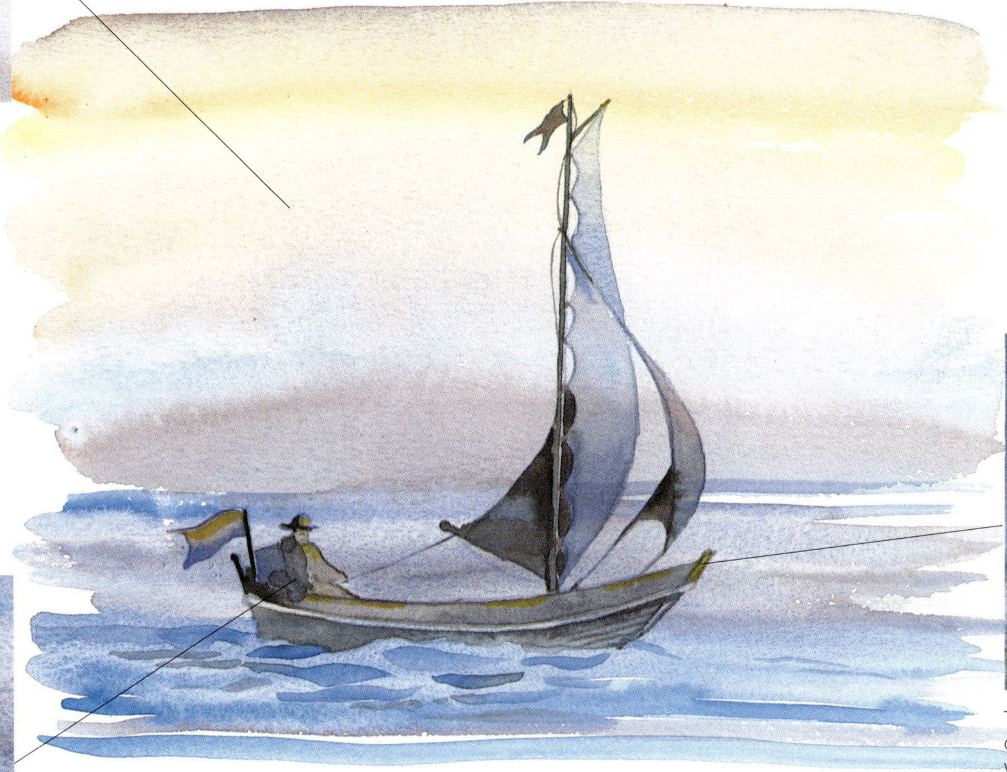

See how a few simple lines are all it takes to give the impression of a figure on the boat, added wet on dry at the end of the painting process.

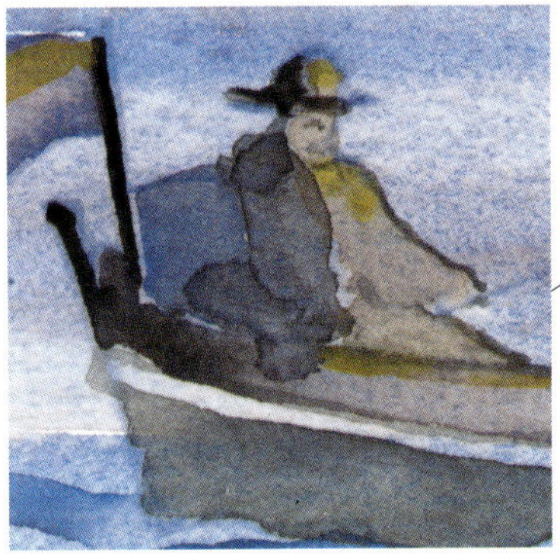

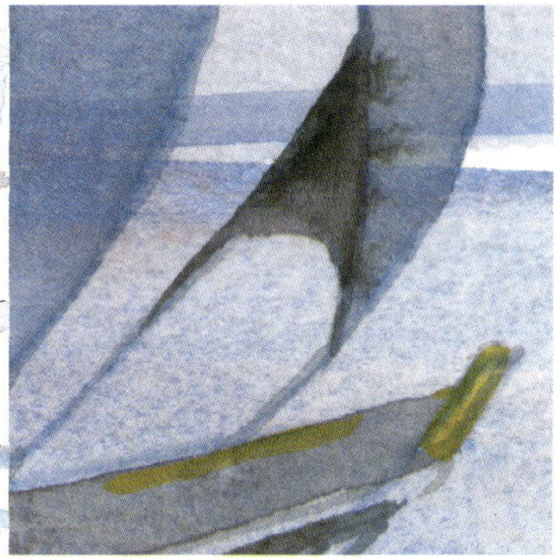

The main sail and boat are painted over the top of the underlying dry wash, using a fine brush and very dilute watercolour paint, with great care and attention. Each layer is allowed to dry before another is added over the top.

Masking Out

Although watercolour paint is translucent and allows the white of the paper to show through, there will be times when you want to leave areas of the paper completely free of paint, perhaps to create bright highlights, or to save an area of the paper for a later application of paint. As watercolour does not like to sit still, if areas to be kept white are not masked off, the paint will seep into them and ruin the desired effect.

There are a number of ways to mask out areas of the composition. A simple paper mask can be used to block out an area of the paper, which is fine as long as the paint is not allowed to come too close to the edges of the mask or it may seep underneath. Alternatively, artist's masking tape can be used by sticking it down on to those areas that you wish to block out. This method is fine for large areas of paper, but is not so well suited to very selective masking. The tape can be cut with a scalpel to create shapes along its edges, but this is not conducive to blocking more fiddly details.

The most suitable choice has to be artist's masking fluid – a medium created specifically for this task. It is the perfect antidote to watercolour paint, as it creates a watertight skin over the paper so that paint cannot seep underneath it. Tinted masking fluid is available and makes the task even easier as you can still see the fluid even when you have painted over it. Masking fluid is applied in exactly the same way as paint – with a brush or another painting tool of your choice – so quite fine areas can be blocked out. It is a thicker substance than watercolour paint, however, so cannot be used for hairline masks. In such instances, scratch out the colour with a scalpel blade, once the paint has dried. This will produce finer and more accurate results.

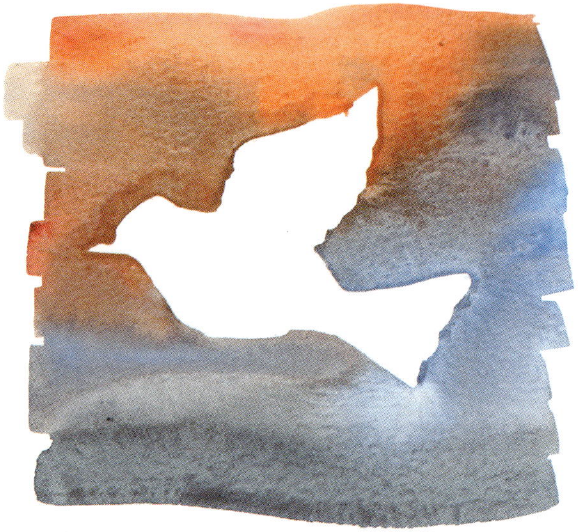

Using a simple paper mask, you can block out an area of your watercolour paper before overlaying washes. You will not be able to produce very fine details around the edges of the mask, however. Use this technique where sharp edges are not necessary.

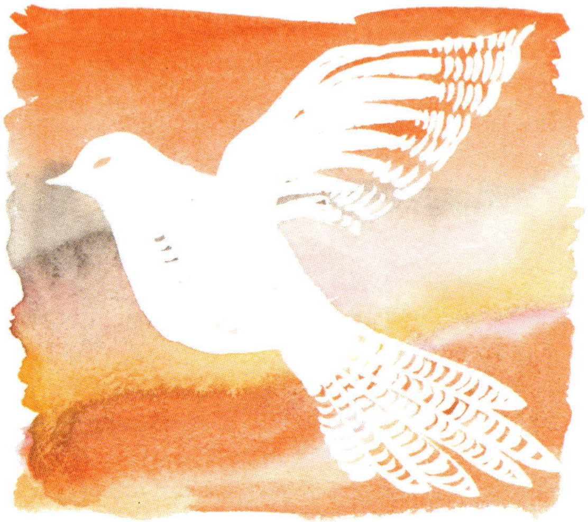

For much more detailed work, you will need to employ masking fluid. In this instance, masking fluid has been used to block out the shape of the white bird. Note how the dark areas between the tail and wing feathers have been left unmasked, so that the overlaid washes of paint can seep into these details and add form and texture.

Once you have painted over the mask, whether it be fluid or tape, ensure that the paint dries out completely before you remove it. Touch the paper with the back of a hand to test for any remaining dampness. Try not to leave tinted masking fluid on the paper for more than a few hours, as it could stain the paper if left for too long. When using tape, peel it away from the paper slowly so it doesn't tear the surface of the paper.

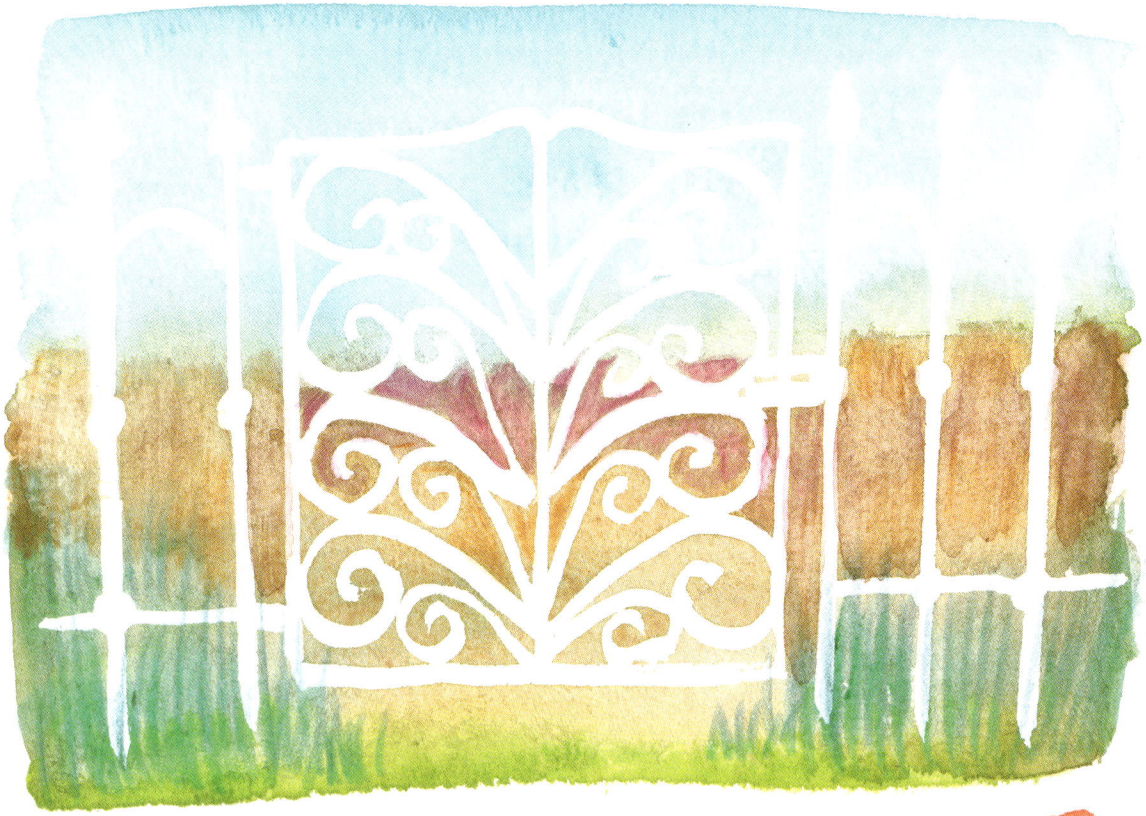

LEFT You can use masking fluid to produce fine, white lines and intricate edges, such as this gate-post. Ensure that the paint has dried out completely before you remove the masking fluid, or you might damage the sharpness of the edges.

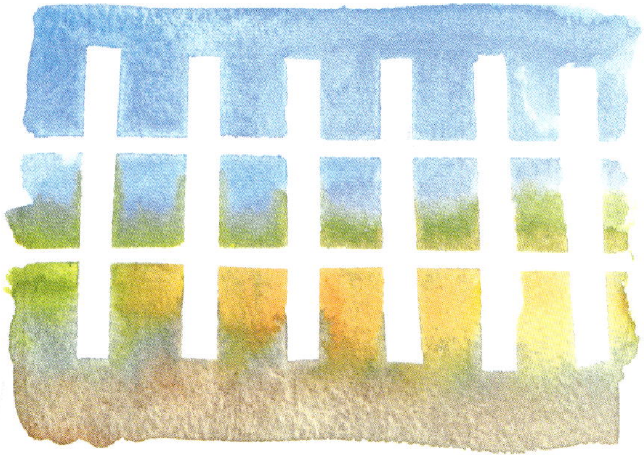

ABOVE Using masking tape in strips, you can block out very definite lines, as in this fence. Once the paint has dried, remove the masking tape. Be careful to pull it away from the paper gently, or it might damage the paper surface. Once you have removed the masking tape, you can fill the white area with paint.

How masking fluid works

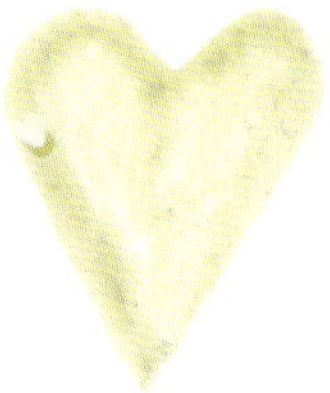

1 Paint the shape you want to mask out using masking fluid and a brush. Leave it to dry.

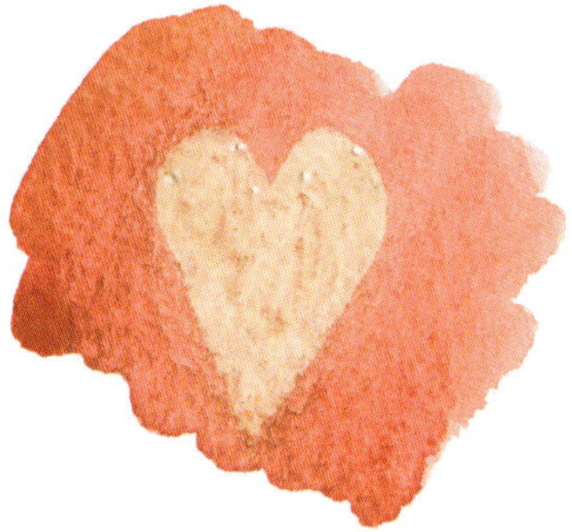

2 Wash paint over the masking fluid and surrounding paper, as required.

3 Leave the paint to dry, then rub the masking fluid away to reveal the white paper beneath.

Helpful Tips

- A word of warning: once masking fluid has been applied to a painting, the brush should be washed out immediately, or it will be ruined. Use warm water and soap to do this, and make sure that the brush is really clean between the bristles. It is worth keeping an old brush handy for this task alone.

Pen and Ink

Although the unexpected effects that watercolour washes provide can be very enjoyable, there may be times when you want to tighten up a painting with a little more structure than the paint alone can provide. An underdrawing can help. It can be done with pencil, but to produce lines that have more substance, and do not look simply like an underlying sketch, experiment with pen and ink.

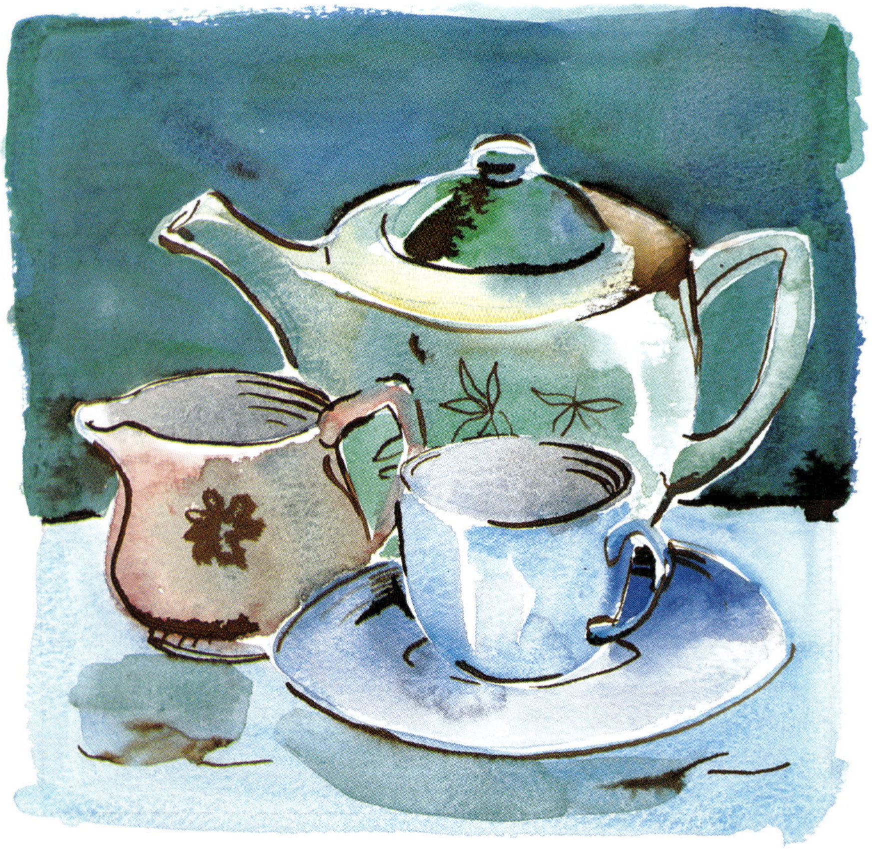

You can use pen and ink in conjunction with watercolour to produce less definite lines and areas of colour. In this example, brown ink has been used as a wet medium in conjunction with washes of watercolour, to produce softer contours and less definite edges. The pen-and-ink marks continue to provide a structure to the loose washes, too.

Pen and ink lines have been associated with watercolour painting for hundreds of years. They can be done either with water-soluble ink, ensuring that the drawing blends into any wet paint added over the top, or with waterproof ink, which will stain the paper and remain stable, however much paint is applied over it. A highly detailed underdrawing can be done with pen and ink, or it can be used to add fine detailing to a painting while it is in progress. Pen-and-ink lines can even be introduced at the end of a painting to add a few final touches, or to redefine a few areas.

Pen-and-ink lines don't need to remain fine. They can be blended into the paint while it is still wet to produce interesting shadows and dark tonal areas, or the ink can be diluted with distilled water for softer effects. Alternatively, ink can stippled onto areas of the picture by holding the pen at a right angle and dotting over the surface of the paper. Crosshatching lines will produce a further interesting effect.

When choosing a nib, it is worth investing in a good-quality steel one that won't blot ink over the paper. Fine lines can be created by holding the pen as if you were writing, and wider marks by turning it and using the nib on its side. By using both techniques in conjunction, you can produce a wide range of effects.

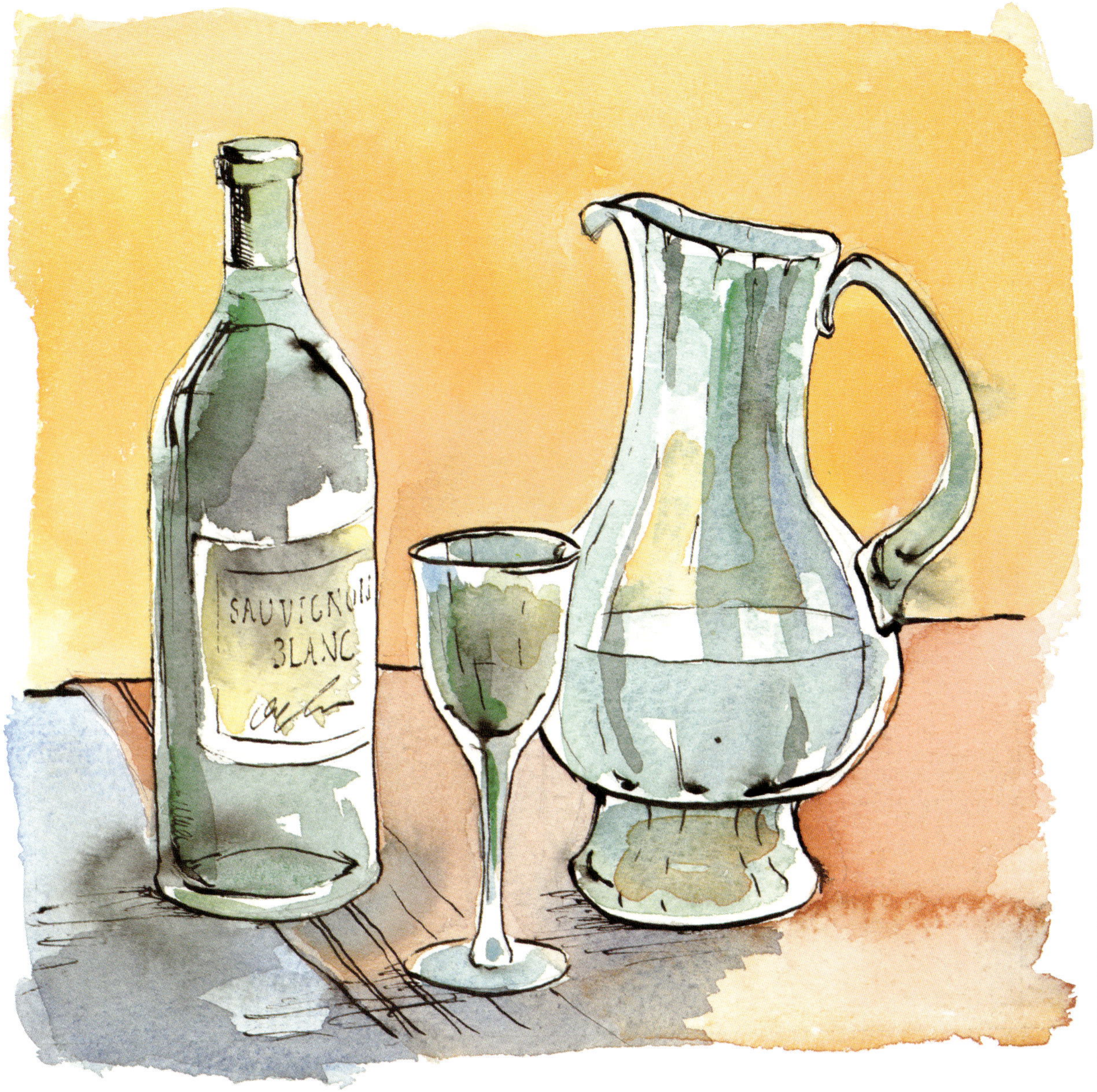

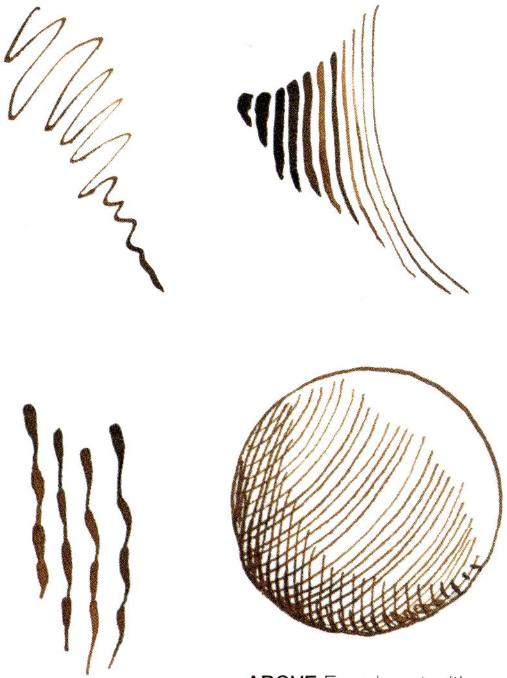

ABOVE Experiment with pen and ink to see what marks you can make. If you turn the nib on its side you will produce far thicker lines than if you hold it upright and use the point. Here are some ideas to get you started. Remember, too, that you can smudge water-soluble ink and use it to produce areas of shadow and tone.

LEFT You can use pen and ink as an outlining instrument, as in this example. Use permanent black ink to draw in the structure of the objects in your still life. Once dry, wash in watercolour paint over the top. See how the pen and ink has produced a sharp outline for each of the objects, and given the painting a tight structure.

Body Colour

Watercolour's natural transparency is one of its greatest attributes – in most situations. There may be occasions, however, when you feel limited by the translucent range of colours and would like to add a more opaque element to your work. In such instances, help is close at hand. Body colour – which usually means gouache paint – is the perfect opaque partner for watercolours. Gouache is also water-based, so it can be applied in very thin, semi-opaque layers. Because it is made of a thicker, more chalky consistency than pure watercolours, however, it dries flatter on the surface of the paper than the more easily absorbed watercolour paint. As a result, it can be used to block out a watercolour mistake, or to add highlights over dark layers of watercolour that have been laid down previously. Used too freely, however, body colour can deaden the freshness of watercolours.

The most useful tube of gouache to have is Chinese white. Used sparingly, it provides the 'missing' white in the watercolour palette. Used too heavily, it will appear at odds with watercolours, and make your work look clumsy. White gouache can be mixed with any colour in your palette to give it an opacity, or semi-opacity, depending on the percentage of body colour added. As the name suggests, the gouache will add more 'body' or substance to pictures.

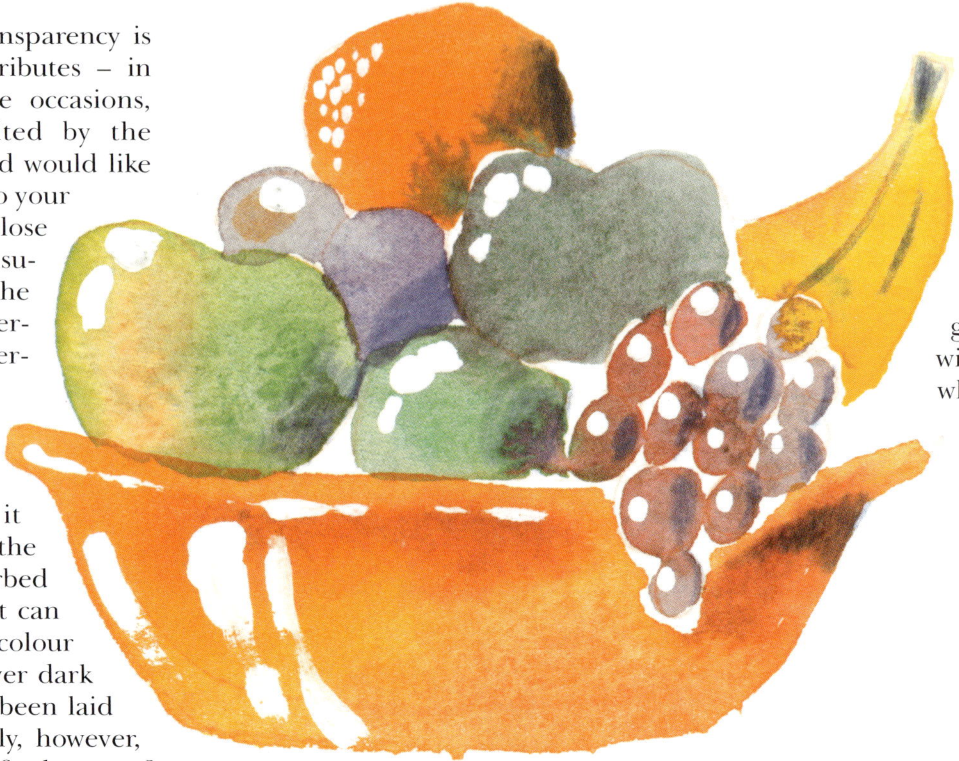

You can use body colour to produce highlights. In this case, the fruit and the bowl are brought to life by the touches of Chinese white body colour, which adds form and suggests bright highlights.

Body colour can be used thick, straight from the tube, or thinned with water for semi-opaque renderings. It is particularly well suited to subjects such as clouds or spray on the tops of waves. If you want to work on a coloured ground, mix all the colours with white gouache, or use a whole range of body colours to ensure that the ground does not dominate the colours laid over it.

Helpful Tips

- Make sure that any underlying watercolour is completely dry before adding white body colour over the top for highlights.

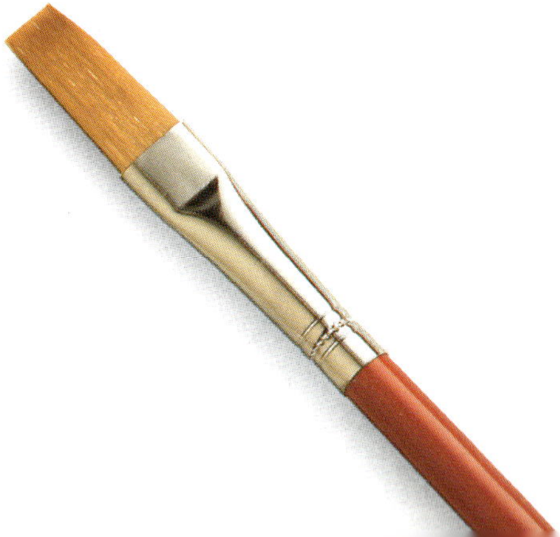

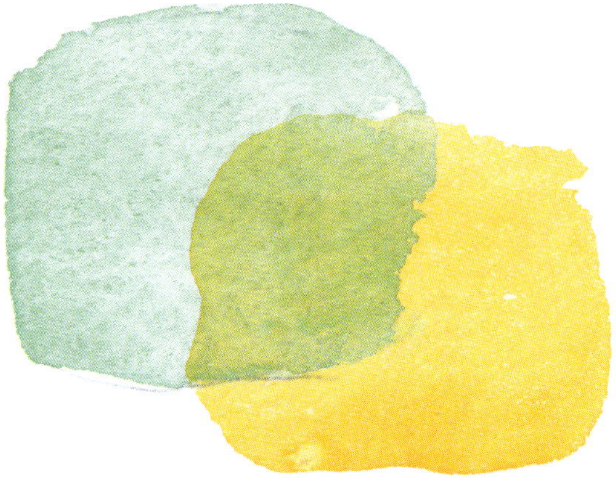

ABOVE Body colour blocks any underlying colour because it is opaque. Here, a block of lemon yellow watercolour has been painted over the top of viridian watercolour. The viridian shows through the lemon yellow paint.

ABOVE Some Chinese white body colour has been mixed in with the lemon yellow watercolour. When this is laid over the viridian green watercolour, it blocks out the underlying darker colour.

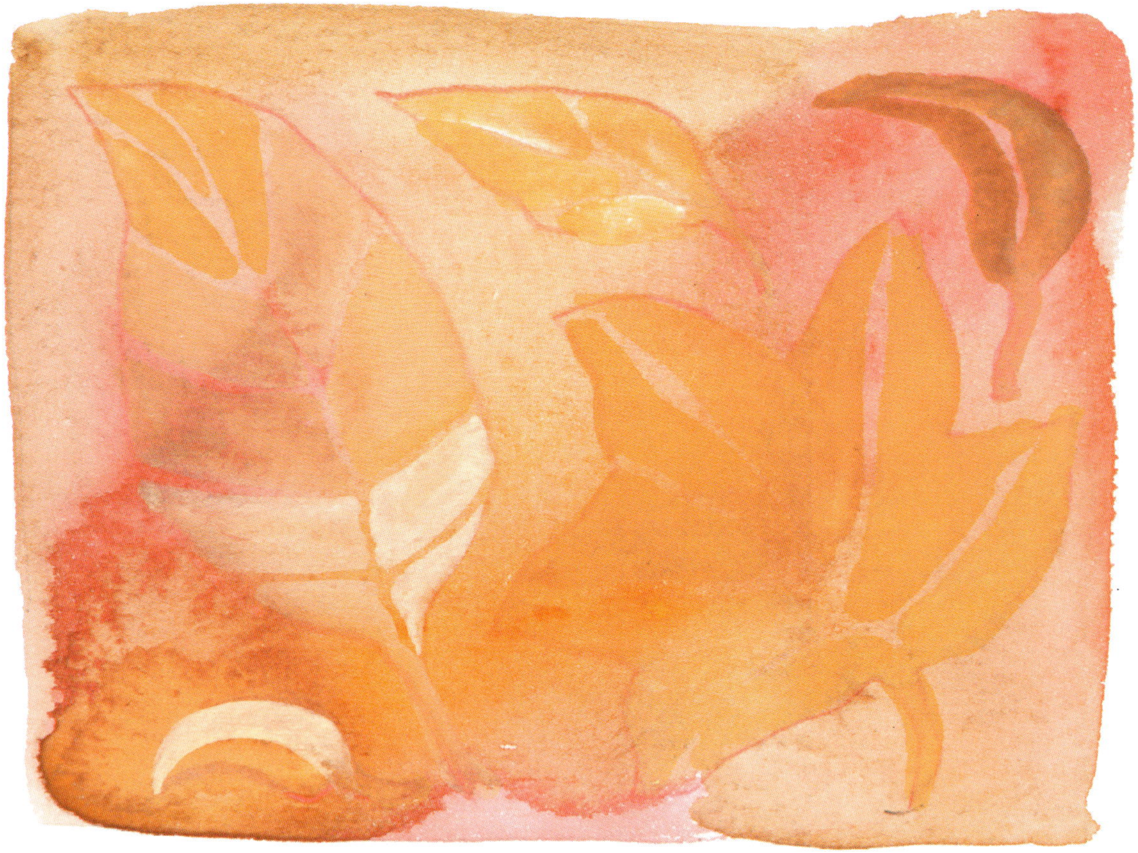

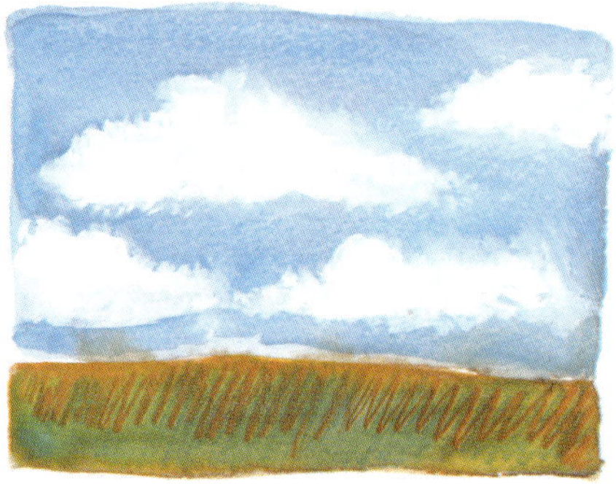

LEFT You can use body colour to overlay watercolour paint, and add in white elements. In this instance, Chinese white gouache has been painted over a damp cerulean blue wash in the sky, to produce the effect of soft, scudding clouds. Note how it completely blocks out the underlying blue colour.

ABOVE Body colour can be mixed with watercolour and used as a subtle part of your painting process. In this case, some of the washes are translucent, because no body colour has been added to the paint mixes, while others appear more opaque, because Chinese white body colour has been blended into the picture.

Lifting Out

Highlights can be made in a number of ways. Areas of the paper can be left free of paint. Alternatively, masking fluid can be used to screen the paper from paint applied over the top of it. Another method, and one that is equally useful, is lifting out. It is a more random way to produce white or very light-toned areas, and relies on working swiftly while the paint is still wet. Lifting out is exactly as it sounds. Wet paint is lifted off the paper before it has had a chance to be absorbed. It is often difficult to remove the paint completely, and traces of the pigment will probably remain. As a result, this is not the best method to use where you want to create crisp areas of white. It is a lovely method, however, for producing softer, more abstract effects.

Paint can be lifted off the paper with a variety of lightly dampened materials. A soft cotton rag is a good choice, as it can be washed out and re-used. Alternatively, try using a piece of kitchen paper or a cotton bud. Any highly absorbent material will do

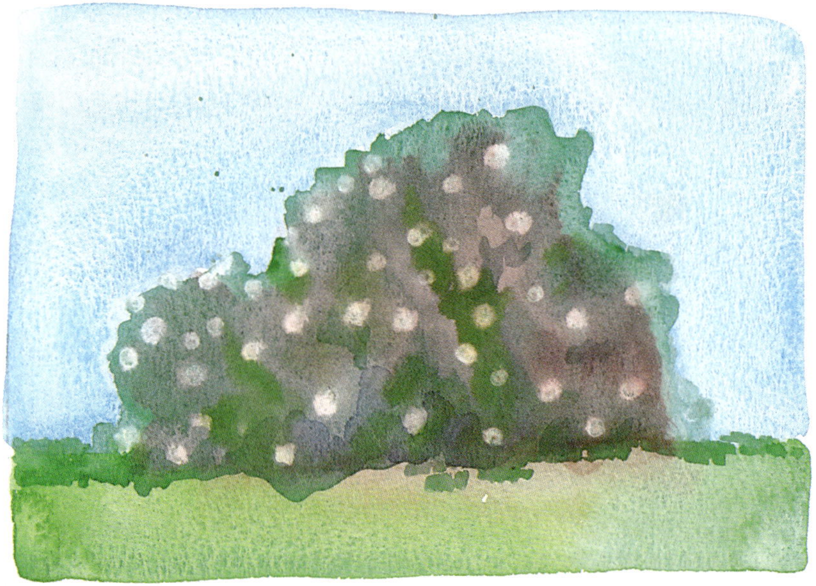

ABOVE You can use cotton buds to lift out specific areas of colour. Wet the cotton bud if you want to lift out more colour, or leave it dry for very fine lifts. In this instance, a dry cotton bud was used to lift out small dots of wet paint, so producing highlights suggestive of fruit and flowers.

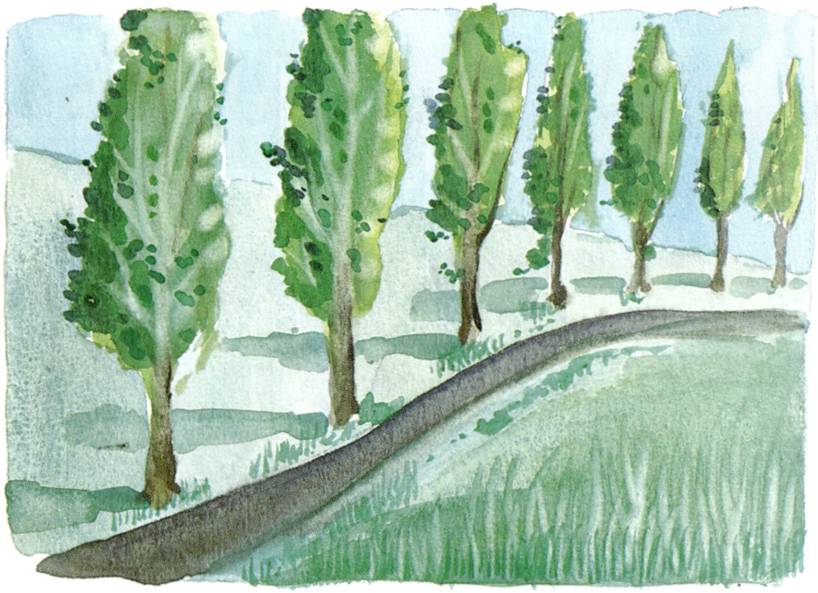

ABOVE You can use a dampened brush to lift out colour, with equal effect to any of the other techniques suggested here. See here how the tree trunks and branches have been lifted out with a wet brush to leave these details paler than the foliage.

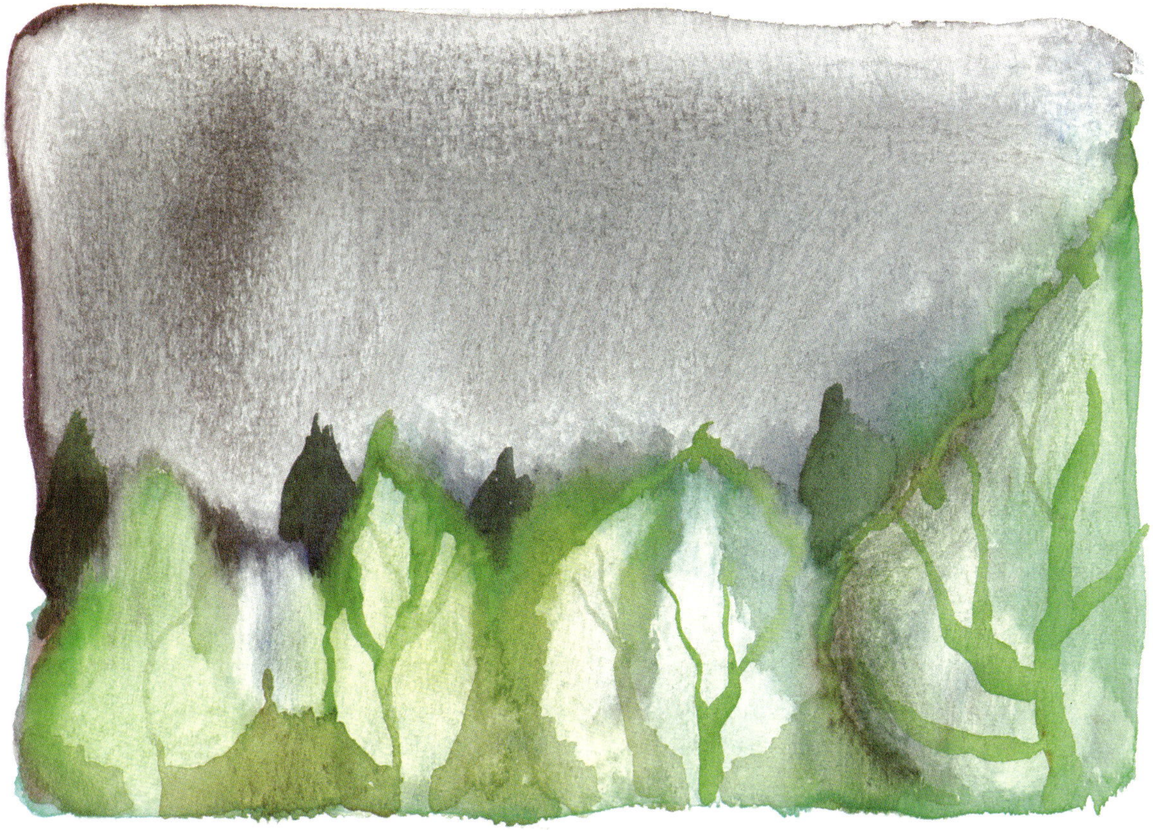

ABOVE Lift paint out with a damp cotton rag to produce misty, atmospheric areas of paler paint. Here, the rag has left soft, pinker areas of colour, because the red pigment in the colour mix used was more permanent than the grey and has already stained the surface of the paper.

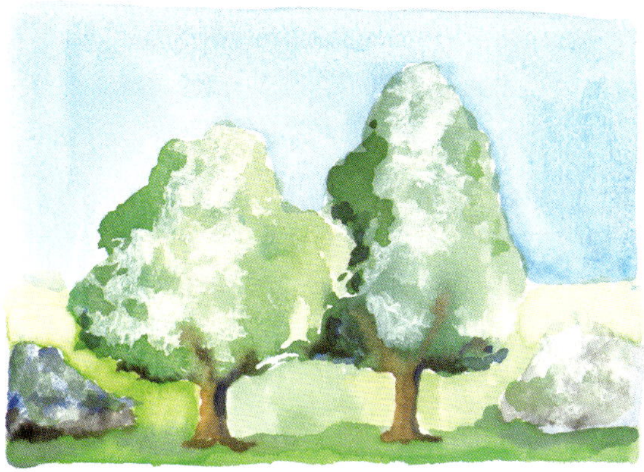

ABOVE Use crinkled-up tissue paper to produce a less soft result. In this example, the crinkled-up paper has been blotted on to wet green paint, which has then been lifted away to reveal the white of the paper below. The edges of the blotted areas are much more crinkly than in the previous example.

the trick. Cotton buds are particularly useful in instances where you want to lift out only small areas of paint. For larger areas, a rag will be more suitable.

Lots of objects do not have stark highlights, and will be better suited to soft lifting out than crisp-edged highlights. Examples include water and skies, the fur on an animal, or the sheen on fabric. Combining stark lifts and softer ones will give you further scope.

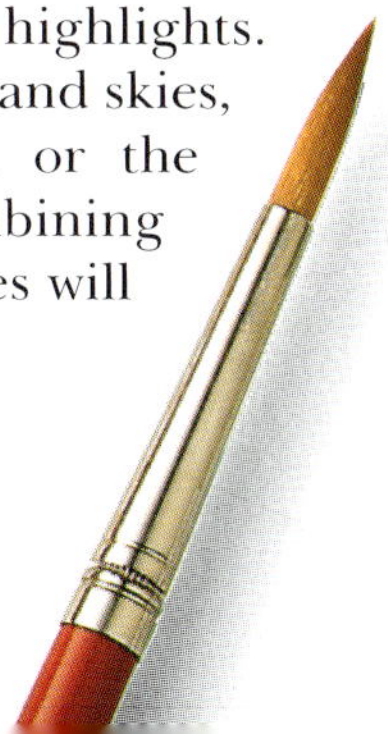

Helpful Tips

● Lifting out can be a useful trick when you have laid down too much paint – even if you aren't intending to make highlights. Just allow a rag or paper to absorb any extra paint that you have accidentally laid down before it has a chance to dry.

Watercolour Pencils

Watercolour pencils provide some of the same effects as watercolour paint. They are an invaluable asset – used either on their own or with paint.

There are a number of ways to apply watercolour pencil to a painting. They can be used dry to create underdrawings, or overdrawings, in the same way as pen and ink. Of course the colours will melt when they come into contact with wet watercolour paint, so as underdrawings they will not create such rigid foundations as permanent ink. This can be of great benefit as it provides a firm structure on which to build the painting, and which loses its force when paint is applied. Alternatively, pencils can be used to draw in details and add textures and shading over the top of dry paint. Pencils can be applied to paper and then blended with a damp brush to make them look like a wash. By combining this method with the previous ones, you will get the most versatile use out of pencils.

It is usually more convenient to apply watercolour paint than pencil as a wet medium from a palette. On location, however, it is easier to create a wet palette from a range of watercolour pencils. To do this, make some swatches of watercolour pencils on a spare piece of thick paper or card before going out. Pack them in your bag with a medium-sized brush – a no. 8 is probably the most versatile size – a jam jar of water and a sketch pad. Once settled in front of the subject, dampen the brush and work it into the swatches of colour pencil.

Try graduating from one colour into another to produce a dry, 'variegated wash' effect.

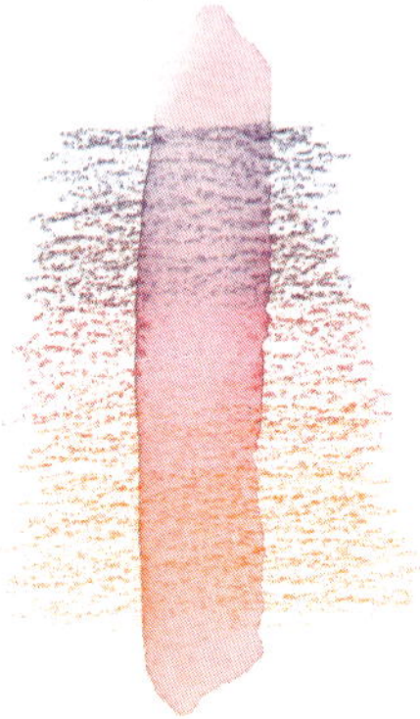

Work dry watercolour pencil over wet washes of watercolour to produce interesting textures.

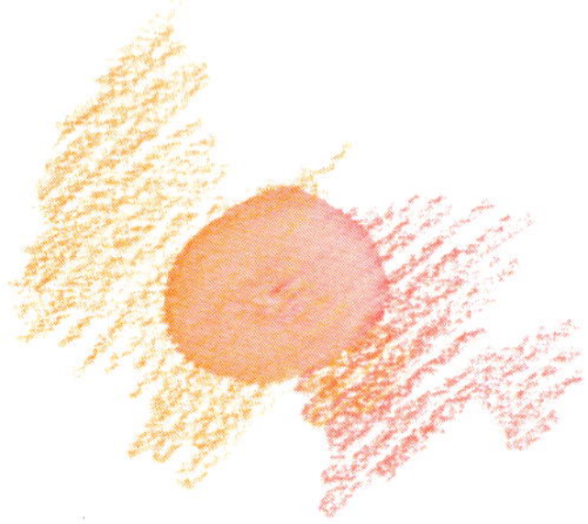

Use different colours and scribbles in conjunction with watercolour paint to achieve a sense of movement.

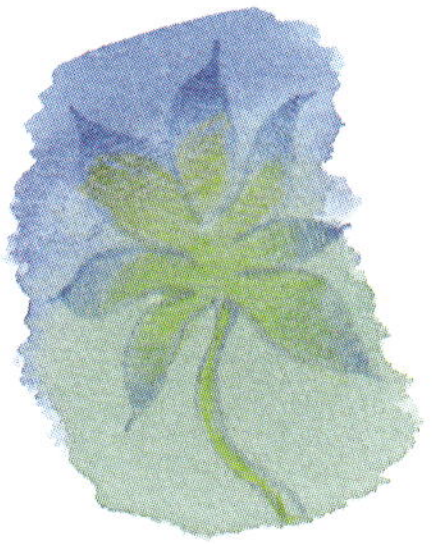

Combine wet paint with watercolour pencil to achieve definition and detail.

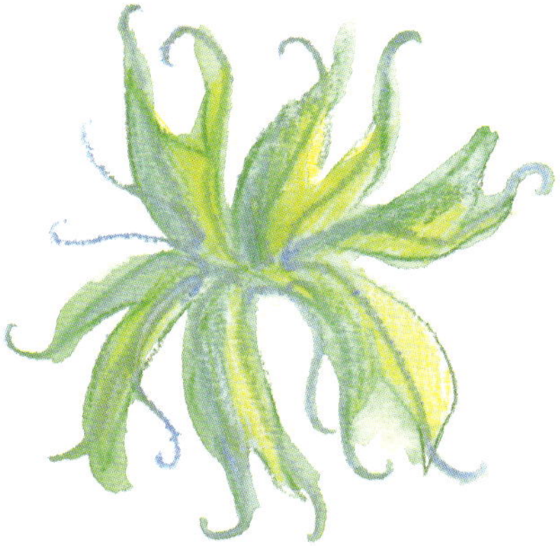

Use watercolour pencils to give the work an outline.

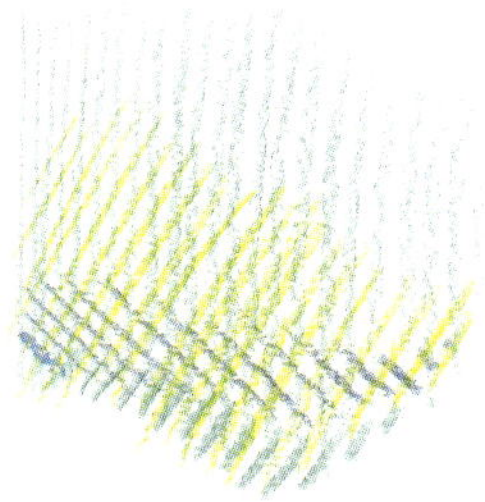

Crosshatch watercolour pencil lines to produce depth and movement.

ABOVE The range of possible pencil marks is wide, even when they are used on their own, and the range can be further increased by combining them with watercolour paint. Experiment with your pencils to see what effects you can achieve.

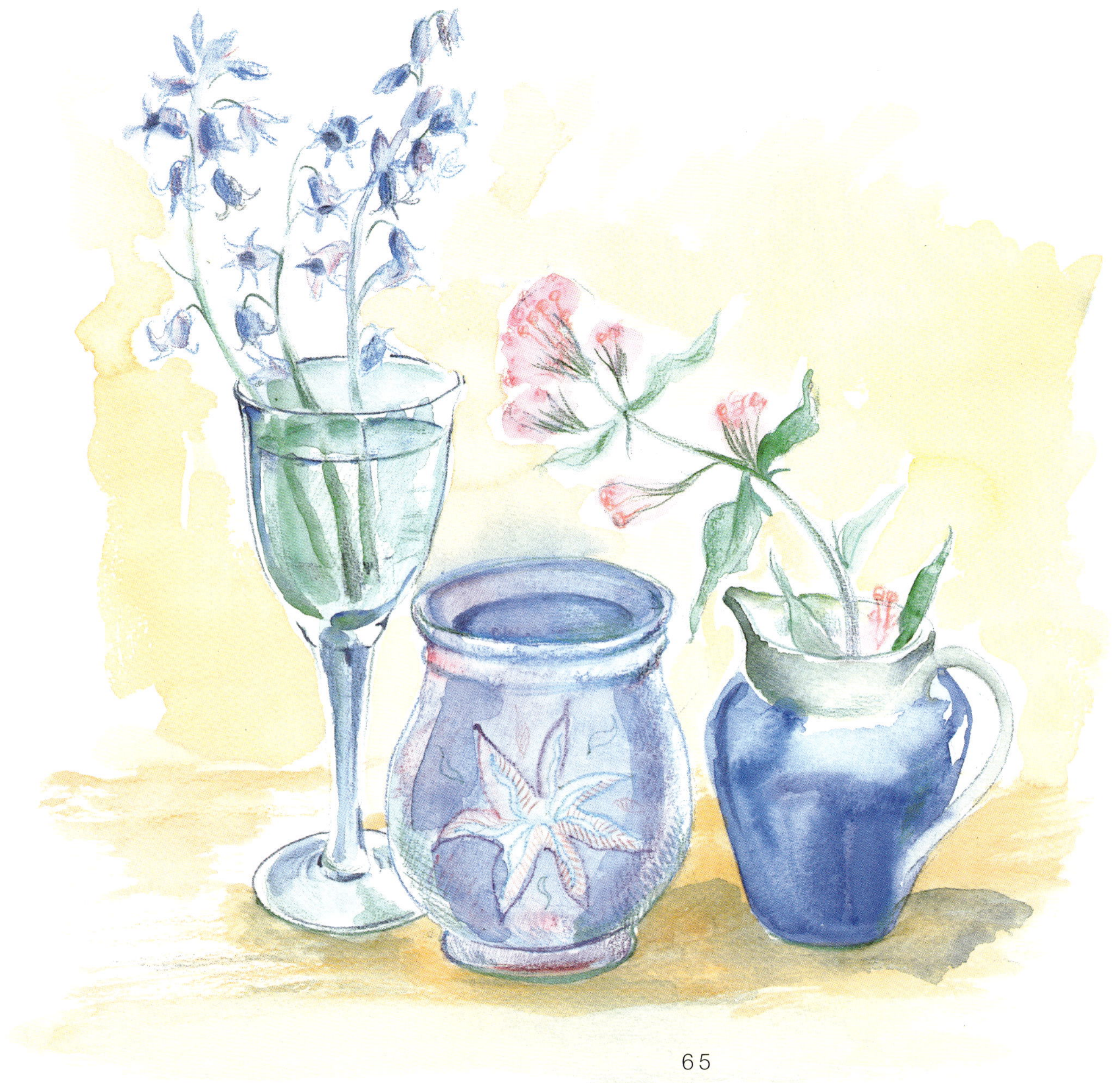

Watercolour paint and pencils can be used together to achieve loose, wet watercolour effects that still retain a degree of form and detail. Allow the pencil to define the shapes of the objects in your composition after you have laid in the colour washes. Create interesting decorative motifs and fine flower heads or leaves and stems with the pencil.

Wax Resist

Watercolour, like any other water-based substance, will not mix with oil. This can be used to advantage with watercolours as there are many oil-based media that can be used in conjunction with watercolour paints. Any picture made of such combinations is known as mixed-media.

Wax is the most suitable oil-based medium to combine with watercolour painting because it resists the paint. It can be used to map out the underlying structure of a picture before applying watercolour paint over the top. A white candle can be used for this as it creates a 'skin' that masks the paper and stops the paint from being absorbed into it. If coloured wax crayons or oil-based pastels are used, the wax resist performs a second task, adding new colours and different textures to the work. By contrast, dark tones can be used to add a greater impression of depth contrast to the picture.

Wax can be used for another watercolour technique, known as sgrafitto, that is good for creating patterns and details. Wax crayon or oil pastel is applied over a dry watercolour wash, and a suitably pointed instrument – such as the end of a brush, a scalpel blade or a toothpick – is used to scratch through the crayon or pastel to reveal the colour underneath. This technique is most suitable for producing patterns and rough textures.

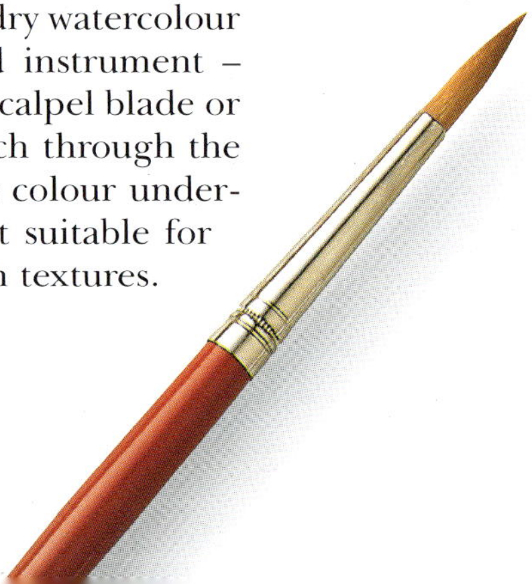

1 First paint a background colour to your design.

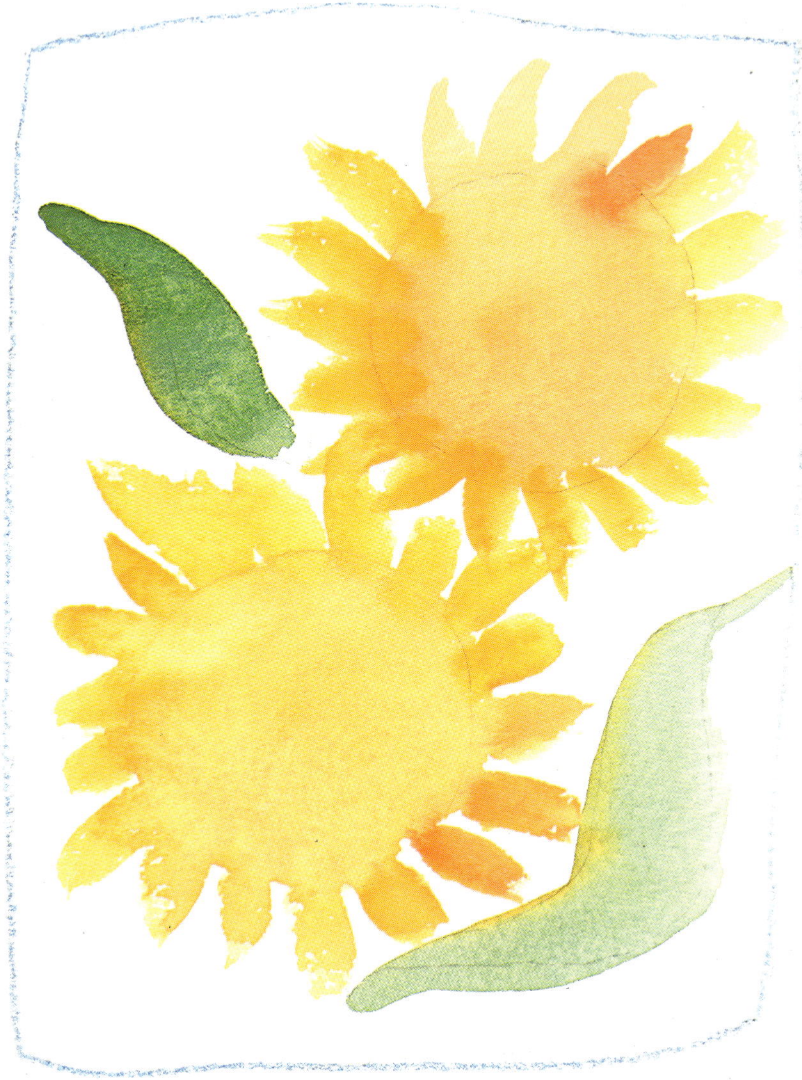

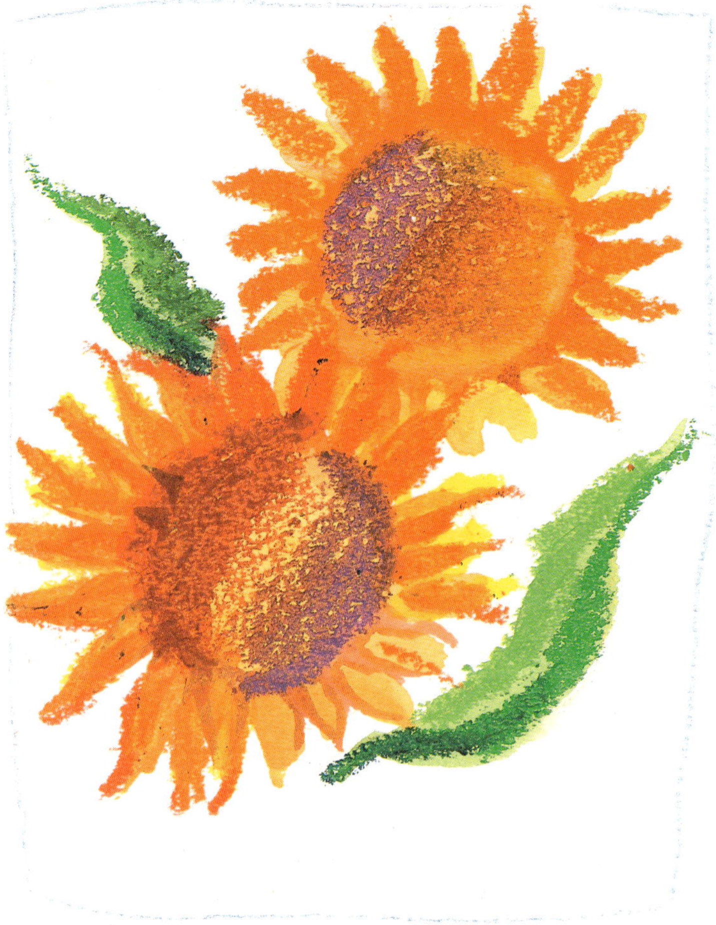

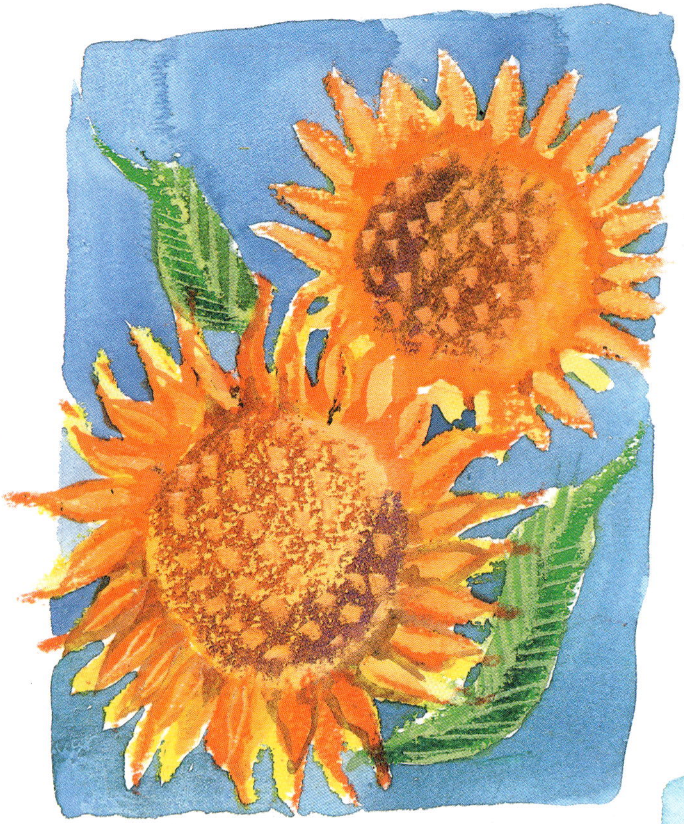

3 Add more crayon and watercolour to your picture to produce a final image that is full of vibrant colours and textures.

2 Once the paint has dried, use coloured wax crayons to enhance the colours and textures of your design. The watercolour base will show through the wax, giving depth to your picture.

Helpful Tips
- Wax resist can be applied in a number of ways. For interesting results, try combining oil pastel and wax crayons in a mixed media painting.
- Two or more crayon or pastel colours added over the paint produce the most beautiful sgrafitto effects.

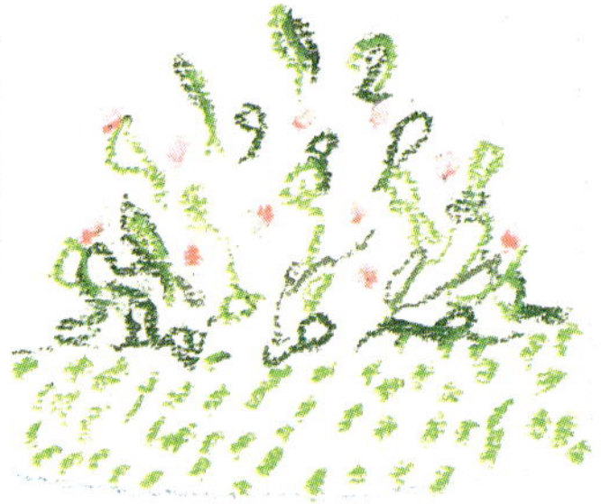

1 Draw in the basic structure of your painting with wax crayons, keeping it fresh and simple.

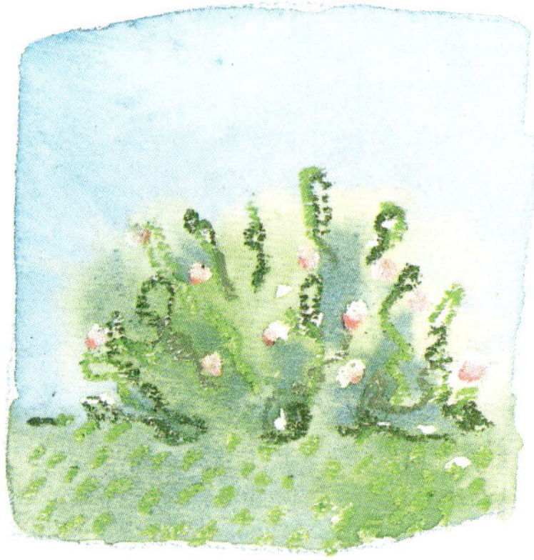

2 Now paint watercolour washes over the top and see how the wax shows through, defining details.

Additives

Although watercolour does not have the thick consistency of oil or acrylic paint, its consistency can be altered to make it more textured. There are a number of additives available that will make the paint thicker and more glue-like. These include glycerin, which will slow down the drying time of the paint, as well as making it look more glossy than normal. Process white, a medium generally used by photographers to retouch black-and-white stills, will thicken the paint and make it completely opaque. Honey will make watercolour paint thicker, but it may also make your brush sticky! When used effectively, it also makes paint more glossy and intense in colour and luminosity.

Watercolour can be made more viscose, which is useful for impasto painting – the technique of painting in thick swirls – in order to give pictures a degree of surface relief. This technique is good for defining a dense area in a picture, or making a textured surface appear more three-dimensional than watercolour on its own can do – for example, when painting ploughed fields or tree bark.

To make watercolour paint more granular, as well as thicker, combine sand with one of the thickeners listed on pages 22–5. This makes an interesting change from the more conventional, flat quality of the paint. The additive will ensure that the sand sticks to the surface of the watercolour paper.

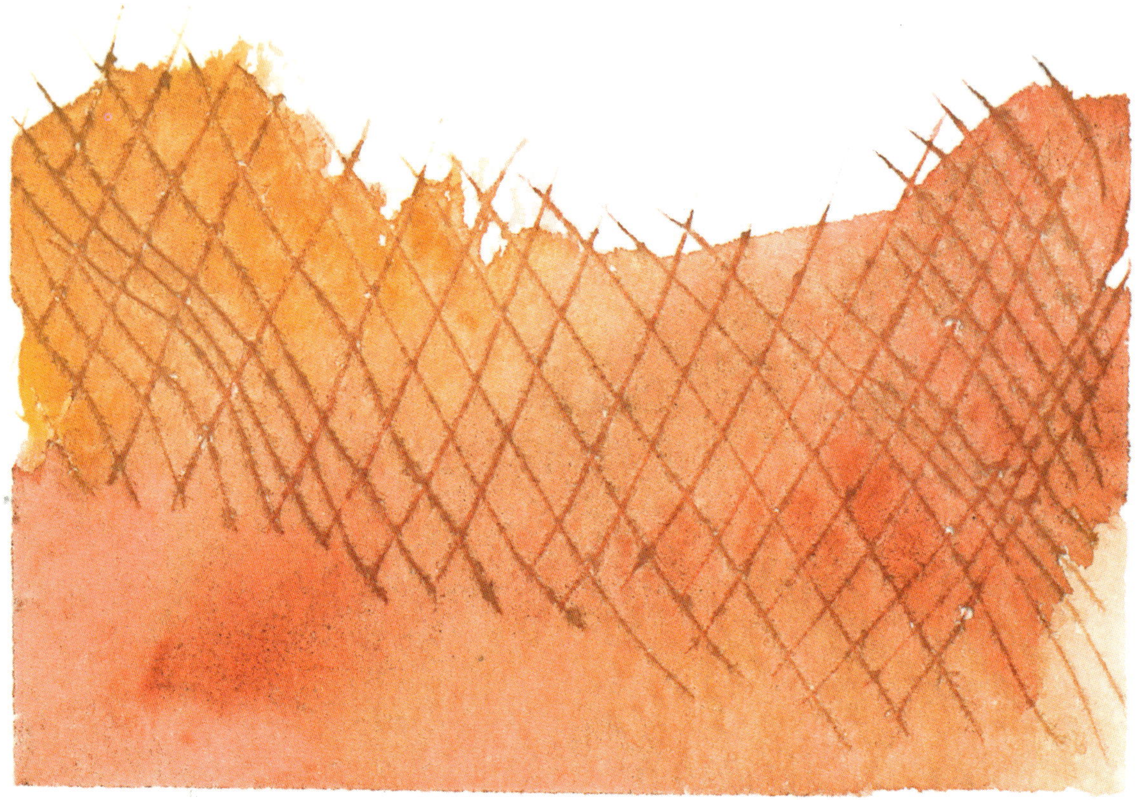

Helpful Tips

- Mix the paint and additives with an old plastic picnic knife. Anything more valuable will get ruined!
- If you have any old, dried-out pans of watercolour, place a drop of gum arabic or honey on top and let the old paint absorb it, which will soon bring the paints back to life.

ABOVE Scoring into the paper will create indentations that will attract more paint than the rest of the paper surface. In this instance, crosshatched score lines are marked in with a craft-knife blade. Then watercolour is washed over the top of the lines. The lines appear very vivid where the paint has pooled.

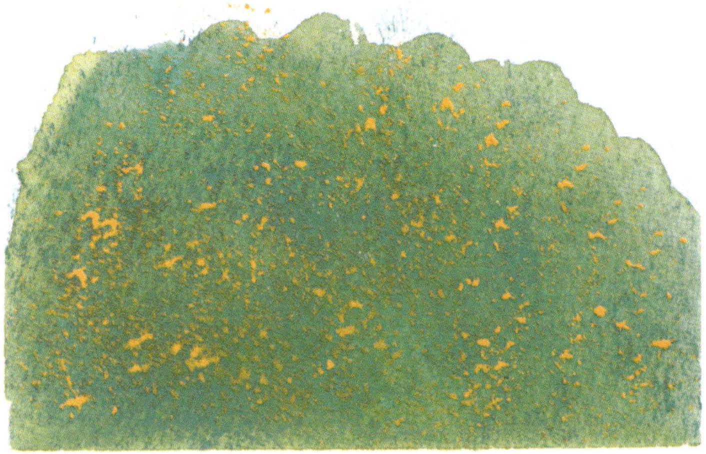

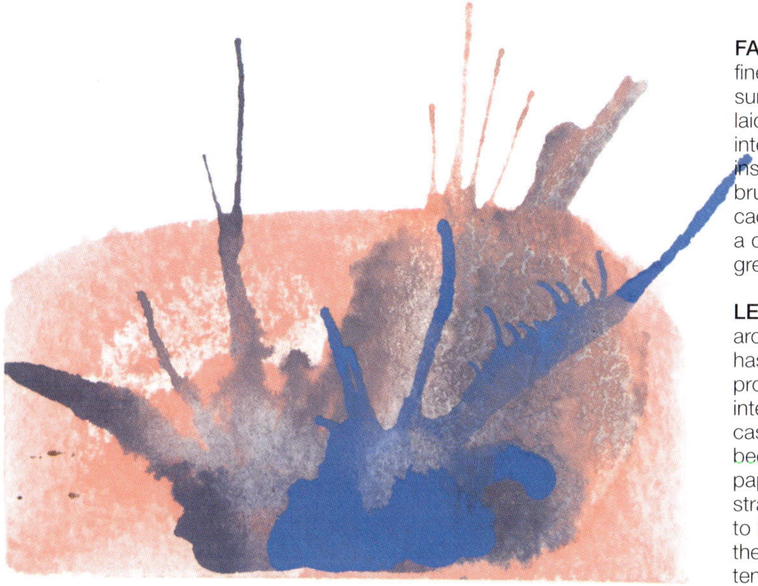

FAR LEFT You can stipple fine dots of paint over the surface of a colour already laid down to produce interesting textures. In this instance, the end of the brush is used to stipple cadmium yellow paint over a dry wash of Hooker's green.

LEFT You can move paint around the paper once it has been laid down to produce some very interesting effects. In this case, three colours have been dropped onto the paper, wet into wet. A straw has then been used to blow the paint around the paper, producing tendrils.

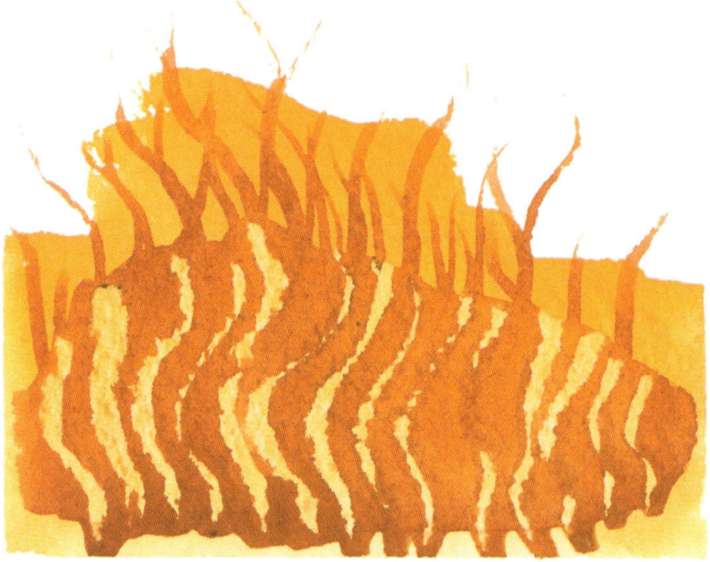

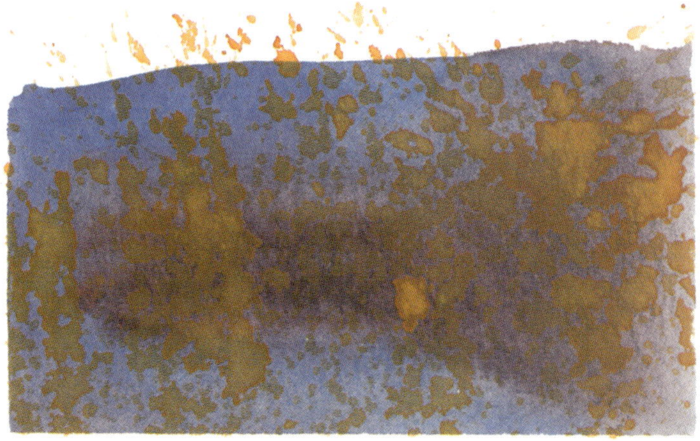

FAR LEFT You can scrape into wet paint to produce some marvellous effects, especially if there is a dry colour underlying the wet colour you are scraping into. In this instance, a comb has been used to scrape through an overlay of deep cadmium red, to reveal the paler orange wash lying underneath.

LEFT Spattered paint produces interesting if random effects. Here, cadmium orange has been spattered over purple with an old toothbrush to produce interesting rust effects.

Using Textured Surfaces

If you don't want to alter the quality of the paint before using it, you can give it more texture by altering the surface of the paper before or after applying the paint. Score into the paper with a scalpel blade before applying paint, and the wet paint will pool in the score lines and dry to a more intense colour there than on the flatter surfaces. Stipple the paint onto the paper with the end of the brush to make interesting textures, or spatter it with a toothbrush to create random sprays of one or more colours.

Alternatively, run a comb through the paint on the paper while it is still wet to make curving parallel lines – perfect for hair or ploughed fields! Similarly, scrape the edge of a piece of card or a plastic credit card through the paint to add interesting patterns to the surface. Pour salt crystals on to wet paint, and allow the paint to dry before brushing the salt away to create a mottled texture. Finally, leave the paint to dry before scraping out some of it with a scalpel blade to produce grass effects or sharp highlights. There are no hard-and-fast rules to watercolour painting – experiment with these and any other techniques you can think of to find what textural effects can be achieved.

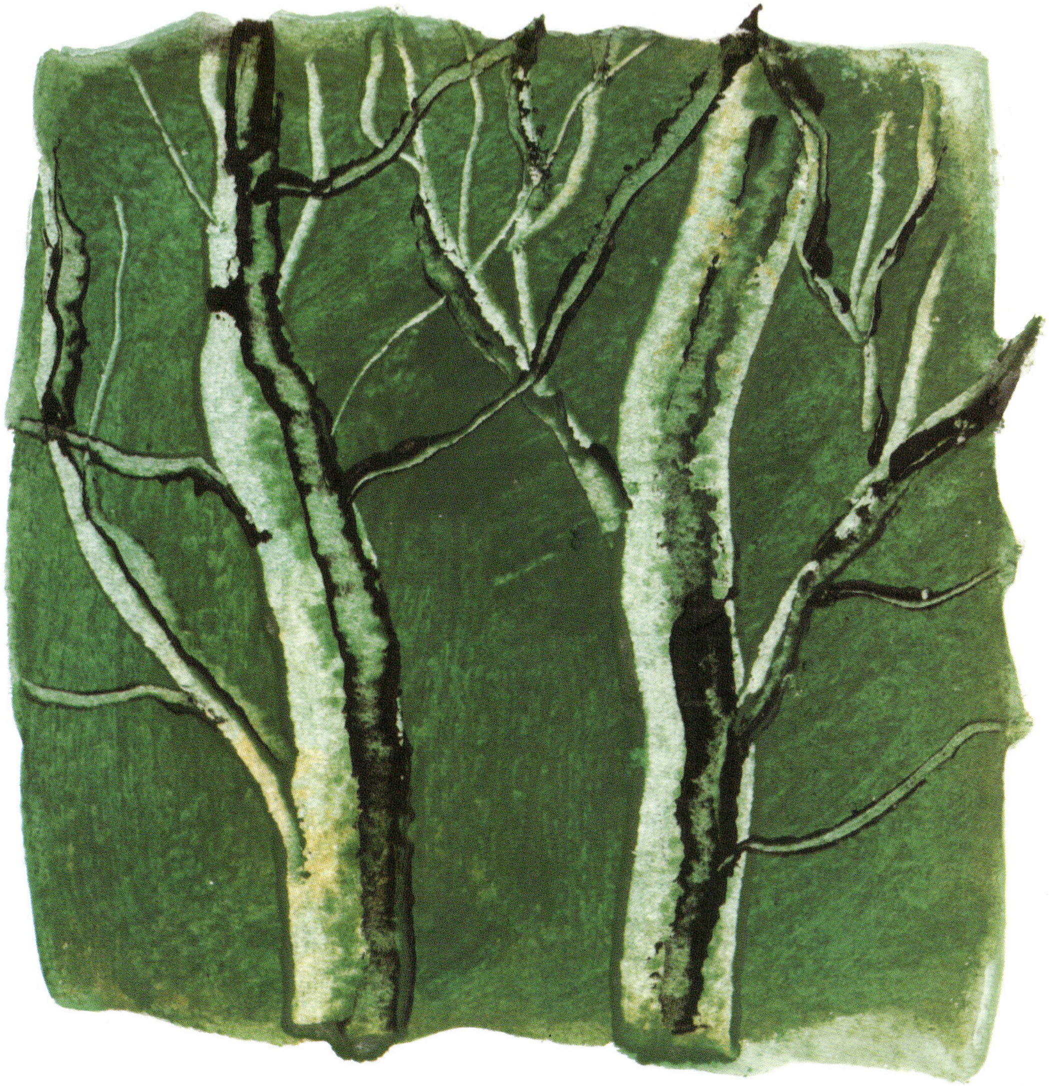

RIGHT Watercolour is mixed with process white to make it opaque and thicker. A wash of the viridian and process white is laid down, then scraped back with a blade. Details are then superimposed with pen and permanent India ink.

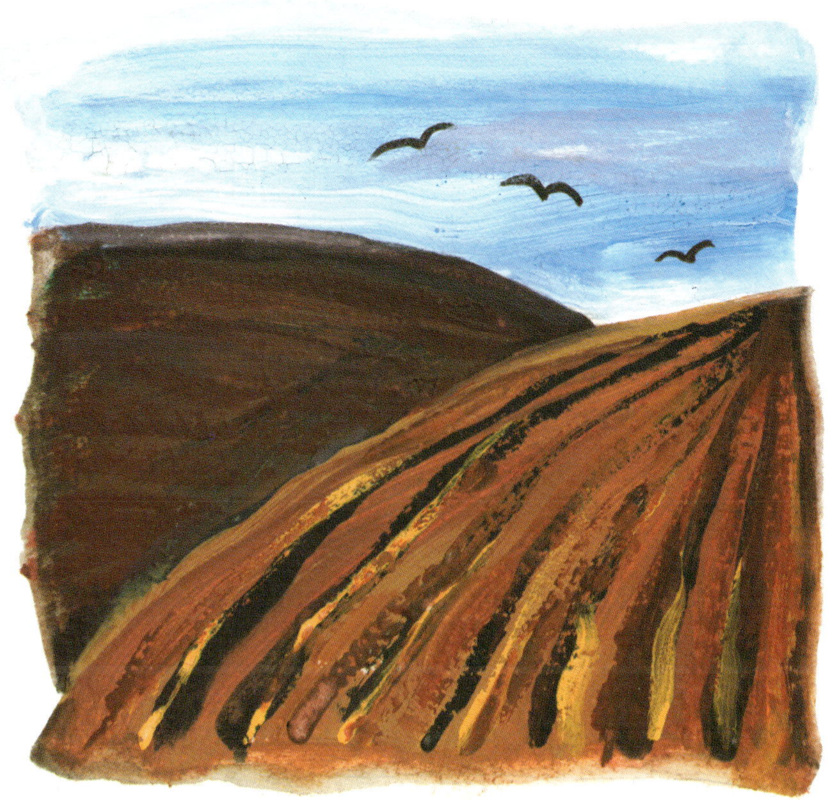

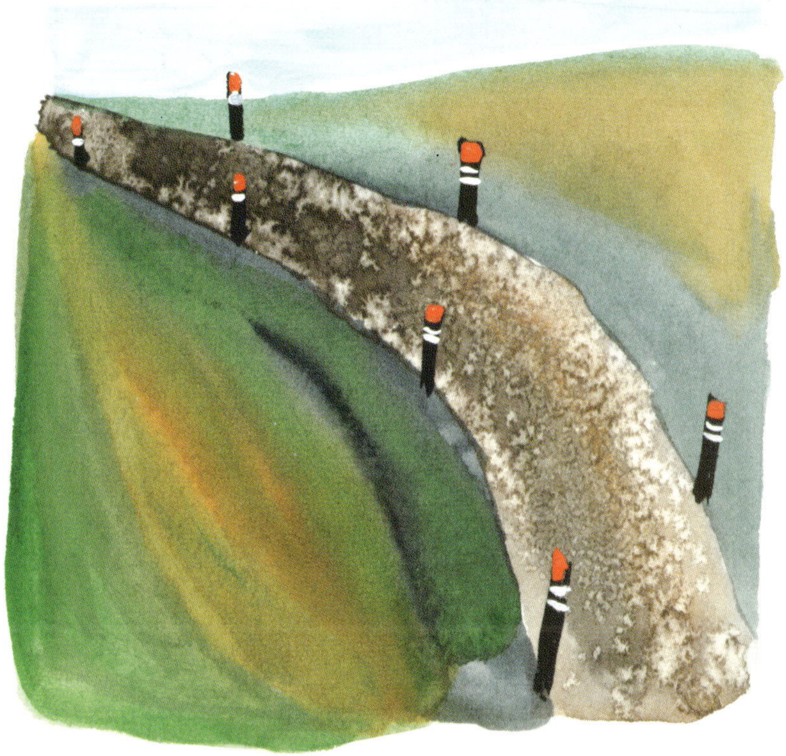

ABOVE Use watercolour mixed with gum arabic to make it thick and viscose. Lay it down with a brush, to produce a textured surface, such as this ploughed field, building up the image with continuous overlays of colour.

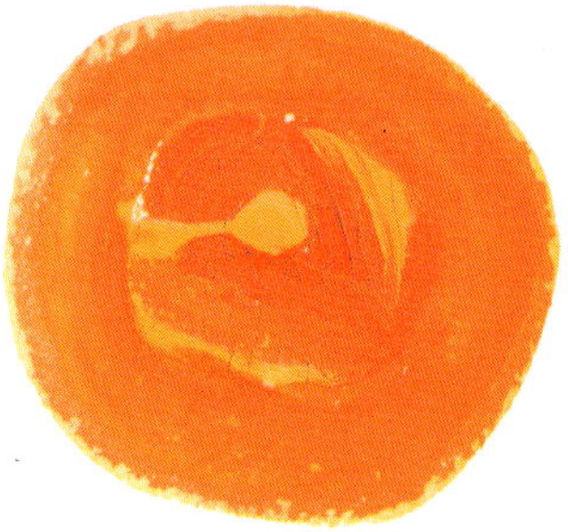

Two paint colours are mixed with process white then applied to the paper with a brush.

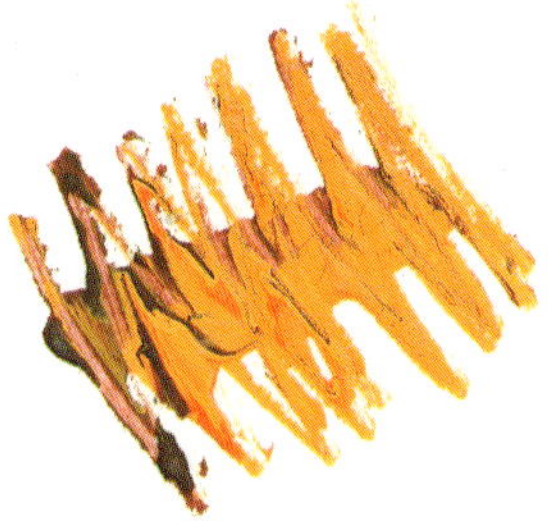

Two colours are mixed with white body colour, then laid down and scraped into with the end of the brush.

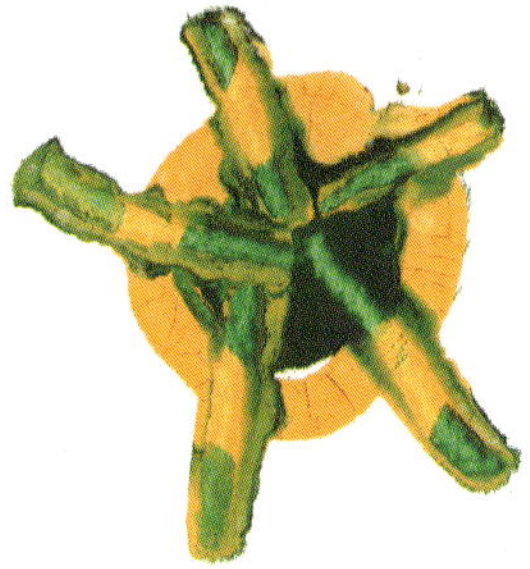

Two paint colours are mixed with gum arabic and laid down with a brush before being scraped with a knife.

ABOVE Additives can be added to the watercolour once it has been laid down, just as effectively as when it is in the palette. In this instance, salt has been sprinkled over the road area as soon as the watercolour had been laid down. Once dry, the salt was removed to reveal texturing in the surface of the paint.

Mixed Media

Many other mixed-media techniques can be used with watercolour in addition to those already described. Any oil-based medium will act as a resist to watercolour paint (page 66), and touches of iridescent oil pastel can make dusk or dawn scenes look quite radiant.

Soft pastels and charcoals add a different mood to watercolour paintings. They are atmospheric media that can be used to create very soft effects. As a result, they are particularly useful for emphasizing atmospheric effects such as mist, stormy seas or soft clouds. Charcoals can be used in the same way as inks to create soft shadows. Remember to ensure that the paint is completely dry before adding dry media over the top. Water-soluble charcoal pencils are available, and these can be incorporated with wet or dry watercolour paint.

Any other painting media can be mixed with watercolour to produce alternative effects – even biro can be used to scribble over the paint! Again, there are no hard-and-fast rules with watercolour painting, but just remember that certain media are going to complement a picture, while the addition of others, such as felt-tip pen or conté chalks, will make a painting muddied or jarring in its range of textures and hues.

Helpful Tips

- Rub a combination of wax crayon, soft pastel and oil pastel over the surface of a piece of paper, then scratch into it with a plastic palette knife. Flow watercolour paint over the top and watch the marvellous effects that appear as the paint settles into the grooves and the other media show through.

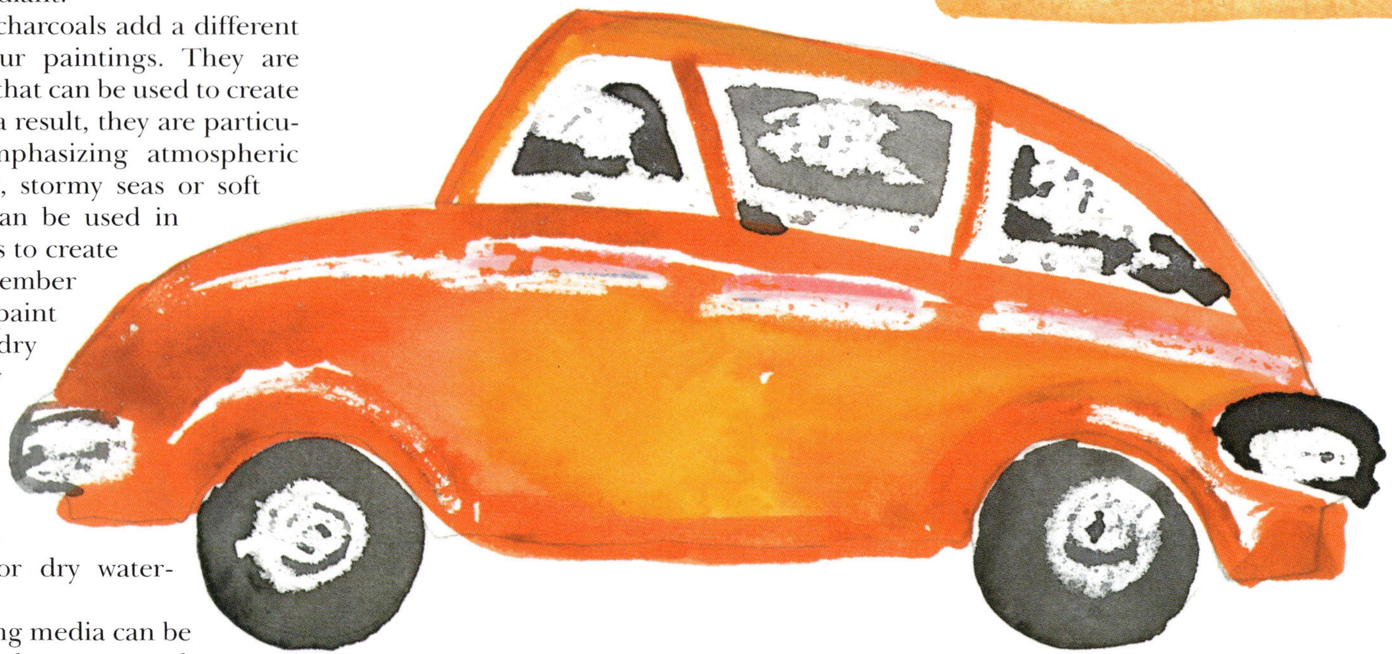

ABOVE You can use mixed media to produce highlights. The car is painted with watercolour and allowed to dry. Oil pastel is then added over the top to produce bright highlights in the windows and on the chrome and wheels.

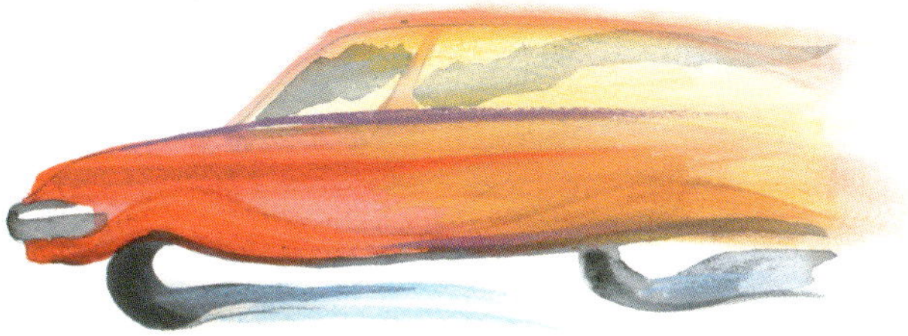

ABOVE Mixed media can help to soften watercolour effects already laid down in order to produce the impression of speed. Here, soft pastels are blended with fingers over the top of dry watercolour to make the car appear as if it is moving.

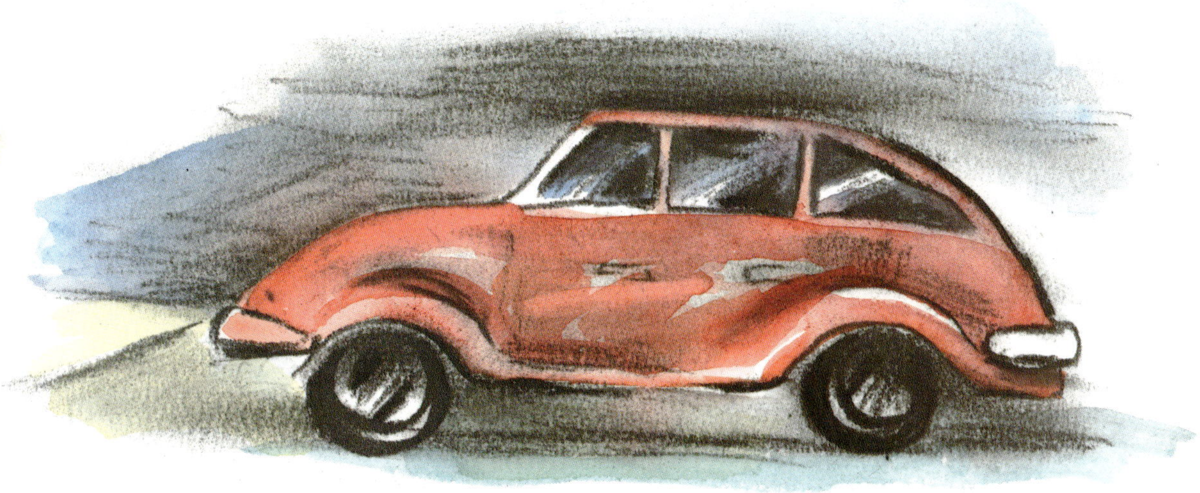

RIGHT A moody atmosphere can be created by adding charcoal to watercolour paintings. In this instance, the charcoal is applied once the paint is dry, to give the impression of dense fog.

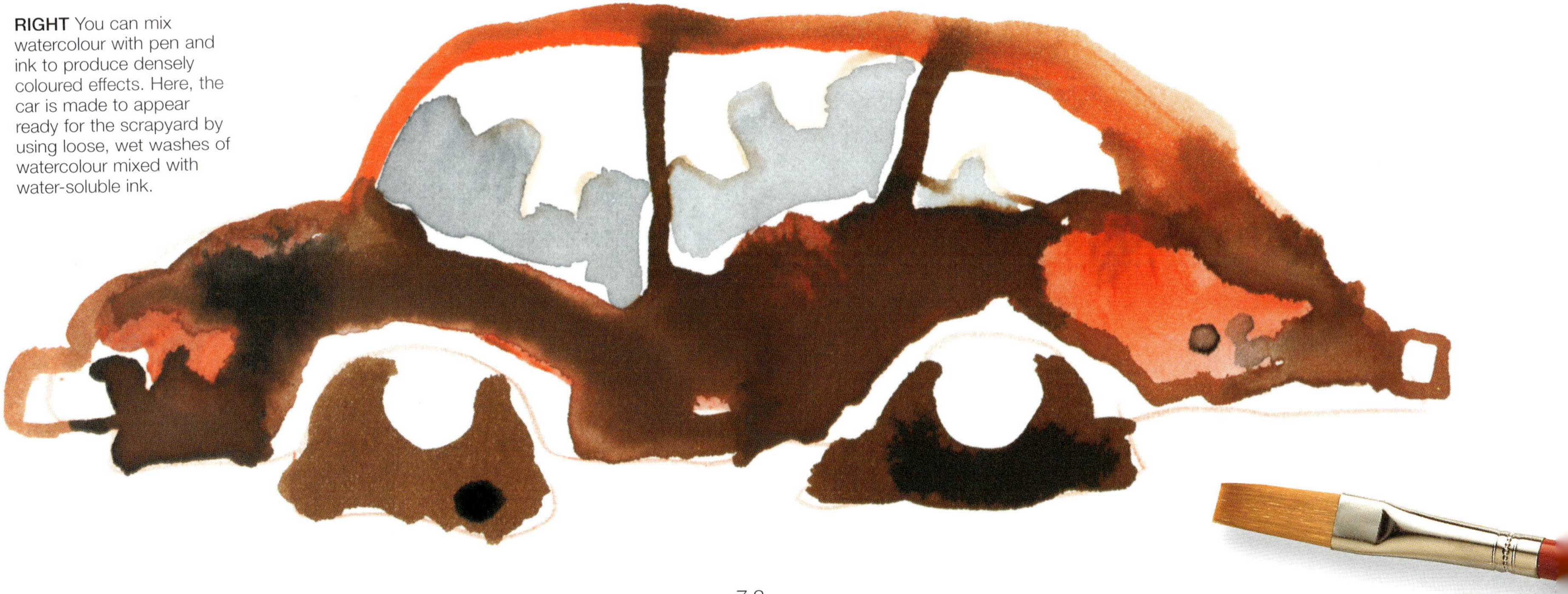

RIGHT You can mix watercolour with pen and ink to produce densely coloured effects. Here, the car is made to appear ready for the scrapyard by using loose, wet washes of watercolour mixed with water-soluble ink.

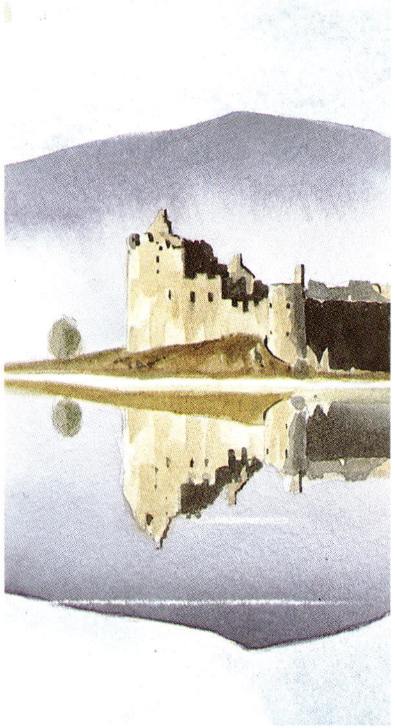
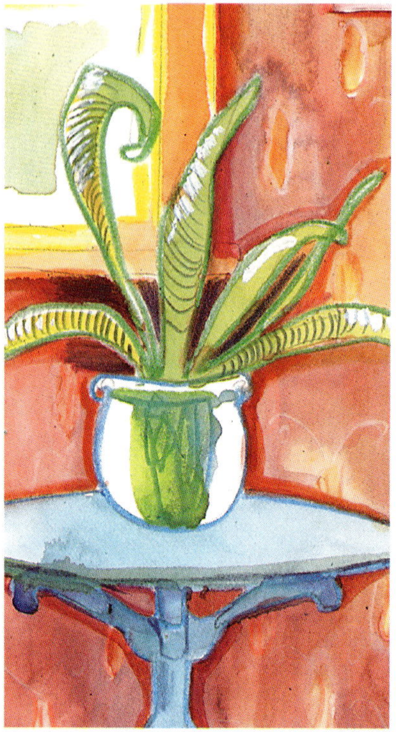
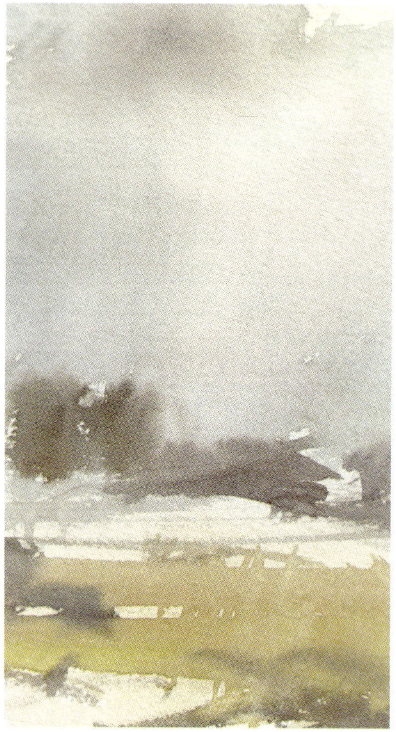
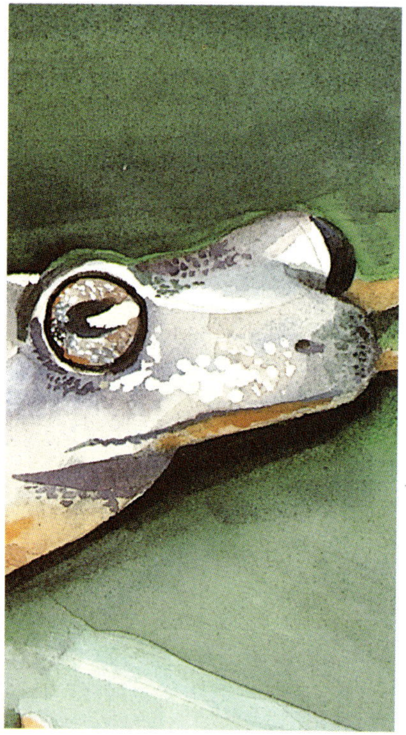

Projects

Whether it is your dream to paint a panoramic landscape, atmospheric still life, clouds scudding across pale blue skies, or waves rolling across endless oceans, these projects will set you off on the right course. Each project has been designed to introduce you to a different aspect of watercolour painting. If you use them as a starting point, they will encourage you to hone your skills and begin to find your own painting style.

Introduction

Even if you have a knowledge of watercolour skills, you may feel unsure about putting them into practice in a painting. There are no hard-and-fast rules, and your own taste should play an essential role in your choice of subject. Just because watercolour painting is often associated with panoramic vistas, for example, you do not have to paint them. The entire world and all its contents are up for grabs, and the choice is yours. The projects included here introduce the most common subjects for watercolour painting to help you get started.

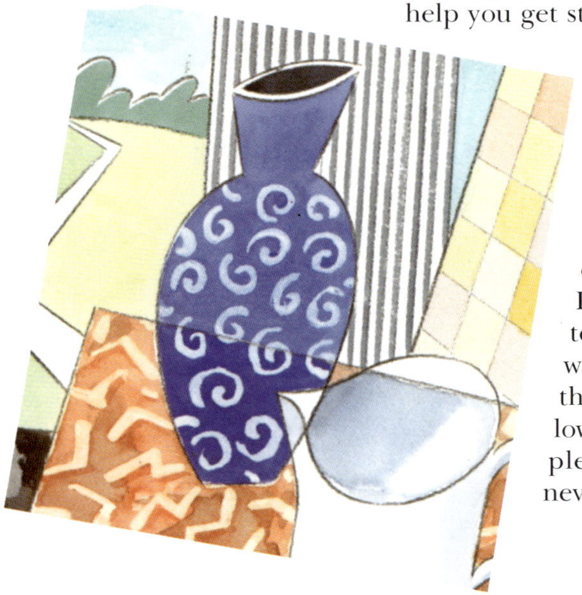

Before starting to paint, make sure that you have gathered together all the materials that you will need, and organize your work space so that you have everything to hand. Refer back to pages 32–3 to prepare yourself for a watercolour session. All of the projects over the following pages rely on a simple selection of colours, never more than 10 being

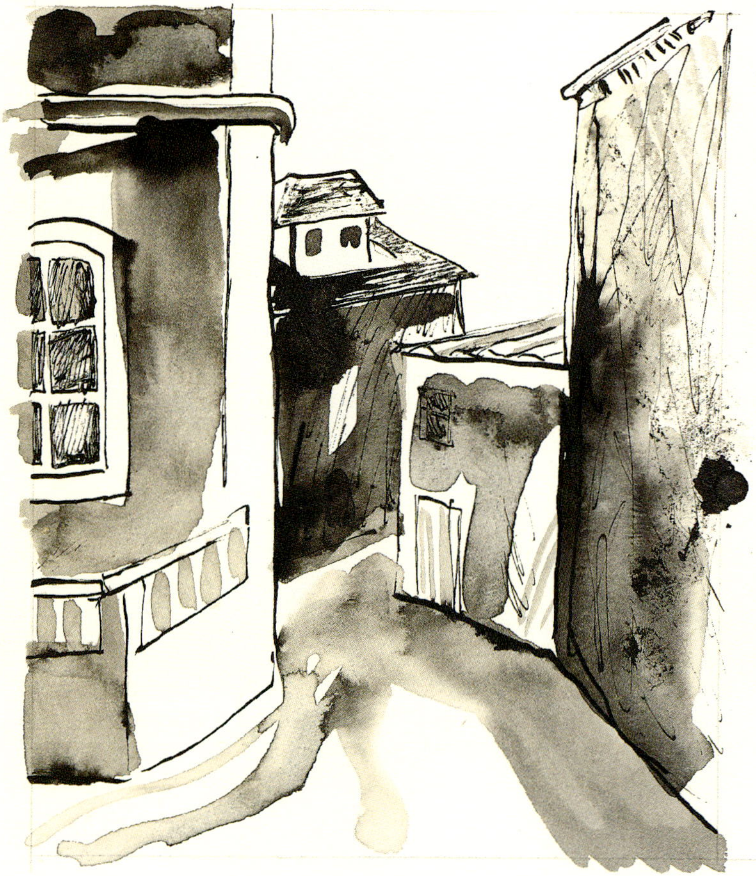

used in any one project. You do not have to select the same colours as are used here, or even the same subjects as those shown, but they will provide a starting point for a number of approaches and techniques.

Allow yourself at least three hours per project. This time can be split between the two sections within each project. The first section considers the particular techniques being emphasized in that project, and you can try these out before tackling the project proper. The second section concentrates on the painting project itself. Two hours spent on this should get you, at the very least, a good way into the project.

You need not follow the projects in the order suggested, although they have been planned to build up skills and techniques gradually as you work through them. Finally, remember that you can always refer back to the previous sections to refresh your memory on how a particular method works – and don't forget to follow the tips that supplement the captions.

The projects are a starting point for further exploration. The wonder of watercolour lies in the medium's versatility – you never run out of new things to try. Taken literally, you should be able to copy the projects as they develop – alternatively, you can allow them to lead you into a world of your own!

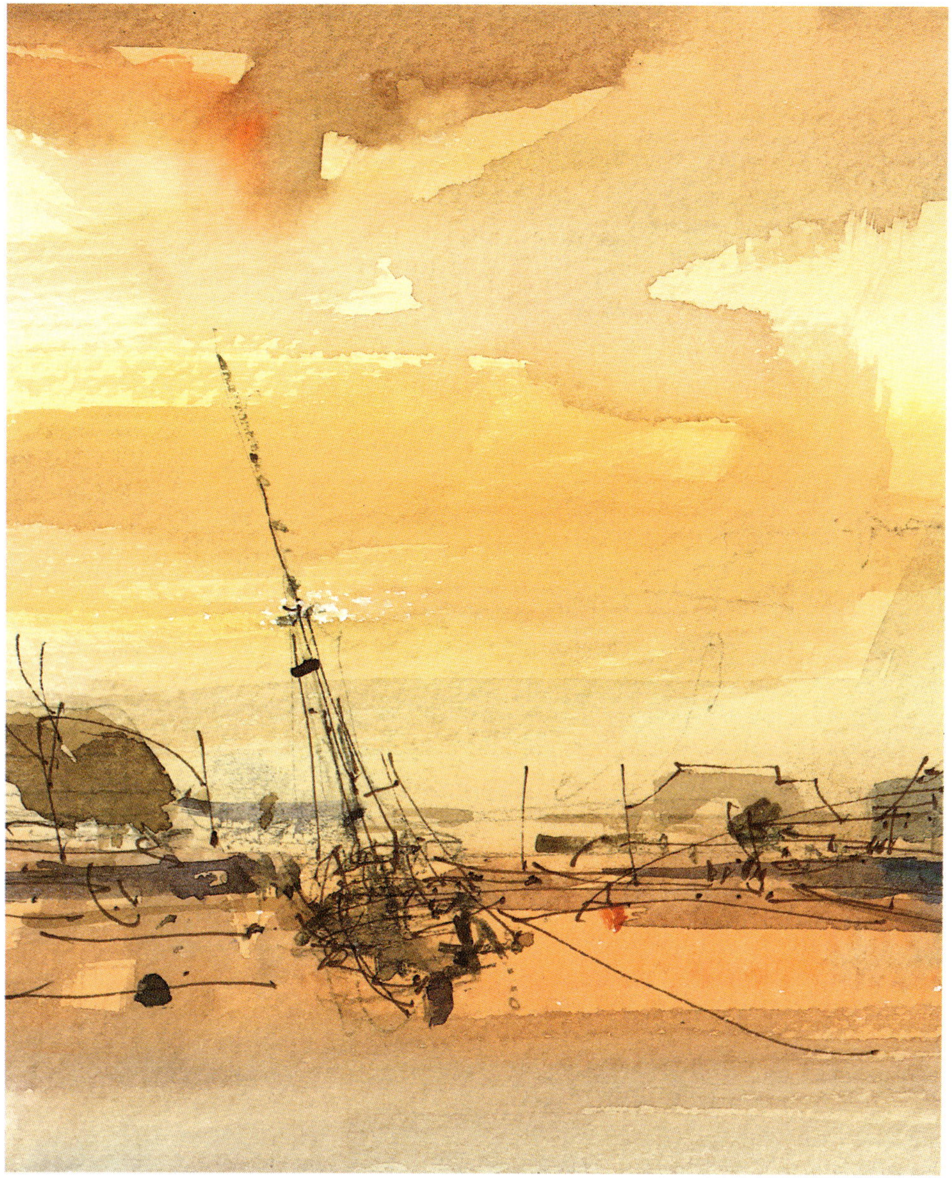

Landscapes

Cool Tones and Foreground Textures

The landscape is a favourite subject among watercolour painters – and with good reason. Not only is it a rich source of subject matter, with each view providing a wide number of compositional choices, but it also contains at least as wide a range of tonal variations as does your watercolour palette.

Watercolour's translucency makes it the perfect medium for capturing natural atmospheric effects, such as mist and rain, shafts of sunlight, and subtle variations in colour and tone. You can never exhaust the range of colour options in your palette, but the landscape will attempt to make you do so!

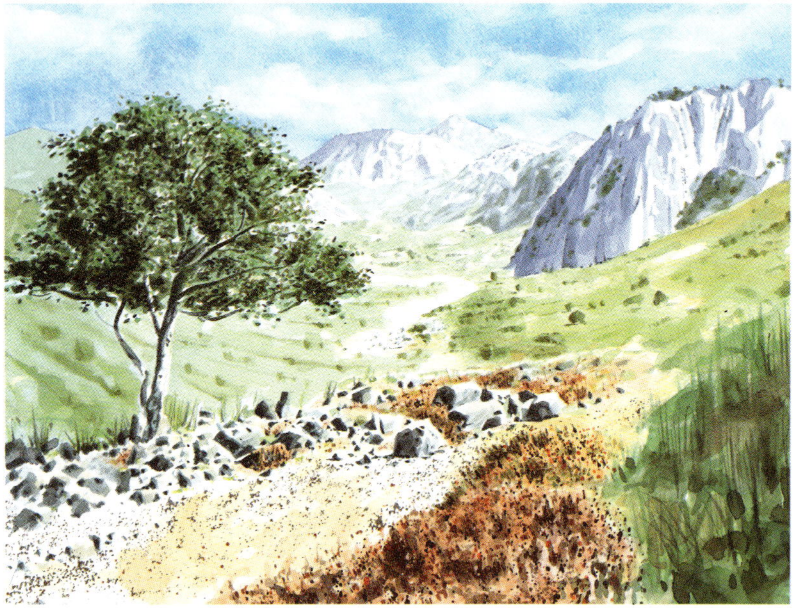

You don't need to work outside to paint a landscape. Instead, you could work from photographs, reference notes and sketches at home if it suits you better. When you do this, however, ensure that you have a range of references to work from. If you try to copy a single photograph, the result is likely to appear stilted. Also, do some provisional compositional sketches to get a feel for landscapes before starting to paint. Watercolour lends itself to capturing landscape textures, so before starting the project, have a go at producing textures in different ways. It is a good idea to have a few textured objects to refer to when painting landscape scenes – a cone, twigs, leaves or grass, or a rock, for example.

This project is based on a cool landscape scene. It shows how the impression of depth in a landscape can be created through the use of aerial perspective, and how foreground textures can be produced with a number of recently acquired techniques. You don't need to follow this landscape project precisely – in fact, it would be better if you use it as a starting point for your own landscape scene.

Also, consider the effect of aerial perspective before you set to work, and use it to create a sense of recession by making the paint more dilute, the details less defined and the colours paler as you develop the scene towards the horizon line. You are in control of the paint, so make sure it does what you want it to do.

Producing reference notes
The value of making reference notes before you embark upon a full-scale painting can never be overestimated as they give you the opportunity to consider the problems that you may encounter before you start painting. In this case, make sure you have grasped the rules of aerial perspective in a quick wash sketch, practise painting light effects to achieve tonal contrast, and consider methods of producing textures and form in the foreground.

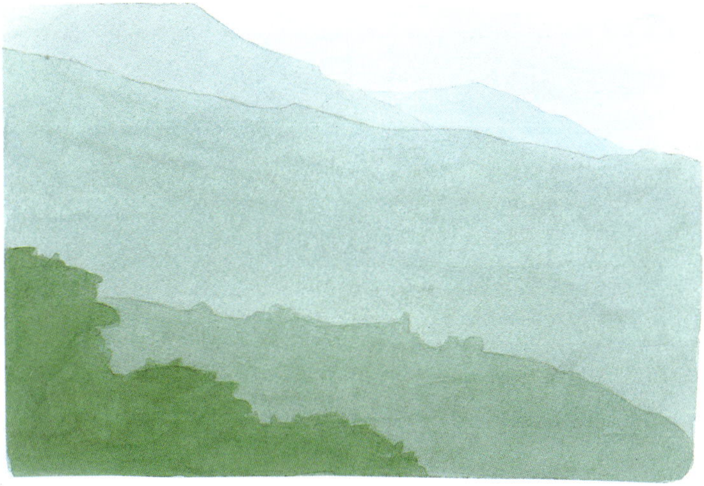

ABOVE French ultramarine blue mixed with Payne's grey has been used to paint an initial wash across the paper. Once dry, successive layers of Hooker's green dark have been applied over the top, becoming darker towards the foreground to produce aerial perspective.

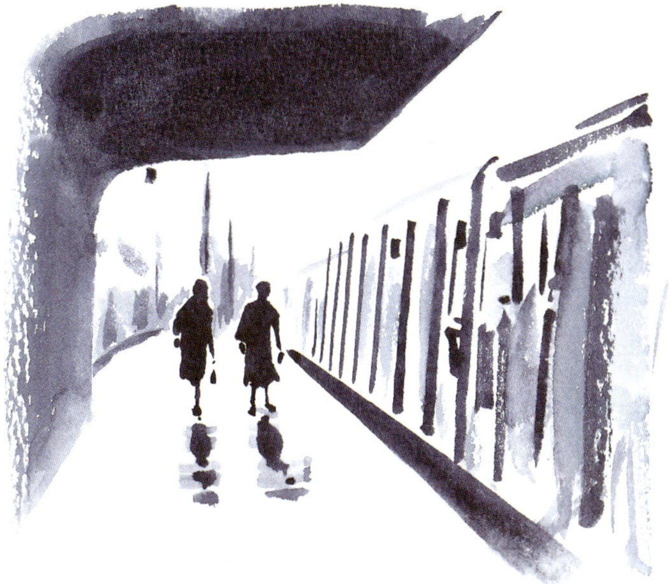

ABOVE Use a single colour to produce a monochrome sketch to refresh your memory of the ways you can achieve form and tonal contrast. See how Payne's grey can be used in a number of intensities, to create stark contrasts between areas in deep shadow and bright sunlight.

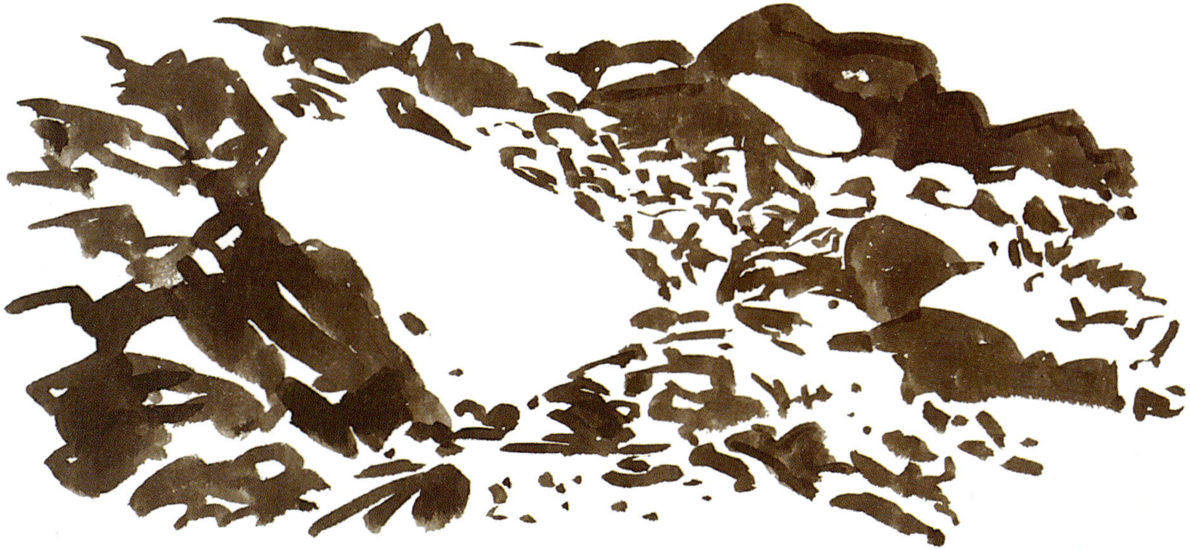

LEFT Again using a single colour, experiment with tonal contrast and changing brushmarks to produce textured foreground impressions.

Space and texture
Use an extended palette of colours to ensure that you have a wide range of colour choices before setting to work on a complex landscape scene. Most landscapes require a wide range of green tones, so pre-plan a range that suits the subject you are choosing to paint. Map out the landscape in pencil before you set to work. Remember to make the colours paler and the details diminish towards the horizon, and use tonal contrasts to develop areas of light and shadow, texture and movement.

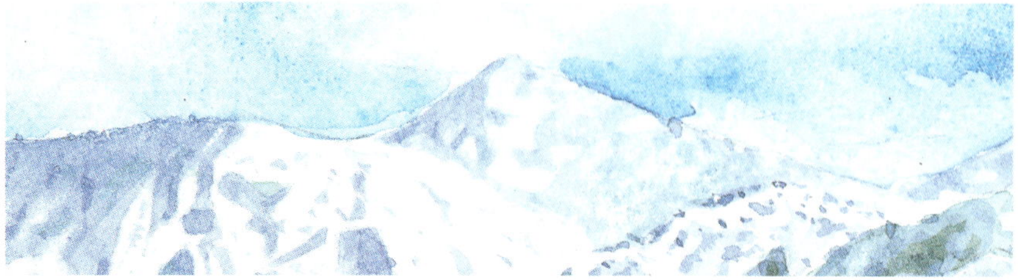

ABOVE The mountains in the distance are painted with more dilute colour, creating the impression of distance towards the horizon line.

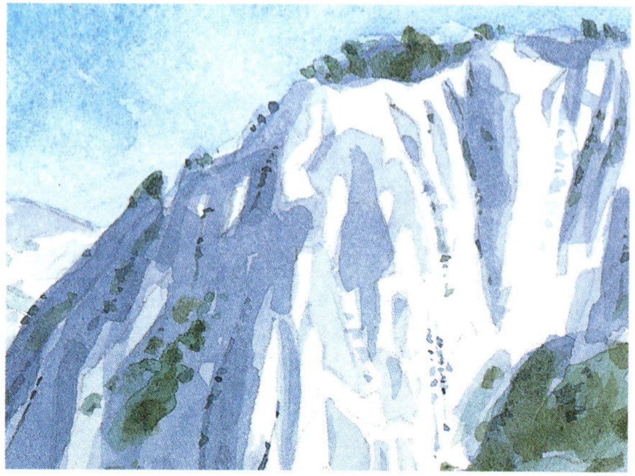

ABOVE The mountain in the middle ground balances the tree opposite, and the use of dramatic tonal contrast further emphasizes the brightness of the sun.

RIGHT Paths are a useful landscape device. Note here how the path winds through the scene, drawing the eye away from the foreground detail towards the mountains in the distance.

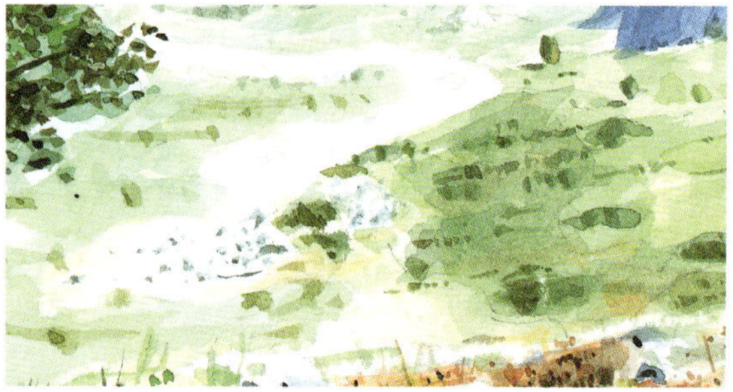

OPPOSITE Warm, bright colours and strong texture in the foreground, set against pale colours and less detail in the distance gives a sense of depth.

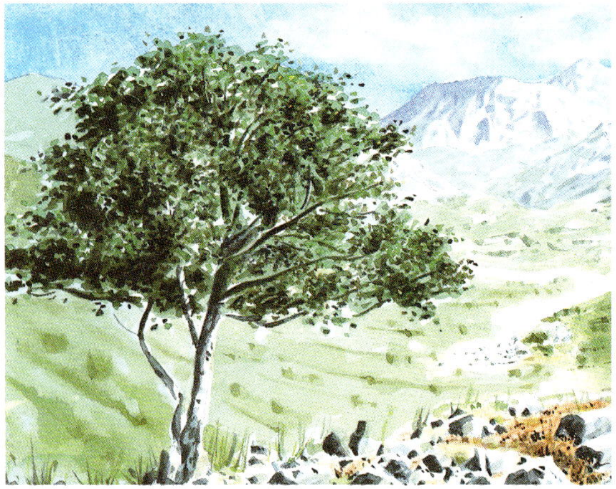

ABOVE The tree to the left of the composition provides a convenient frame to the picture, and also draws the eye into the middle ground. It settles on the side of the path that also draws the eye into the picture. Stippled green tones produce form in the leaves and branches.

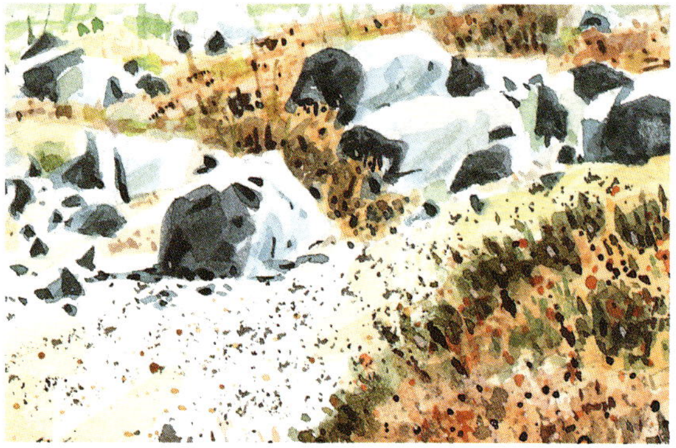

ABOVE Tonal contrast produces stark drama on the rocks, with one side falling into deep shadow, while the other is left white to emphasize the harsh sunlight.

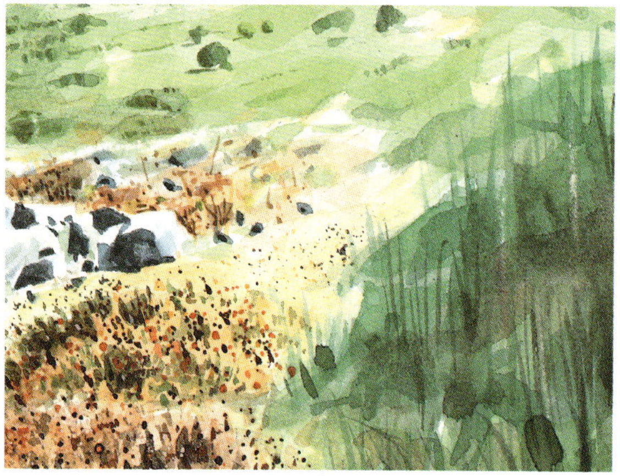

ABOVE You can use a wide range of texturing effects to produce foreground detail. Here, spattering with a toothbrush produces gravel and stones, while green overlays provide a rich area of vegetation. The contrast between the textures and colours adds interest to the foreground.

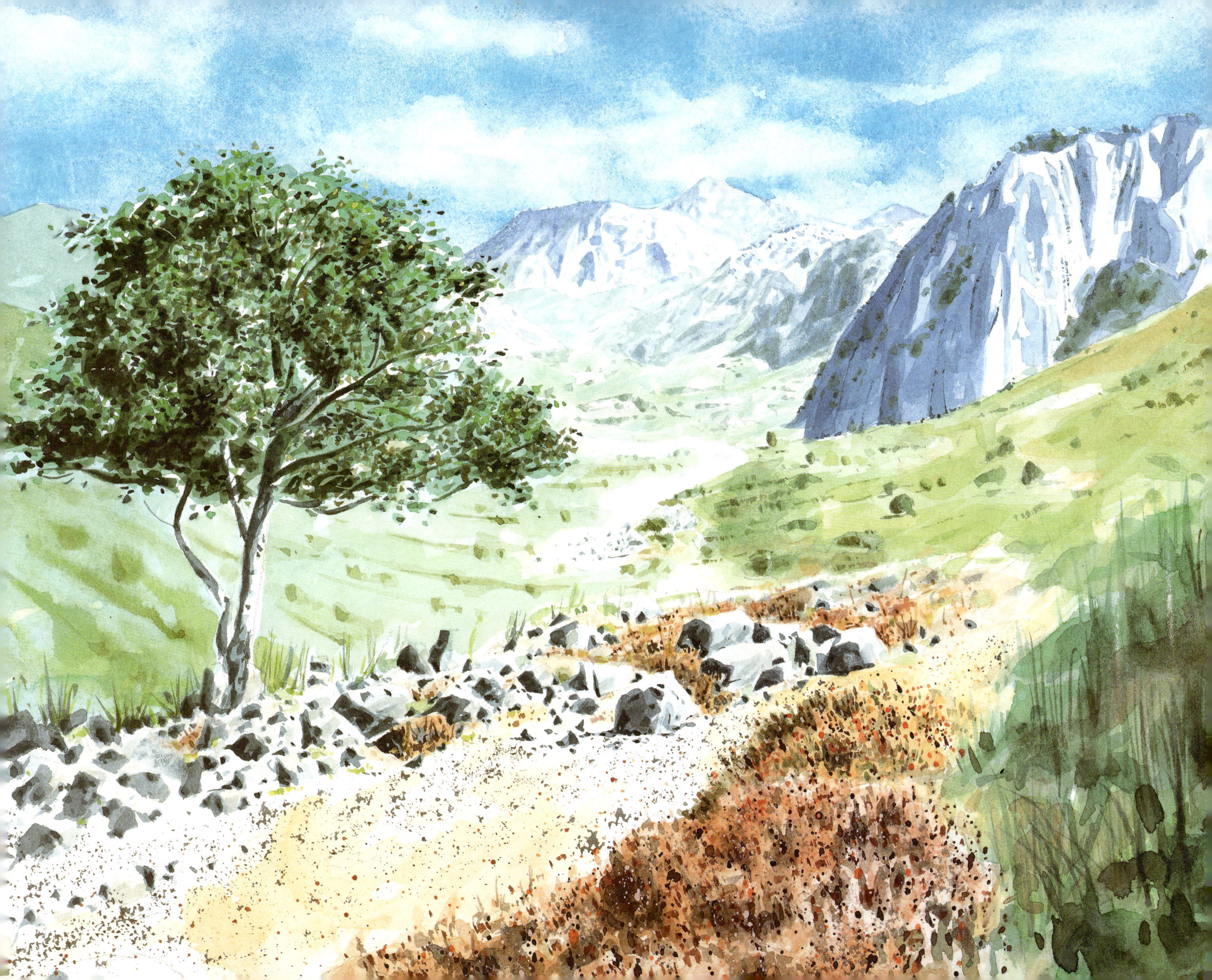

Still Life with Tulips

Limited Palette and Colour Mixing

This simple still life arrangement incorporates five objects, each contrasting in its surface qualities. The red tulips are fragile and their petals and leaves are loosely structured, while the glasses and vase have hard yet transparent and reflective surfaces. The painted pot is matt in appearance, and by contrast the necklace is made of coloured glass beads. Despite these surface variations, the composition has been completed in only seven colours, plus Chinese white gouache. As a result, the objects all contain traces of related hues, ensuring the composition appears harmonious to the eye.

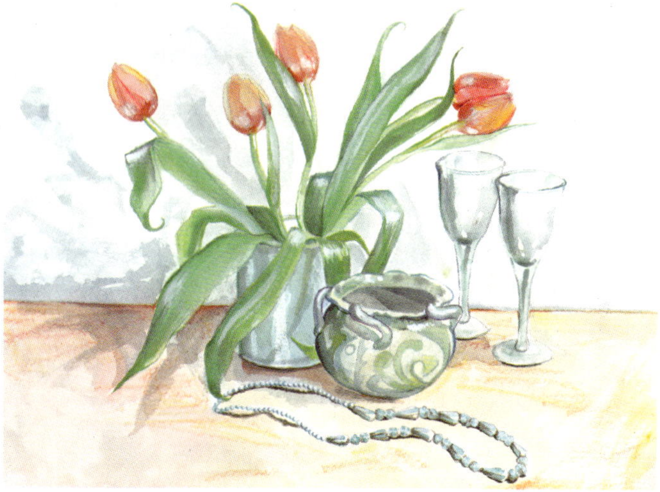

Many artists feel that they need to use a wide palette of colours and a range of fancy techniques to achieve a 'finished' looking picture. They could hardly be further from the truth! Often, the best pictures are those, like this still life with tulips, which use a very limited palette and simple range of watercolour effects, carefully selected to complement the subject of the painting. It is easy to overwork watercolour, especially when you are first starting out. By limiting the range of colours and techniques you use in any one picture, you will be forcing yourself to simplify, and, most likely, improve your work.

Employing a wide palette can make you lazy. Rather than mixing the perfect hue to capture the tulip's stems, or the varying colours of light on the glasses, it is too tempting to select the nearest colour to the reality from your paintbox and make do with it. It is a mistake to do so, for each paint colour you see is only the concentrated amalgamation of a whole range of subtle hues, only revealed when you add different amounts of water to the paint. As you will have discovered on pages 32–4, the three primary colours, red, yellow and blue, come in two biases, one leading towards a warm temperature, and the other towards a cool. When selecting a limited palette, remember to incorporate a primary of each leaning, to give you the widest secondary and tertiary colour-mixing options.

To paint such an effective still life, choose objects which complement one another, but do not fight for attention. See in this painting how the curling tulip leaves relate to the curving rims of the glasses and bowl, as well as the necklace which lies in the foreground. These repetitive rhythms help to unify the composition, and act as a device to lead the eye through the picture, from the necklace in the foreground to the tulips leaning away in the background.

Cadmium yellow and orange, warm hues, are mixed with scarlet lake, a cool hue, to create warm and cool oranges, used in the tulip heads.

Indigo and rose madder produce a range of neutral greys and cool purples, used to produce shadows around the base of the vase and glasses.

Warm viridian and cool turquoise are combined to achieve a subtle range of warm and cool greens, perfect for achieving the tulip leaves and stems.

Indigo, viridian and turquoise are mixed to produce blue overtones in all of the still life objects aside from the tulip heads, which retain warmer hues.

Mixing colours
Choose the simplest palette of colours which will pick out the main elements in your composition, and then practise mixing them to develop further colour ranges for your use. Sometimes it is most effective to mix up a colour from two paints in your palette, while at other times, the most effective results will be achieved by laying them on top of one another, or next to one another, direct on the paper. Depending on the nature of the mix (wet into wet, damp or dry), the resulting colour will differ. The most subtle variation in amount of one colour to the next, or water to paint, will effect the mix you achieve.

Below Here are the seven colours used for this still life, and the range of mixes you can achieve with them.

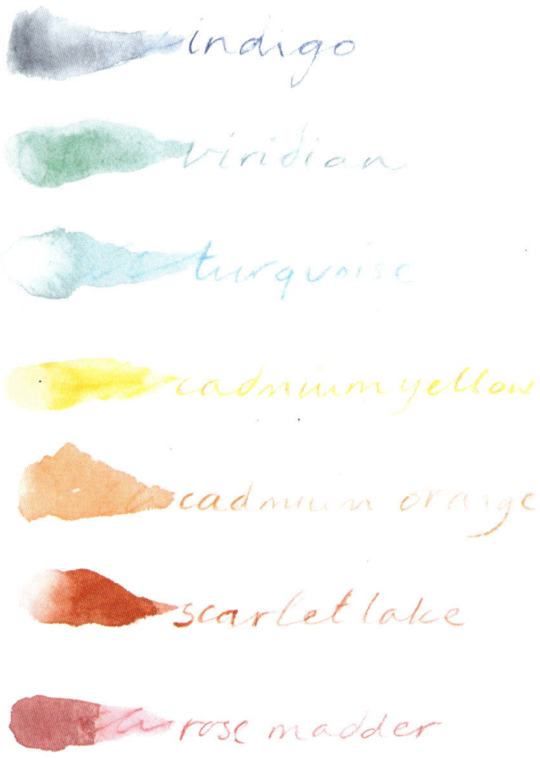

Defining forms

Arrange your still life simply, so that all elements link together, creating unity. Begin by sketching the composition very lightly in blue watercolour pencil, so that you can judge the proportions and spatial relationships between objects. The marks will blend into the picture when they come into contact with water as you work.

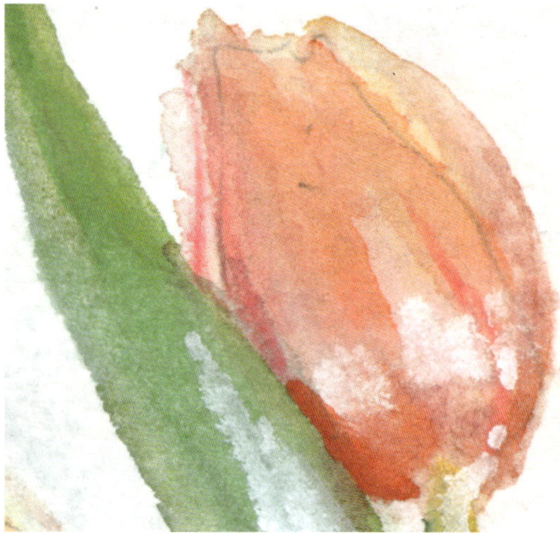

ABOVE Paint the tulip heads with a series of wet over damp and wet over dry layers of colour. Begin with the cadmium yellow, then add cadmium orange and add a touch of scarlet lake last, to give the impression of layers of petals. If you let the paint drip you will lose the form of the flowers. Leave the highlights free of paint or add touches of Chinese white gouache to enhance the petals' fragility. The warm hues in the tulips contrast with the cool green tones in the adjoining leaf suggesting freshness.

Helpful Tips

- Keep your colours fresh by rinsing out your brush between each application of paint.
- Define the most detailed areas of the picture in watercolour pencil, and use a wet brush, free of paint, to blend the pencil marks into the rest of the picture.

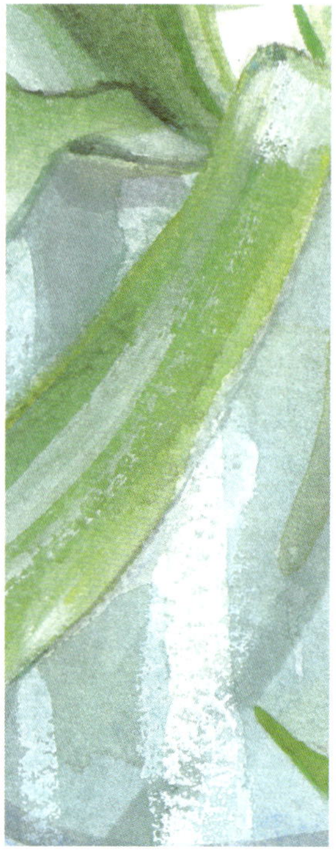

LEFT Add touches of Chinese white gouache onto any areas of your picture, for example your vase and pot, to create additional highlights.

OPPOSITE The painting has been kept fresh and simple. The limited range of colours, mixed together skillfully on the paper, produce a coherent and unified composition.

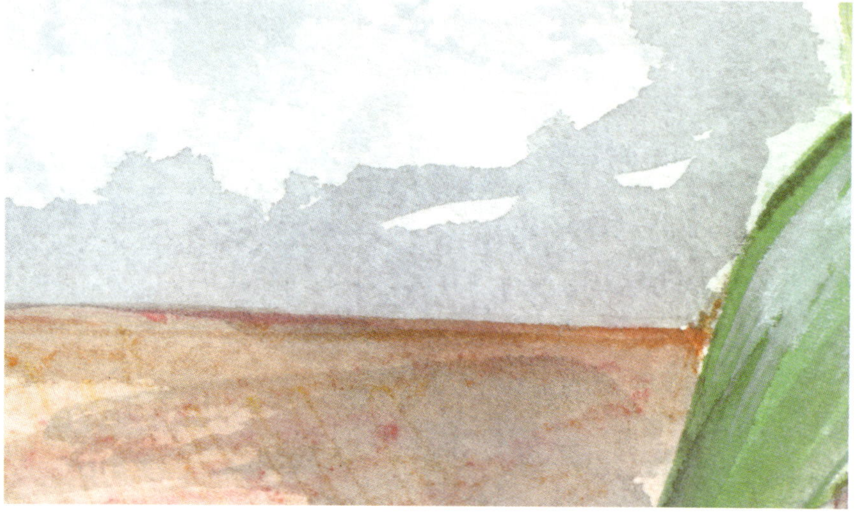

ABOVE Wash in the background last, using very light washes of cadmium yellow and orange in the foreground, and a few touches of indigo in the background. Use the neutral mixes of indigo and rose madder to develop shadows beneath the leaves and around the base of the glasses and pot.

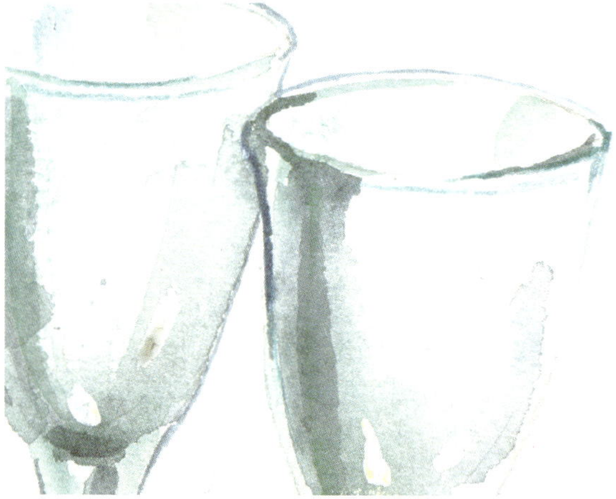

LEFT Keep the glasses fresh by using very light touches of paint, wet in wet, within clearly defined parameters. Notice here how the outlines of the glasses have been clearly defined with blue watercolour pencil before the paint was added, to enhance their shapes.

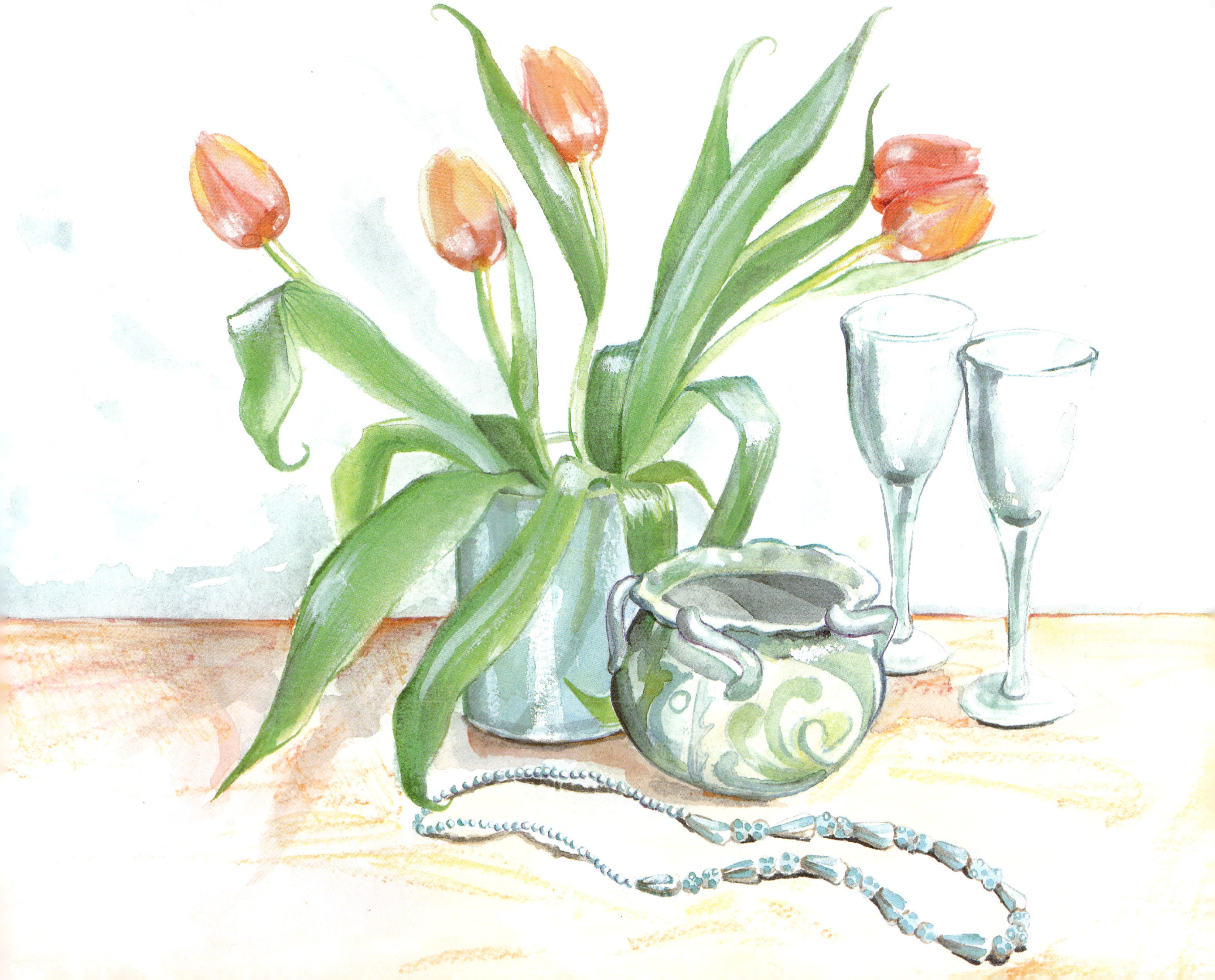

Townscapes

Painting Buildings and Textures

The town and city offer plenty of scope for the watercolourist, and paintings can provide far more interesting reminders of holidays than a postcard or photograph. These reference materials will also be useful for any studio paintings you want to produce of towns or cities that you have visited, so always remember to collect visual references when you visit places of interest.

Paintings of townscapes will bring your perspective skills into play once again. The most useful of these is likely to be linear perspective (see pages 44–5), as you will be working with series of geometric shapes. Before you begin, establish the eyeline in the picture and remember that converging lines meet at a vanishing point on the eyeline.

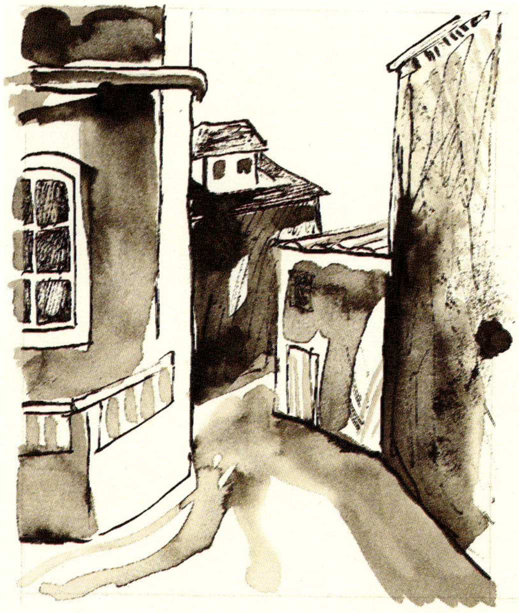

When you are looking down a street with buildings on both sides, all the perspective lines converge towards the same vanishing point. When deciding what viewpoint to take, try to position the vanishing point slightly off centre in order to make the composition more interesting. Don't, therefore, take a position where you are looking down the middle of a street. Stand to one side or the other so that the buildings along one side of the road take on a sharper focus, and a more central role, than those on the other side. If your street scene includes steps up or down, plot the horizontal lines of the steps in pencil before you add paint to ensure that the levels and angles are accurate. This will make the painting far easier to complete.

Many watercolourists choose to paint townscapes using pen and ink, both to structure the underdrawing, and to overlay fine details such as window-frames and paving stones. This makes a lot of sense, and will help you to underpin the basic construction of the scene. Once the pen-and-ink underdrawing has dried, the watercolour can be floated over the top to create tone and enhance form. By combining watercolour wet into wet with permanent ink, you can achieve an interesting array of brick and metal effects particularly suited to paintings of buildings, too.

Effective textures for brickwork and other facades will draw upon your texturing skills. Use a combination of effects to produce variation across a painting – from stippling and spattering to some scraping back or lifting out. Used in conjunction with each other, these techniques should provide you with a wide choice.

Compositions and textures
There are a number of ways to create interesting townscapes. Use linear perspective as a guide for the geometric shapes of the buildings and to ensure that features are in the correct scale. To begin with, establish the horizon line, and then locate the vanishing point of the street. Draw in the main lines of the buildings in pencil so that you can rub them out once you have started applying paint. To emphasize certain buildings, or foreground details, bring your texturing skills into play.

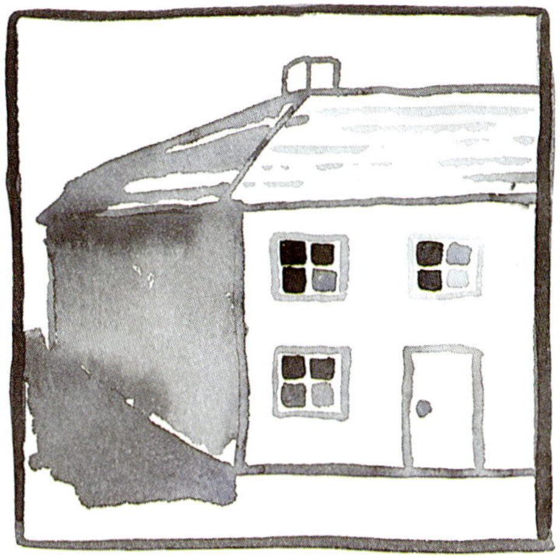

Composing with buildings
For an up-front effect, draw the buildings face on, creating depth by marking in the perspective lines and vanishing point.

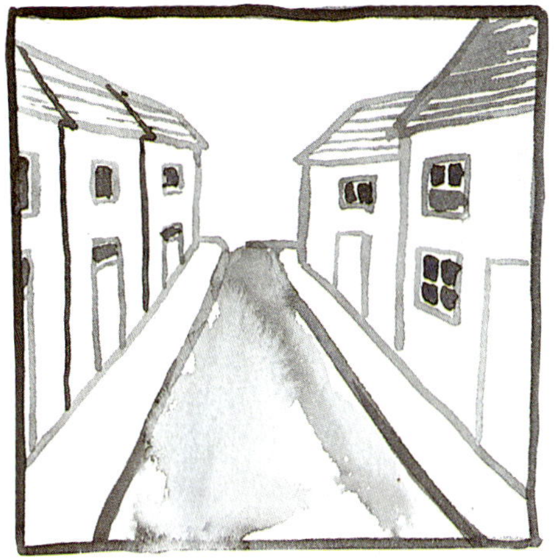

Allow the vanishing point to exist just off-centre to create interest in this linear street scene.

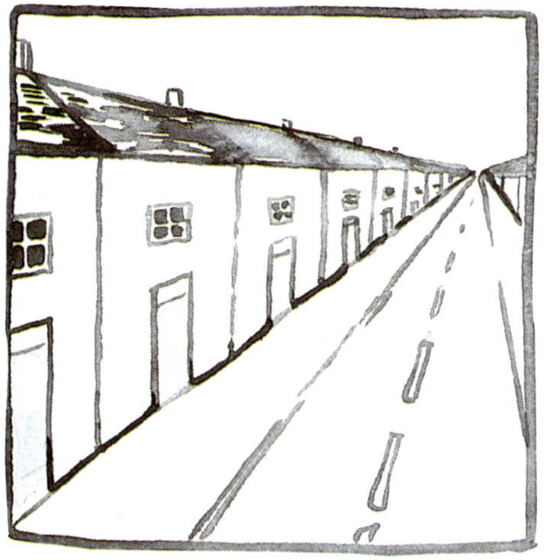

To create the impression of great distance, make the street become narrower and reduce everything in size towards the vanishing point on the horizon line.

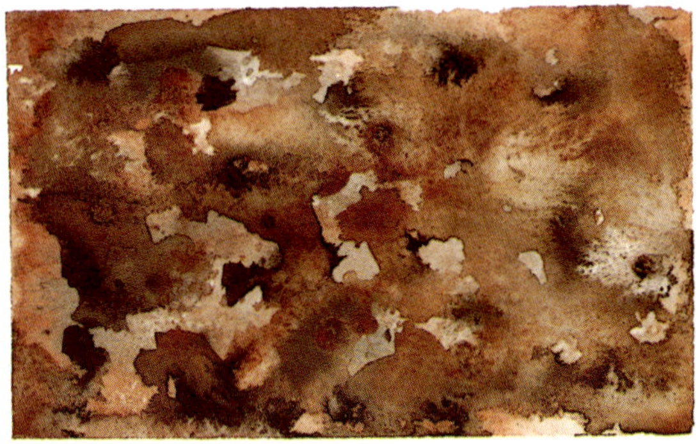

Texturing facades
Lay down a pale, warm wash, such as burnt sienna. While it is still damp, drop black waterproof ink and a thicker solution of burnt sienna over the top and watch how they create a marbled surface.

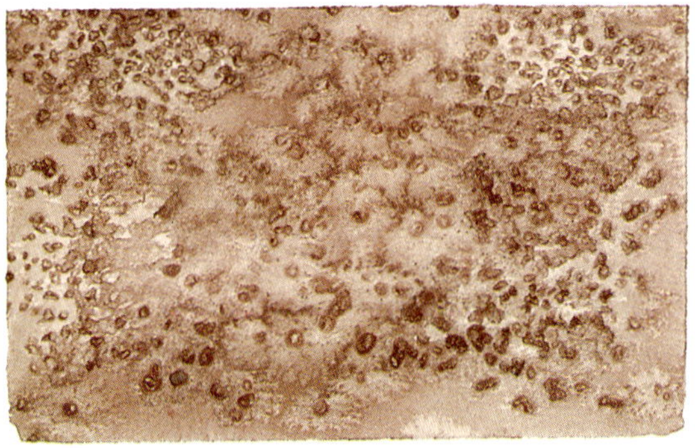

Paint a wash of colour, then sprinkle salt over the surface while the paint is still wet. When it is dry, rub the salt away and you will be left with a rough, cobbled effect.

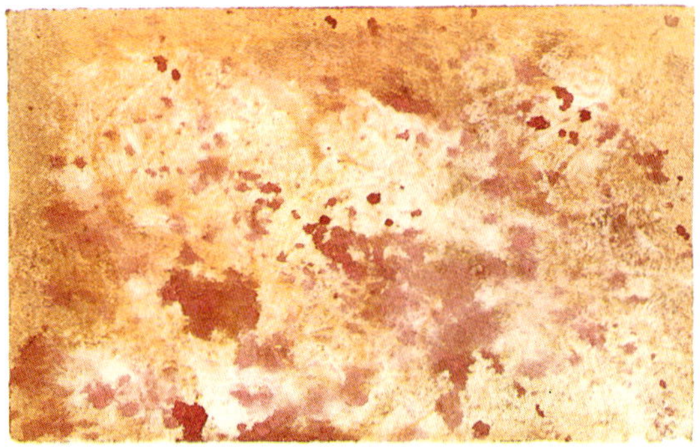

Lay down a flat, warm-coloured wash, then use a crunched-up piece of tissue paper to lift out the wet paint. Now spatter a second, brighter colour over the top with a toothbrush to produce a brick-like surface.

Combining line and wash
A pen-and-ink underdrawing will help you to plan the painting, and you can then fill in the buildings with washes and overlays of watercolour. If you want to retain a clean surface, allow the ink to dry completely before adding any paint. Once the ink is dry, you can overlay watercolour and, as in this instance, add more pen-and-ink lines to create textures and refine details.

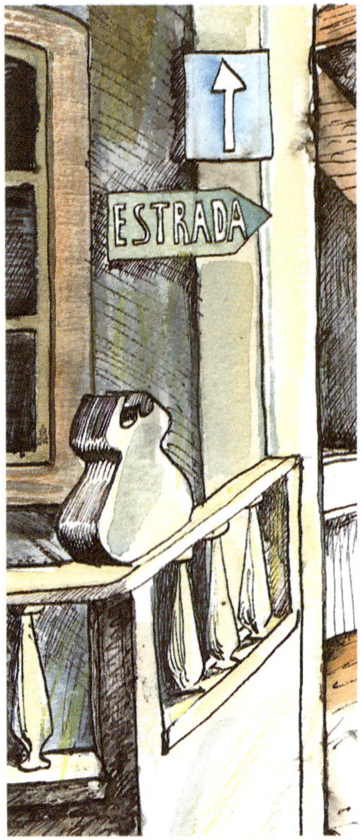

RIGHT Use pen and ink to make an underdrawing, and once it is dry, wash in very pale colours to produce the undertones of the buildings. Once the paint is dry, overlay pen-and-ink lines in this area to produce very clear details.

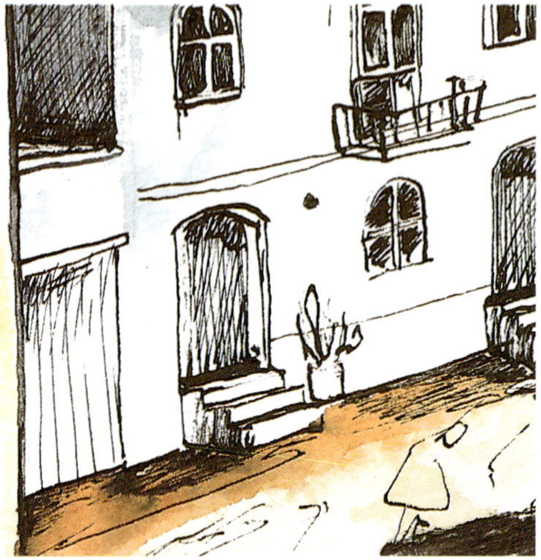

LEFT Keep the centre of the painting light in tone to contrast with the darker walls on either side. This will encourage the onlooker's eye to travel down the winding street to the middle ground. Parts of this façade are left completely white to enhance the effect.

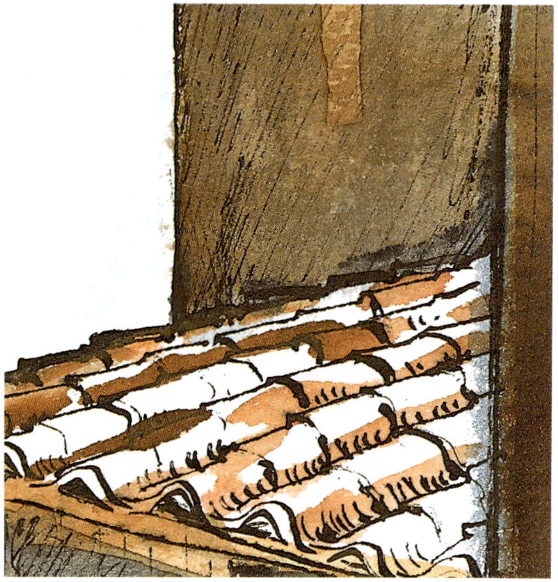

ABOVE By mixing burnt umber and permanent black ink together, wet-into-wet, you can achieve a rust-like texture suitable for old, crumbling walls on the side of a street, such as here, which have been made filthier by passing traffic. Rub the two media into each other with a finger or rag to blend them.

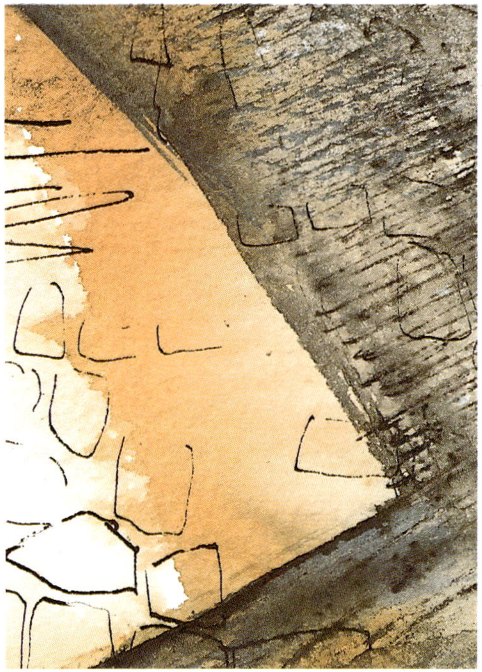

RIGHT Details do not always need refining. A few suggestive pen-and-ink lines give the sense of paving stones, without making them the focus of the foreground. They help, instead, to lead the eye towards the details further into the painting.

Helpful Tips
- To keep your painting simple, use a limited palette of colours. In this instance only five colours are needed: burnt umber, raw sienna, Payne's grey, yellow ochre and cerulean blue.

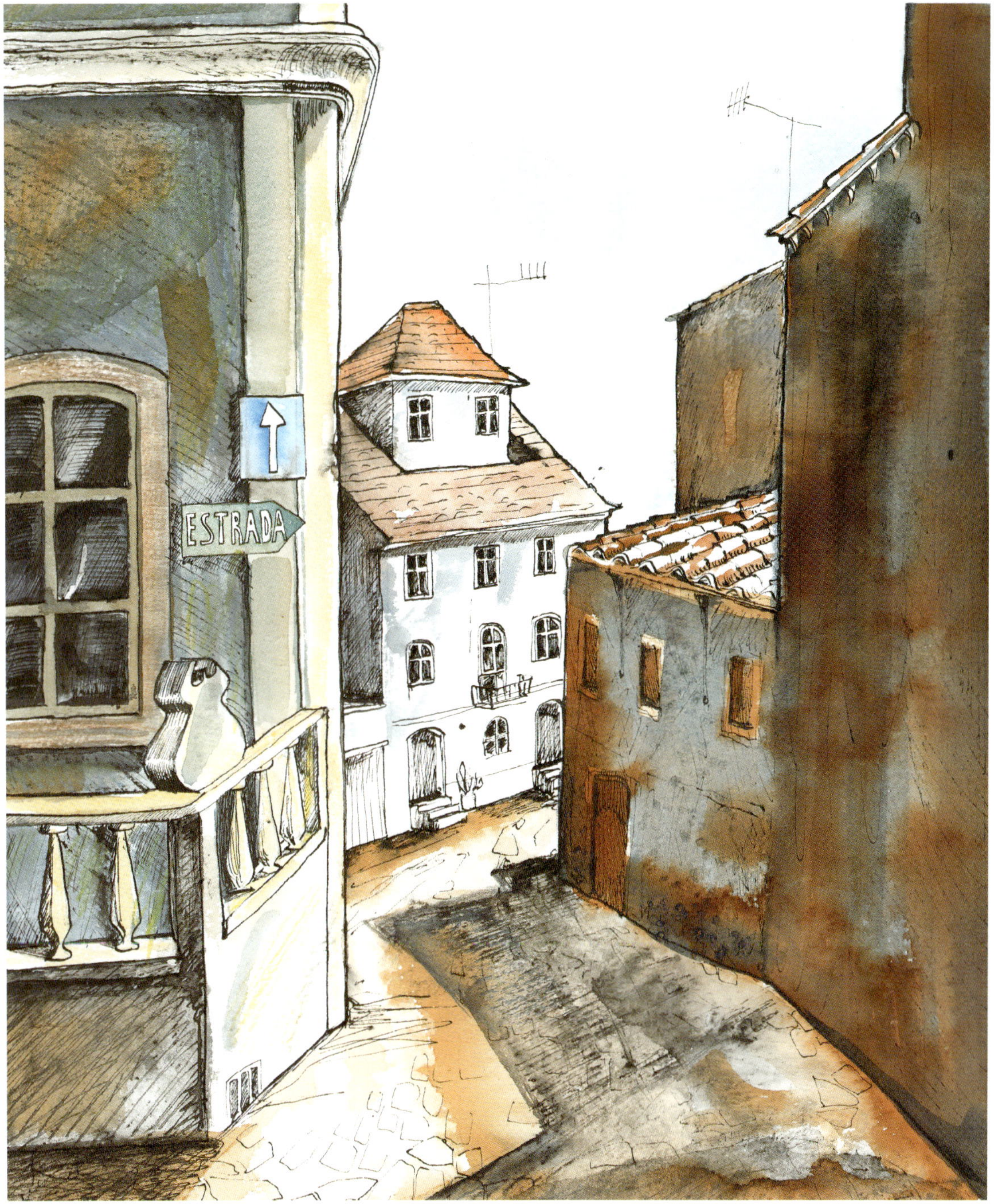

LEFT This painting is composed with only a few colours and pen and ink in order to create structure and enhance textures, using the initial pen-and-ink sketch and a collection of photographs for reference. Note how the viewpoint takes advantage of the angle of the street and the winding road.

Still Life with Fruit

Mixing Complementaries and Neutrals

Unlike a landscape, which you cannot rearrange, the objects in a still-life arrangement need to be positioned by you before you set to work. The selection of a subject, and the arrangement of objects into a composition, requires an understanding of the ways in which you can achieve the effect you want. Do you want your picture to appear random and 'found', or do you want to create a theatrical arrangement? Are the colours in your composition to be tonally compatible, or striking in their discord? Are you going to select objects of a similar scale, texture and tone, or combine shapes and sizes to create a change of pace and emphasis throughout your still-life set-up? All of these factors need to be considered before you begin.

The subject of this still-life project is fruit and vegetables, whose colours and shapes are naturally compatible. Their scale is similar, although their shapes differ, adding a degree of variation to the set-up. When you choose objects, consider their colours, textures, shapes and sizes. Arrange them in a group, not too formally, but so that the onlooker's gaze is led through the painting, from the foreground towards the back of the picture.

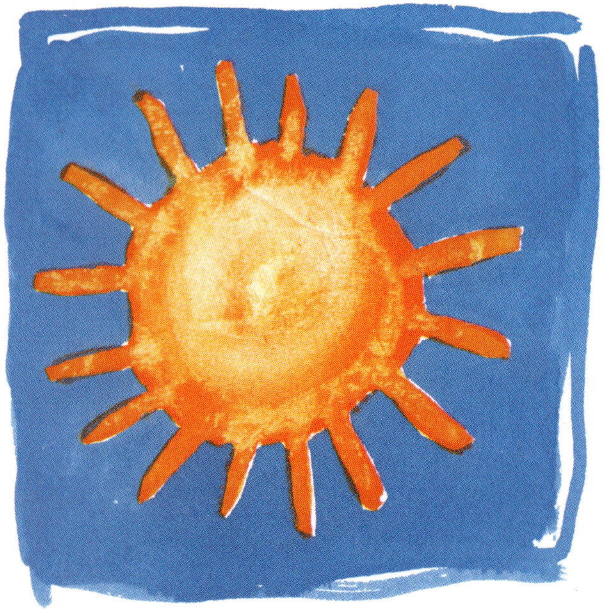

The emphasis within this project is on mixing complementary colours and neutral tones. Refer back to colour mixing (see pages 36–7) to refresh your understanding of the colour wheel and complementary colours. Complementary colours are those that sit directly opposite one another on the colour wheel. When two complementaries are painted next to one another, they intensify each other, making both appear brighter than when each is used on its own. Here, the complementaries are placed close together, so producing a bright, fresh still-life composition.

When two complementaries are mixed together, they produce neutral tones that are perfect for painting shadows. When the effects created by using complementaries side by side and mixed are combined in one painting, the result is a harmonious but colourful painting.

Before you set to work on the still life, you could try some simple exercises to improve your colour-mixing skills. Try painting blocks of two complementary colours side by side and see how each complements the other. Now paint two random blocks of colour side by side and note how much flatter they seem.

Finding complementaries
To find complementary pairs, refer back to the colour wheel (see pages 34–5). The complementary of any colour on the wheel is the one that lies directly opposite it. When you put these two colours next to one another in a painting, each will enhance the brilliance of the other. When you mix them together, they will produce a wide range of neutral colours.

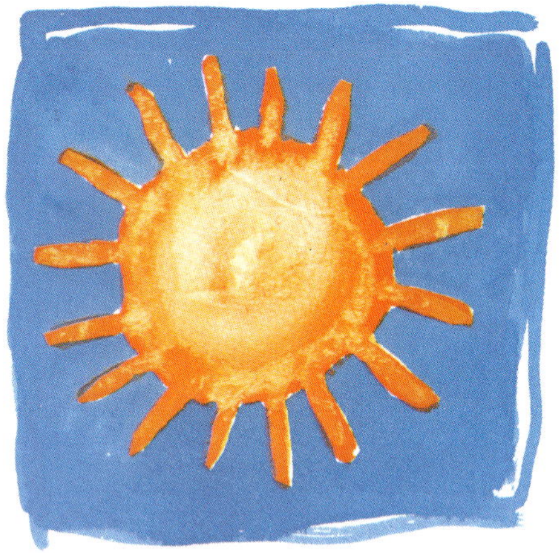

Orange and blue are complementaries, each drawing out the brilliance of the other. Refer to the colour wheel to find the complementary pairs. They sit opposite one another on the wheel.

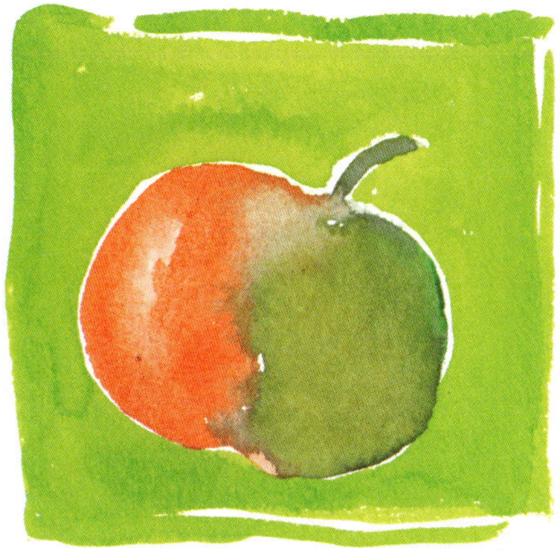

Green and red are complementaries. These two colours often appear together in nature – the apple being a perfect example.

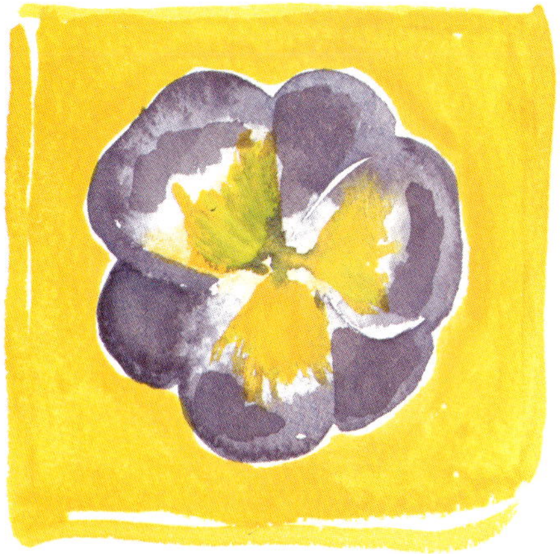

Purple and yellow are very different colours, yet how well they complement one another, both colours appearing equally vivid when painted next to each other.

Helpful Tips
- Keep your complementary colours as clean as possible in order to achieve the greatest brilliance when using them together.

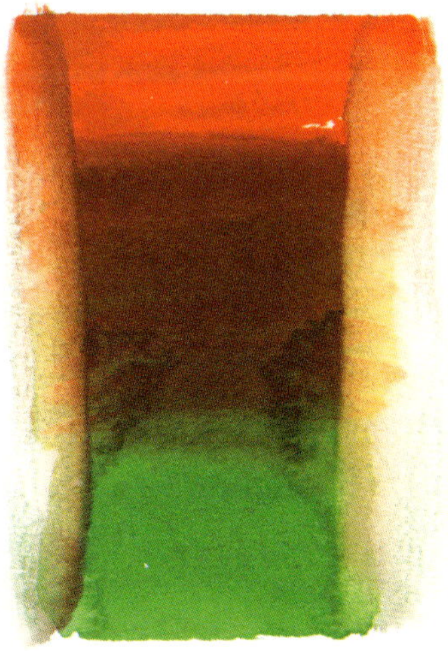

Producing neutral tints
Mix scarlet lake with Hooker's green light to produce a rich, neutral tint.

Mix French ultramarine with cadmium orange to produce a warm neutral tint.

Mix cadmium yellow with purple to produce a paler neutral tint.

Still life with fruits
This still-life project relies on complementary pairs to create harmony and unity across the surface of the picture. Select fruit and vegetables in complementary colours in order to gain the most benefit from their natural compatibility, and mix them together to create neutrals for shading.

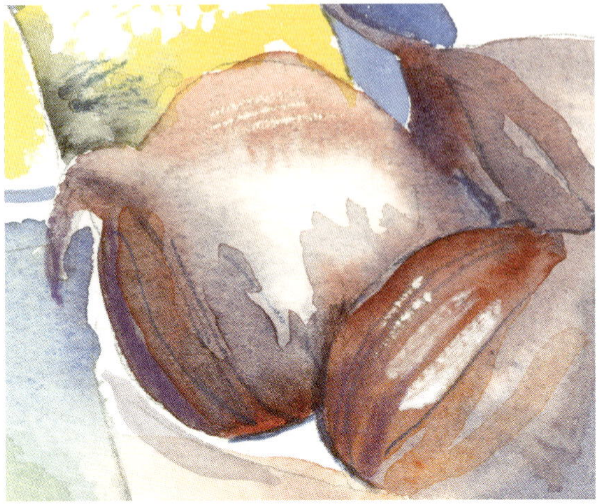

LEFT Place objects next to one another that are complementary – the lemons, although placed in a separate bowl to the purple onions, are overlapped by them so that the complementary colours are adjacent.

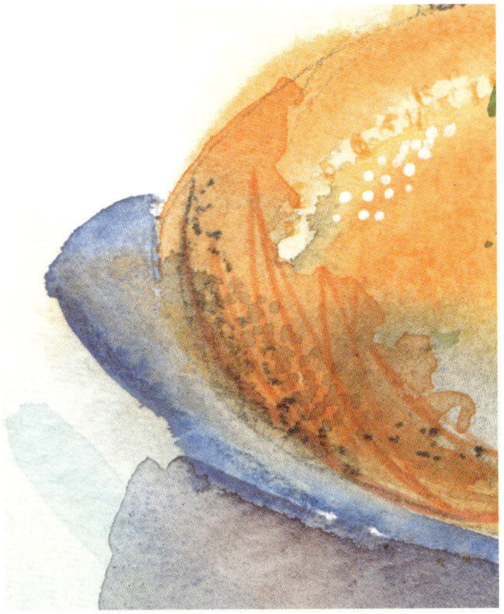

ABOVE Choose a plate whose colour complements the fruit placed on it. This blue plate makes the oranges appear far richer in tone than they might otherwise do.

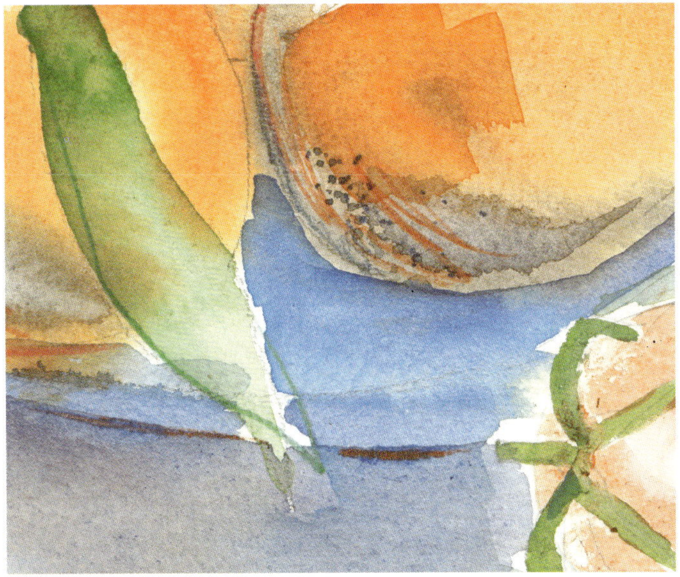

ABOVE Mix neutrals from the complementary pairs to add shadows around the base of objects, which will create depth. Here, orange and blue are combined to produce a cool neutral, suitable for the shadow around the base of the plate.

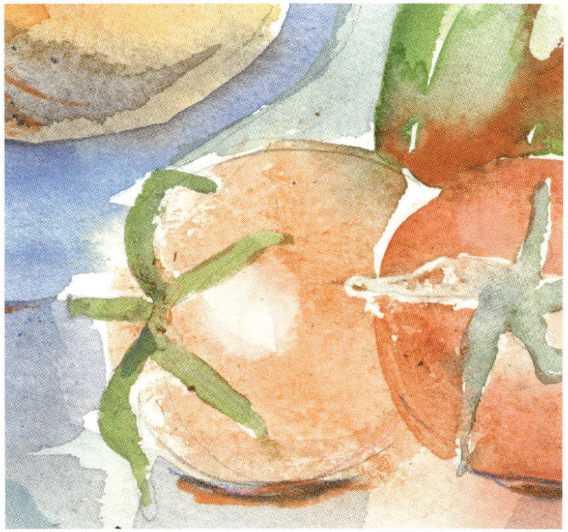

ABOVE Apples and tomatoes are placed next to one another so that the cool and warm complementary pairs of red and green can be juxtaposed. Chinese white body colour is used to add highlights on the apples and make them appear glossy.

OPPOSITE The complementary pairs produce a fresh painting in which all of the colours appear harmonious in tone and hue.

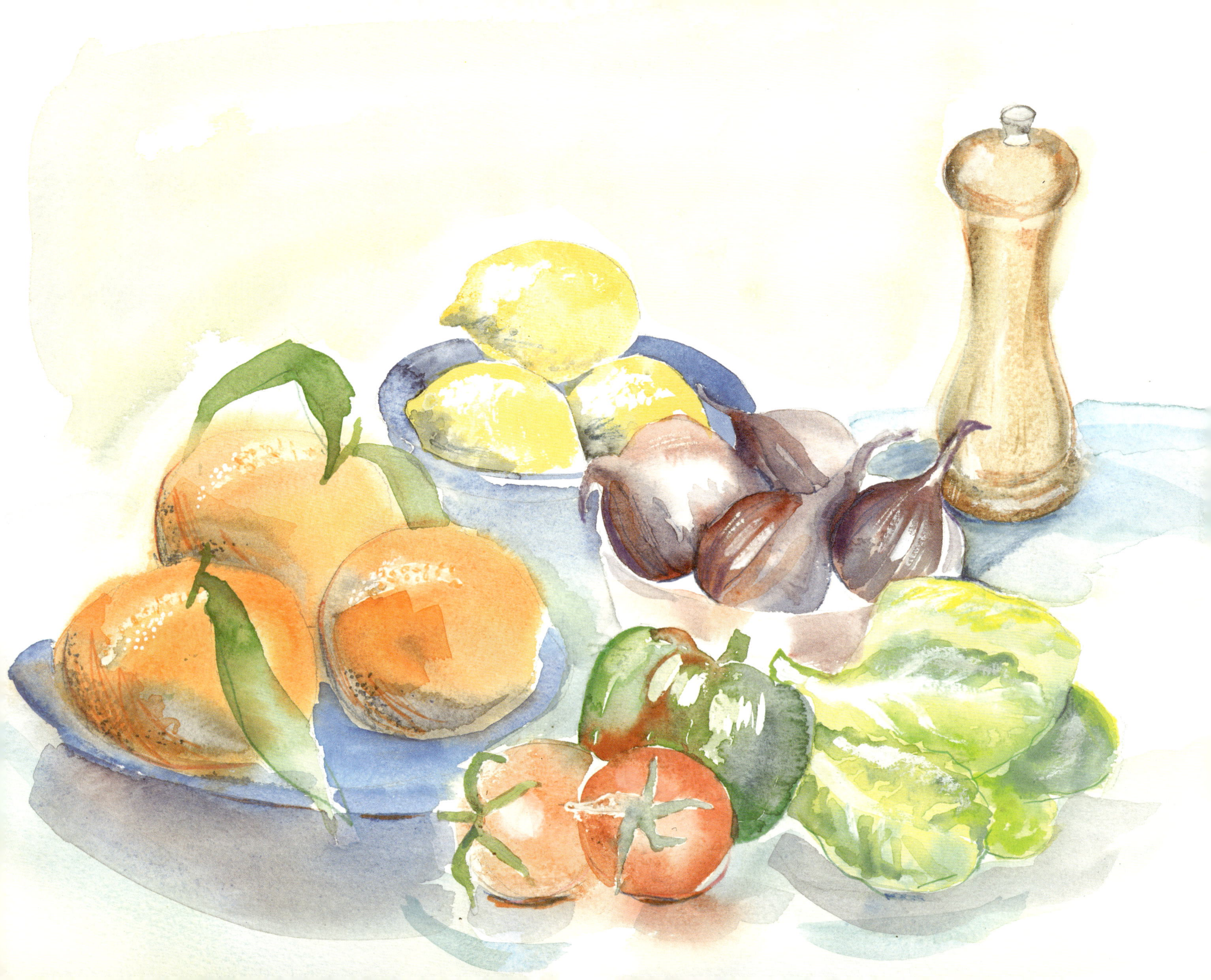

Water

Colours and Types

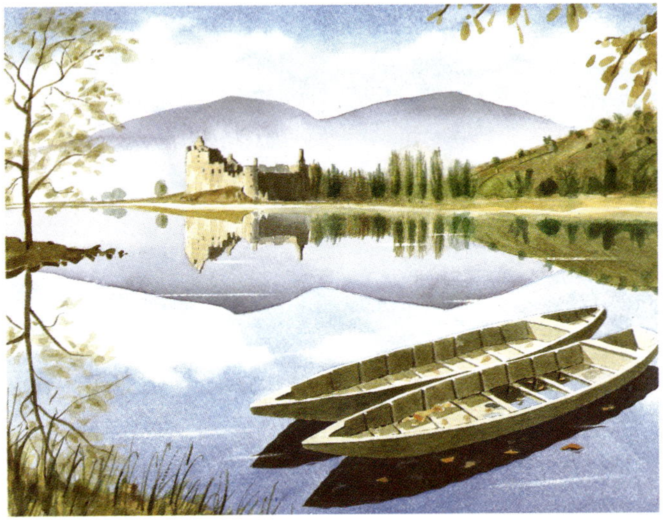

Watercolour is the perfect medium for painting its namesake, the translucent qualities of the paint reflecting water's transparency. To make the most of this relationship, keep your paintings fresh and lively, as overworked colours are the surest way to mar the clarity of water.

A simple way to achieve this translucent impression is by laying flat washes of paint and allowing stripes of white paper to show through. Overlay two or three colours, wet on dry (see pages 54–5), to build up depth, but don't allow the paint to run or melt into the other colours as this will destroy the crisp effect created by this technique, which is particularly suited to depicting still oceans or flat lakes.

If you don't feel confident about leaving areas of white paper, mask them out with fine strips of masking tape or fluid before you begin. To paint an ocean from horizon to foreground apply a gradated wash, making it pale towards the horizon line. For a sunset or sunrise scene over water, use vivid oranges and pinks in a variegated wash to achieve a similar effect.

These techniques are particularly suited to large, open expanses of clear, calm water, but there are many instances where you will probably want to achieve a more moody effect. Wet-into-wet, melted washes of different colours can be used to produce lovely atmospheric effects, suitable for mist rising over rivers, or rain above a lake. To create the effect of ripples, try using repeated calligraphic S-shaped strokes of paint, laid over a very pale wash of the base colour. Make the ripples thinner and smaller as they recede, but retain a rhythm between each line. To produce white crests on waves, use Chinese white body colour instead of watercolour paint at the tip of each wave.

To create more tempestuous effects – for fast-running waters such as river rapids or waterfalls, or stormy seas – you will need to be more adventurous. In such instances, various techniques for creating texture come into their own.

To produce spray effects on waves or rapids, spatters or stipples of Chinese white body colour over washes of paint are particularly effective. Alternatively, a few touches of watercolour pencil can describe movement on the surface. Dry-brush marks over flat washes are also suitable. Use masking fluid to block out areas of particularly rough water, and then stipple colours into those areas once any surrounding paint is dry.

Colours and types
There are many types of water and each has a different mood. Bear in mind that any mass of water will reflect the colours in the objects that surround it – grey skies will make water appear darker and cooler than warm blue skies, which will lift and lighten its tone. Remember to grade water from dark in the foreground to light towards the horizon line in order to make the most effective response to this subject.

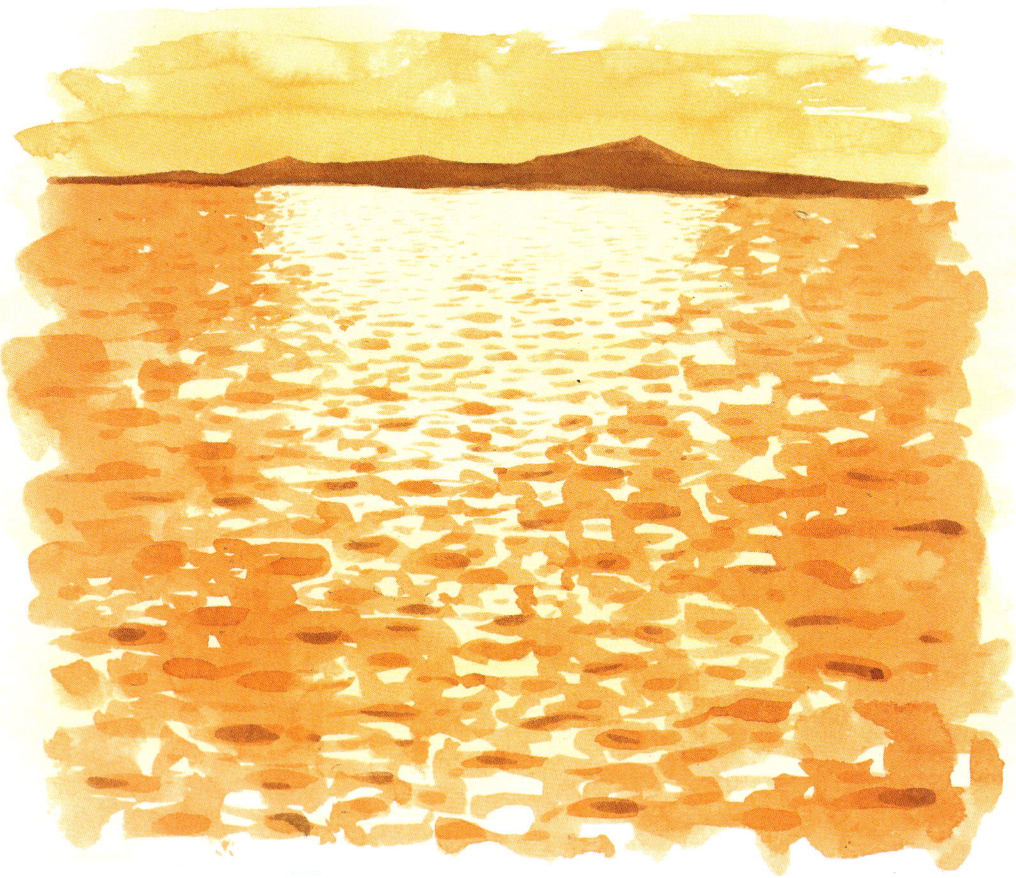

LEFT This warm, moody sunset seascape has been painted with aurora yellow, cadmium orange and burnt sienna. Note how the thick, calligraphic marks of three different tones of orange create movement and rhythm over the choppy surface. To produce a sense of distance, makes the marks smaller as they recede towards the horizon. The sky is comprised of a much flatter wash, which contrasts with the sea and emphasizes the movement on the water surface.

BELOW Variegated washes and overlays of Payne's grey, Winsor violet and French ultramarine blue create a tempestuous sea.

BELOW Use Chinese white gouache to produce random spray effects over the top of water and waves. Here the spray seems to lift up off the surface of the water.

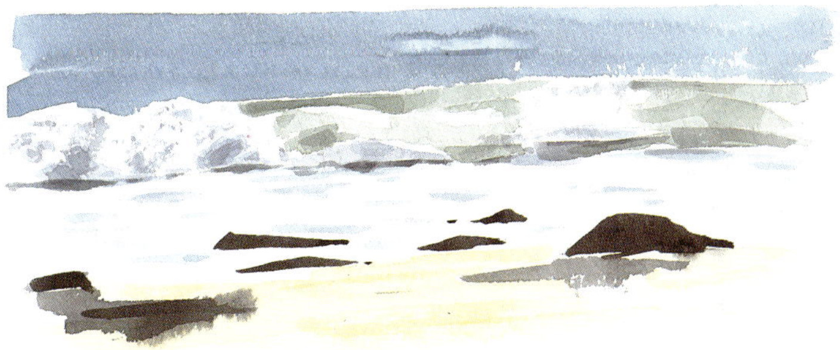

Reflections on water
Water will reflect the colour of the sky and of any objects that surround it. In this instance, the water is completely clear and still, so is depicted only through those objects reflected in its surface.

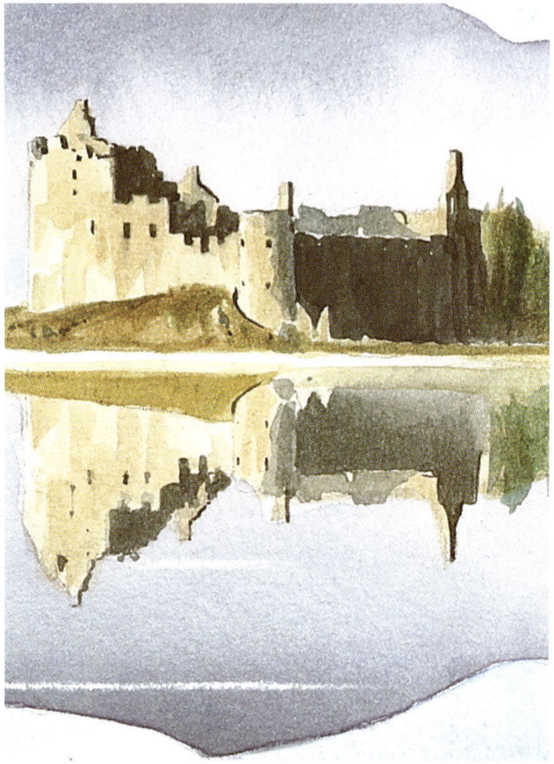

ABOVE The reflection of the castle in the water is less well defined than the castle itself in order to make a distinction between the two forms.

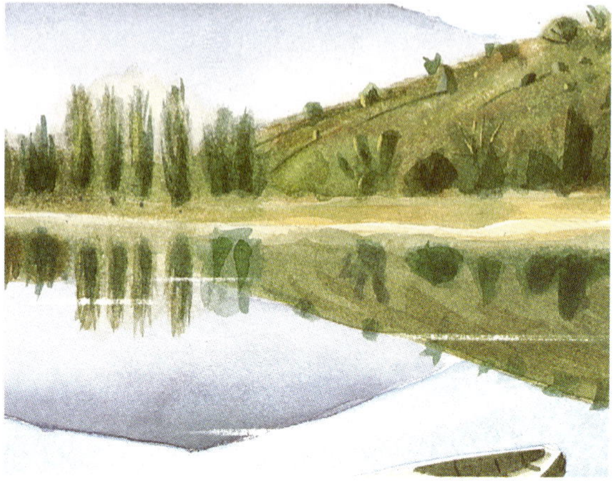

ABOVE There are slight ripples in the surface of the water, shown by fine lines of Chinese white gouache.

OPPOSITE Very clean, fresh watercolours are used to capture the effect of clear, still water through the reflections on its surface. There is a subtle contrast between the more defined elements on land and their reflections in the water, but it is enough to establish the difference between the two.

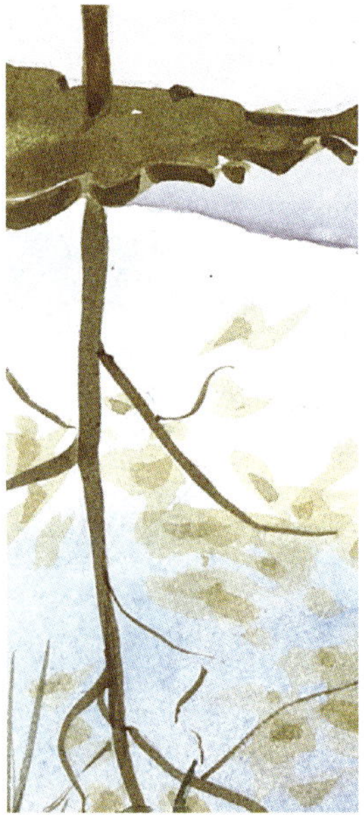

ABOVE The tree and clouds that lie above are reflected in the water. Note how the blue of the water becomes more intense towards the foreground.

ABOVE Chinese white gouache is scumbled over the water to suggest reflections of clouds above.

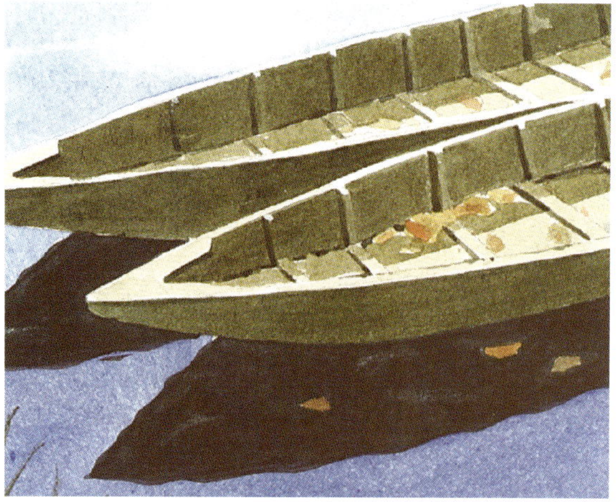

ABOVE The shadows underneath the boats are extremely dark, suggesting the depths of the water below.

ABOVE The water is an intense French ultramarine blue in the foreground.

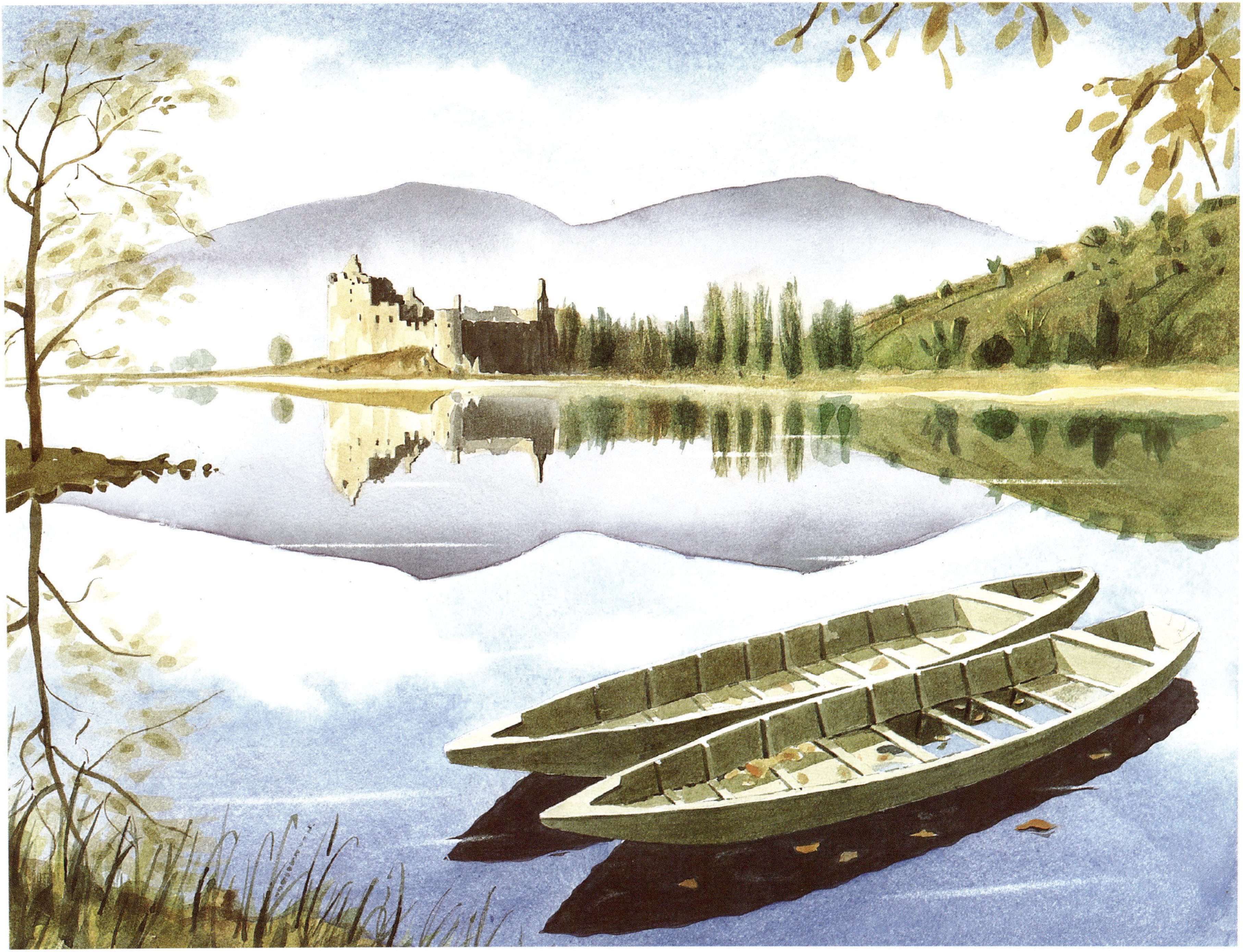

Interiors

Flat Colours and .Patterns

Interiors pose a whole new set of challenges – none more so than what type of composition you should consider. Elements within a room often look compatible to the naked eye, yet when it comes to finding a composition to paint, the whole effect starts to appear disorganized, even random. If this is the case, you need to do some quick rearranging before setting to work.

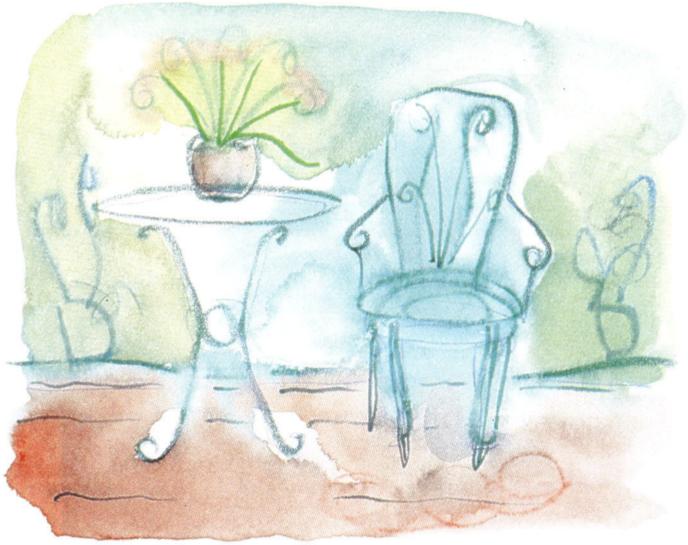

Try to keep the composition interesting, but not too fussy. Take out a standard lamp, or vase of flowers, if it makes the scene too complicated, or add them in if they will provide a decorative element in an otherwise drab room. Contrasting shapes and patterns might well enhance your composition, so don't feel obliged to work with colour-coordinated objects. These can, in fact, look dull, as they provide no change of pace in a picture.

The French artist Henri Matisse (1869–1954) was the master of paintings of this subject. He managed to combine the exuberant colours, textures and patterns of French interiors with an apparent simplicity, producing paintings that were at the same time elaborate yet uncomplicated to look at. The secret lay in his use of colour and composition. Use a limited range of colours, and keep them clean and bright. Don't try to introduce too many tonal contrasts. Instead, work with colours that are either warm or cool. Don't worry too much about creating a sense of depth. Instead, rely on flat patterns and bright colours to carry the mood of the picture. To add the suggestion of depth, follow Matisse's device of including a window in the composition to lead the eye through the interior and towards the window, implying depth and light beyond the picture plane.

Patterns are a lot of fun to paint, and interiors provide ample opportunities to experiment. Wallpapers, carpets, curtains and furniture are usually decorated with repeated patterns and motifs. Try to use a different treatment for each pattern. Use masking fluid to block out one, and perhaps overlay pen-and-ink marks or watercolour-pencil details on another. Watercolours can also be layered in order to build up the tonal differences necessary to create the folds in fabric. Other techniques include mixing media such as pastels and oil crayons over or under watercolour paint to produce varied effects.

Creating interesting patterns

Before you set to work on an interior, practise painting different patterns. They don't have to be done on flat backgrounds. Instead, you can build up a textured ground to work on in particular areas, so producing changes in style between one furnishing and another.

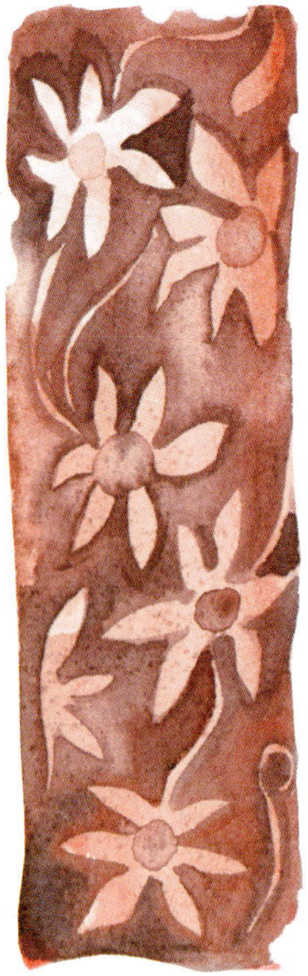

Wet on dry

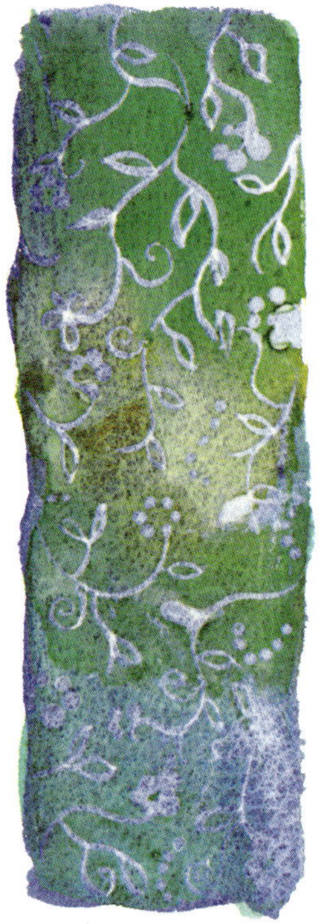

Variegated wash over masking fluid

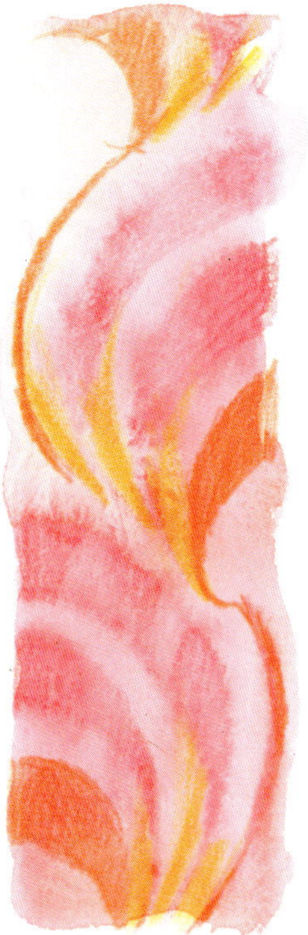

Watercolour pencil over watercolour washes

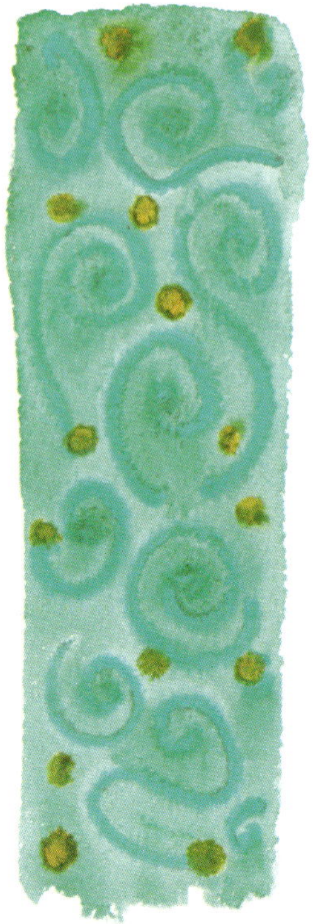

Pencil and oil crayon over watercolour wash

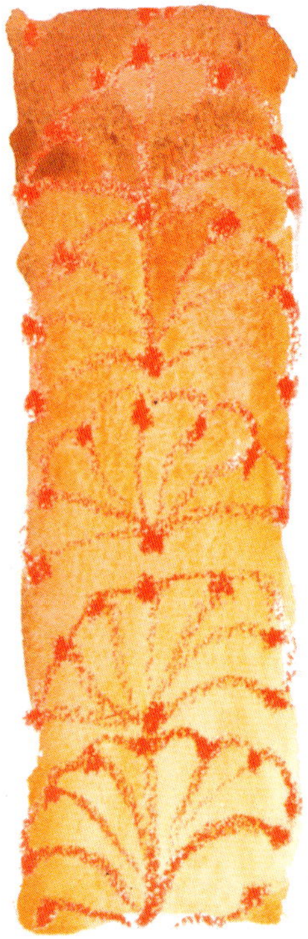

Wash of watercolour over oil pastel to create wax resist

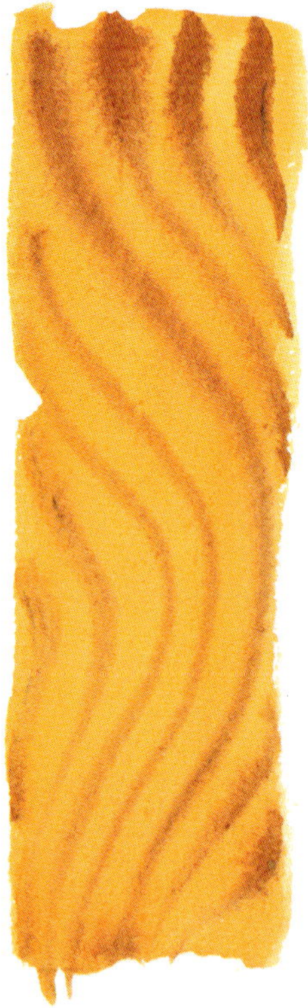

Watercolour paint, wet in wet

A bright interior
Choose a limited range of bright colours. In this instance, the artist has relied on the range selected for the limited palette on pages 32–3. You can use the same range of colours, or extend the palette to make the painting more varied. Make a series of colour sketches to establish the placement of elements in the composition. When you are ready to begin, make a very light pencil sketch of the composition on to watercolour paper, preferably using watercolour pencil.

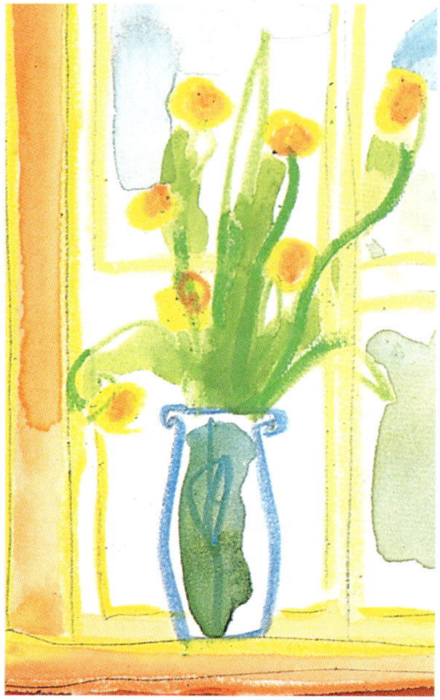

LEFT To produce the impression of glass, touch a very pale, green wash into each pane, leaving spaces white. Then mark in the vase using a watercolour pencil. Put in the flowerheads with a wax crayon, then add watercolour stems and petals over the top. Keep each mark light and gestural.

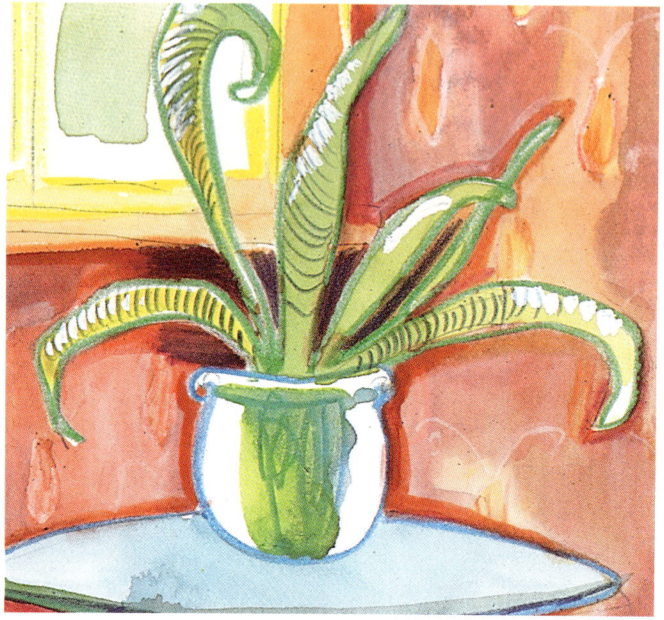

RIGHT The cactus plant dominates the table top. Paint in the outlines of the leaves in a dark green watercolour or wax pencil, then add washes over the top. Once these are dry, you can mark in further patterns using sharp and fine watercolour-pencil marks.

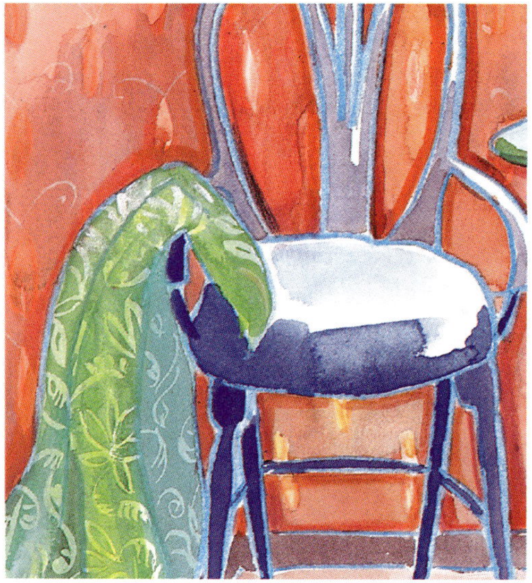

LEFT Paint the outlines of the chair and table in pale blue paint and allow them to dry. Don't worry if the lines are a little unsteady because the inconsistency will add to the naive nature of the painting. Once dry, fill in the darker tones with loose washes of watercolour, ensuring that the paint does not drift outside the painted outlines. Leave bright highlights white. Mask out the pattern on the cloth and leave it to dry. Once dry, wash over different green tones to produce a folded effect, enhancing this by painting strong, vertical blue lines between the folds of fabric.

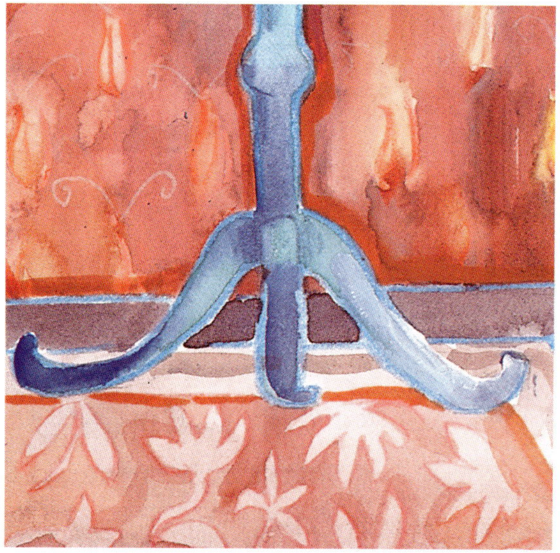

LEFT Mask out the carpet pattern, then paint light washes over the area of the rug. Once the first washes have dried, use fine lines drawn with watercolour, or watercolour pencil, over the top of the washes to define the edges of the carpet. Now rub off the masking fluid and wash a further layer of the same colour over the carpet, which will make the pattern appear less distinct than if areas had been left white.

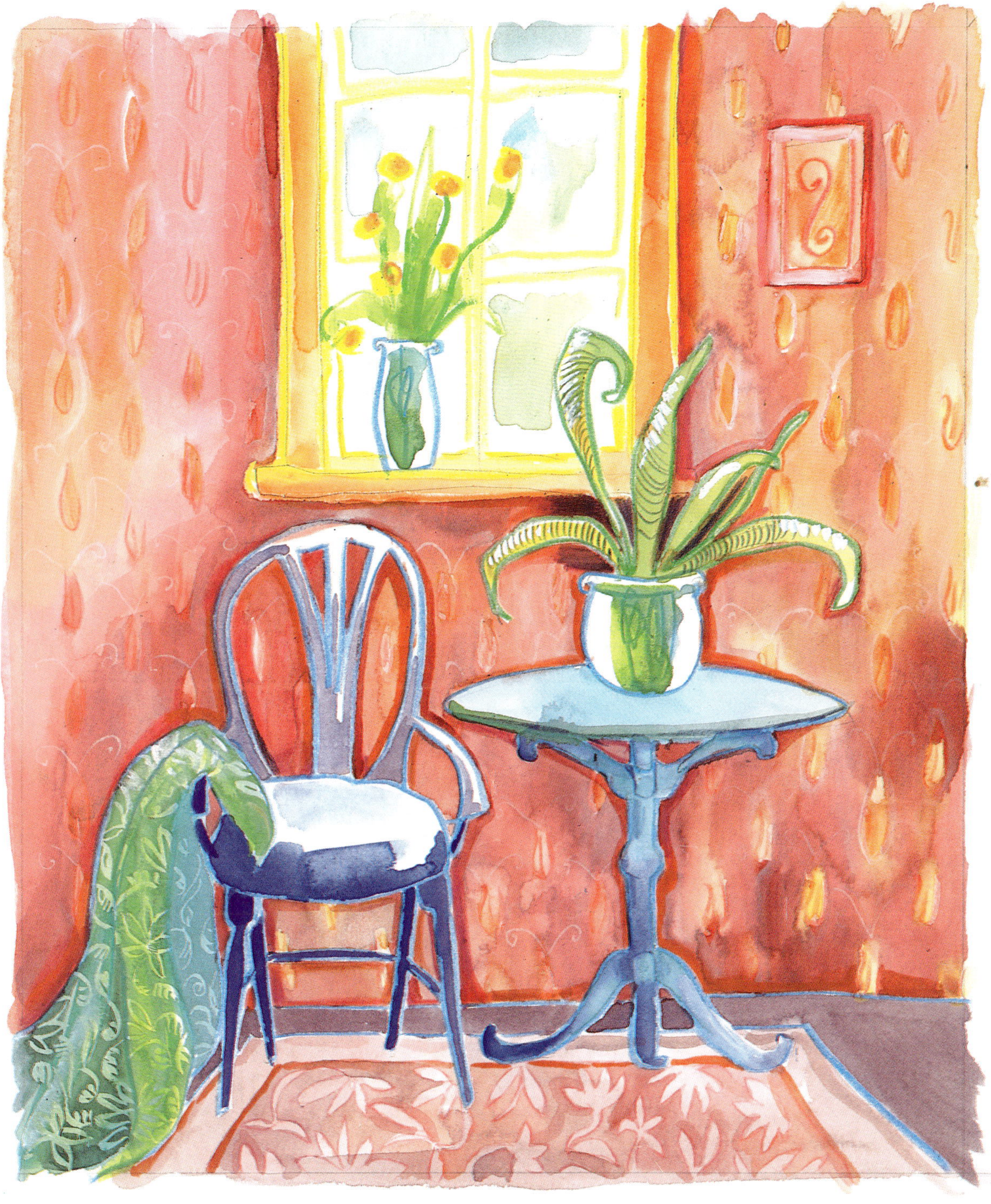

LEFT With the use of bright colours and very little mixing, the painting retains a lively and decorative feeling. The composition appears simple, yet it includes quite a number of interesting shapes, patterns and textures.

Skies

Moods and Atmospheres

Sky, like water, is a natural subject for the watercolourist. No other media can capture the translucent qualities of the atmosphere in quite the same way. No wonder Turner was obsessed by the changing effects of light and the problem of how to capture them with this wonderfully fluid medium. There is nothing more satisfying than laying down a saturated wash and watching it spread and melt over the paper of its own accord. The unpredictability of watercolour is something to be cherished, as long as you are confident enough to enjoy it! Allow watercolour to flood the paper and, provided that you are using a relevant range of colours, it will practically create a sky effect before your very eyes. This is because the sky is as unpredictable as the medium. Sit and observe it for more than a second, and it will reinvent itself as you watch. You will never be able to freeze an impression for long enough to copy it accurately.

Instead of attempting a copy, aim to capture the sky's mood. Is it a cool, grey day or a bright, warm one? Is the sky an endless blue, or a patchwork of slate and charcoal greys? Are the clouds high in the sky, or thunderously low? Where is the light source – is it overhead, or perhaps shining from behind the clouds? If you observe the sky you will soon come to appreciate that it is never a single colour. Even the clearest blue sky includes areas of variation, and it almost always gets lighter towards the horizon line.

Try to produce a range of dark, intense hues in night skies to produce depth. Prussian blue and Payne's grey are two watercolours that create a wide range of deep purple and blue hues, perfect for stormy or night skies. Use touches of bright colours like cadmium yellow to produce lights in the sky.

Gradated and variegated washes are as successful for applying skies as they are for water. Alternatively, a wet-into-wet technique incorporating backruns works equally well. Don't be afraid to make skies dramatic, either, and use a wide range of colours to capture the atmosphere.

The night sky can be an exciting challenge to paint. The sky is never completely black, so you can render it in watercolour without having to reach for black inks. Mask out stars and the moon before working dark washes across the sky, then rub the fluid away once the watercolour has dried. You can then add in touches of yellow or orange to achieve the impression of shining lights.

Painting the sky
The sky should be an integral part of the painting – it should not be an afterthought that gets filled in at the end. The sky tones should reflect the overall values in your painting – even if you want the effect of the sky to be a subtle one. If you paint a wash over the whole paper before adding details, you will create a natural unity between the sky and the land mass below. Enjoy allowing the watercolour to do some of the work for you – you will never be able to paint the same sky twice!

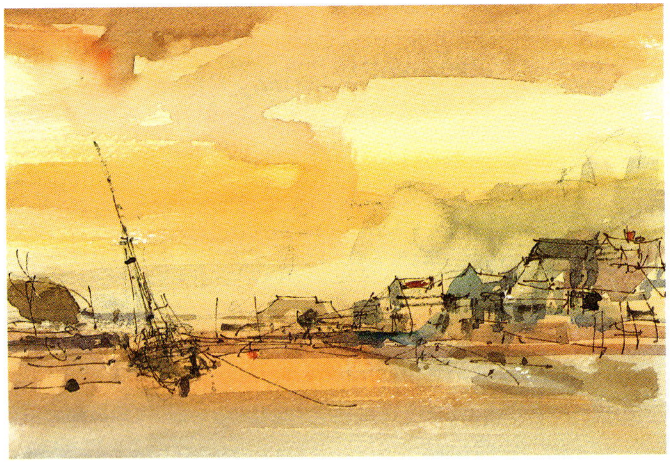

ABOVE Use oranges and browns to produce a richly toned dusk sky. Although the sun is absent, its effect is felt in both the sky and water.

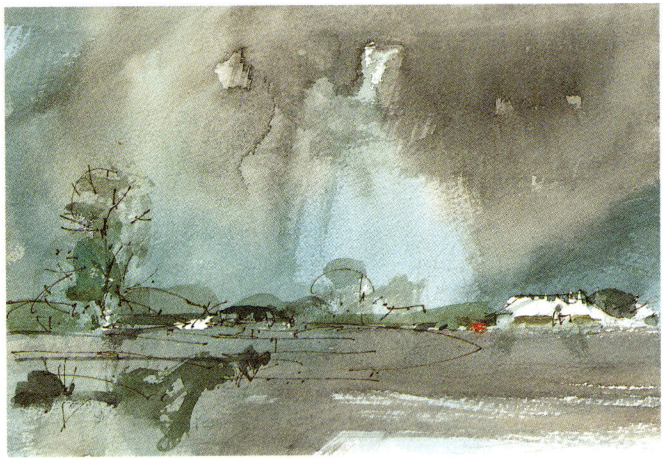

ABOVE As clouds form the sky darkens, and the suggestion of falling rain is produced through washes of watercolour across dry paper.

Helpful Tips
● To paint clouds, leave areas of paper white; or, if you want a really concise effect, mask them out before applying washes. Chinese white body colour overlaid on to damp washes will make effective soft clouds, and on to dry washes will produce more clearly defined tones. Another trick is to lift out paint with a damp sponge!

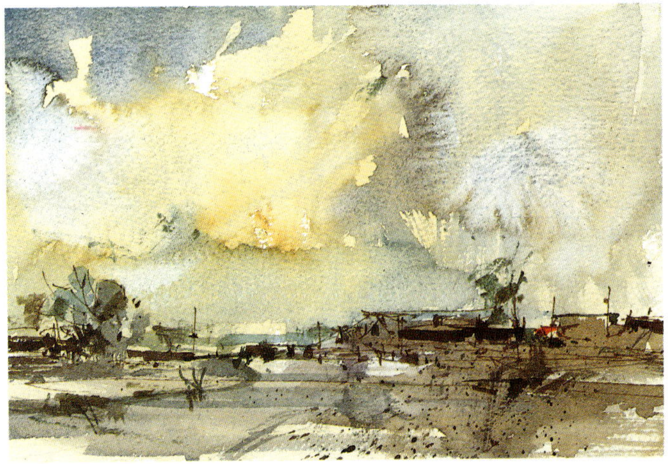

ABOVE Use a wide range of tones to develop a dramatic sky. In this instance, the colours range from dark blue to white.

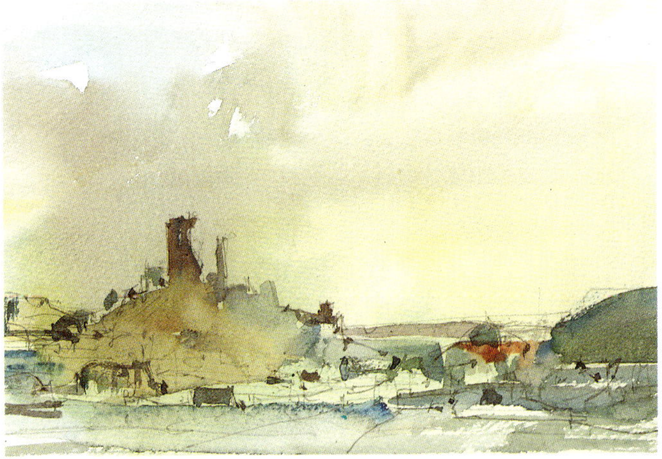

ABOVE Negative space can be as important as positive space – see how this very simple seascape dominates the composition.

Painting dramatic skies
The sky does not have to play a secondary role – in this example it is the subject of the work, taking up two-thirds of the picture surface. There is very little detail, but the composition feels complete. Washes of water applied over the paint create backruns that flood the paper, giving an appearance of rain.

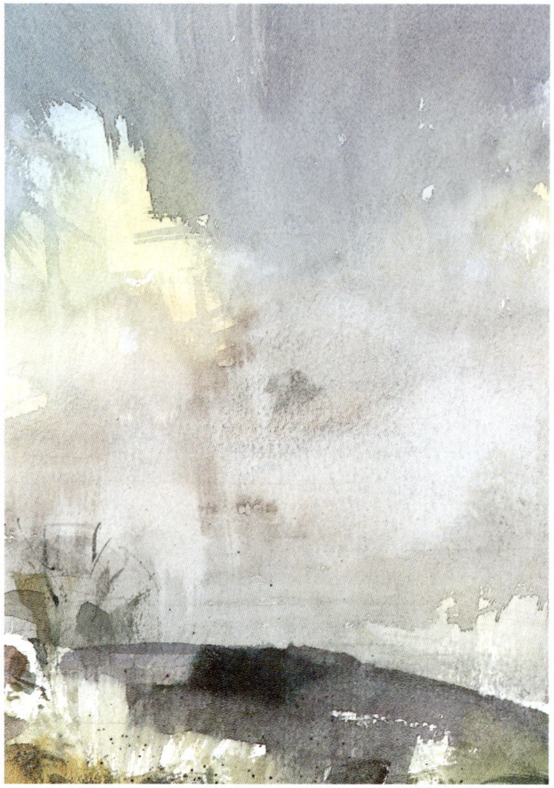

ABOVE By brushing paint diagonally across the paper, you can suggest the impression of rainfall. Notice, too, how burnt sienna is mixed with French ultramarine blue in the sky. It also appears in the hills on the horizon line, enhancing the unity of the painting.

RIGHT The atmosphere of the sky is enhanced by the use of broad brushstrokes, and areas of the paper are left free of paint to create bright light behind the tempestuous pink and purple clouds.

BELOW The horizon line is low and the sky darkens as it recedes towards it.

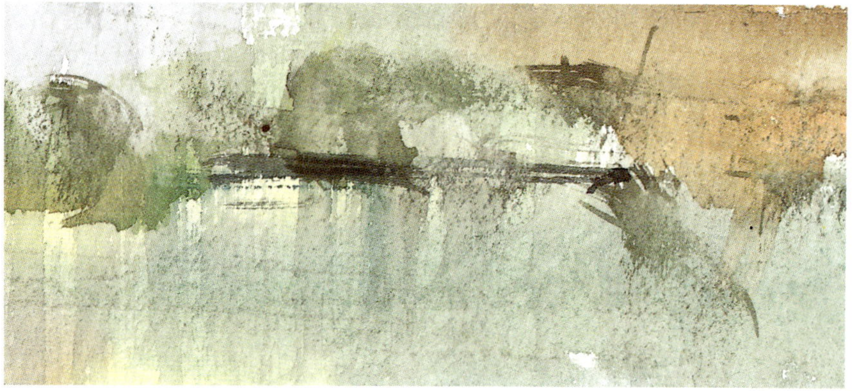

Helpful Tips
● Build up layers of watercolour dark over light, and make sure that you don't block out all of the underlying colours. Add Chinese white body colour light over dark – it is opaque so will block all colour beneath it.

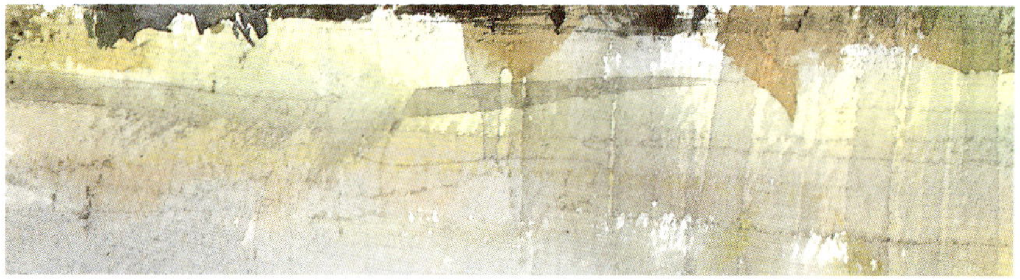

LEFT The foreground is painted with the same colours as the sky to achieve unity.

OPPOSITE Negative space is as important as positive elements in this semi-abstract skyscape.

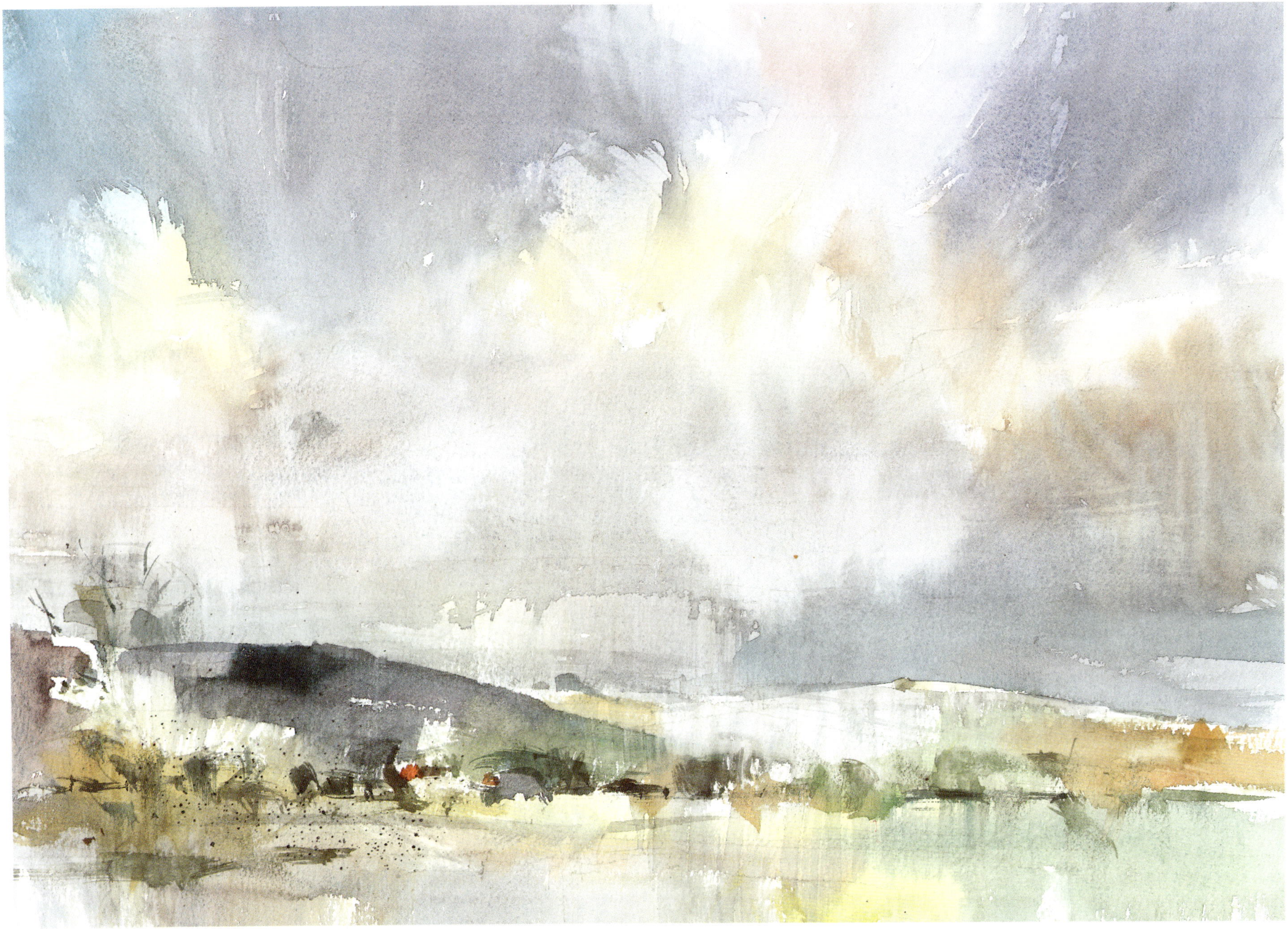

Wildlife

Movement and Colours

The many beautiful birds and animals in the world provide wonderful subjects for your watercolour paintings. Wildlife displays all of the colours and patterns of nature in myriad ways – crying out for representation in your watercolour work.

Of course, it would be wonderful to go off on a safari in order to get acquainted with some suitable material, but for most of us this is out of the question! Instead, we have to refer to books and television for inspiration. Nature programmes are a particularly useful source, especially as the camera often magnifies the subject many times over, making an analysis of detail far easier than from life.

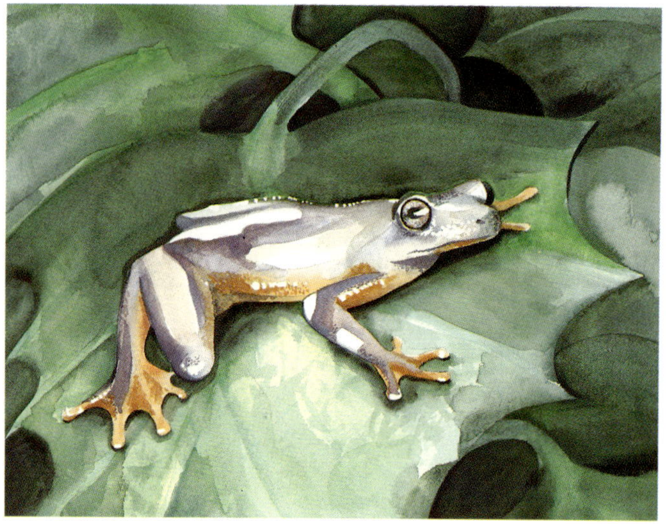

Down to detail. Don't worry if you find it hard to paint fur or feathers accurately. Just as the landscape can be edited, so your representations of wildlife can be simplified. An animal can be brought to life just as effectively by capturing its poise or exact colours as by reproducing every last hair on its coat.

A tiny insect can be the subject of an elaborate painting project, and you can always try painting a large animal in a very small space. It is a real artistic challenge to see how deftly you can paint an elephant in a small area, or fill a piece of paper with a painting of a bumble bee!

If you have any wildlife films on video, try freeze-framing the screen on the creatures of your choice and makes quick sketches of them to work from. In the same way as with photographs, don't try to copy a creature too accurately from a frozen image, or you will be likely to paint all of the life out of it. It would be better to sketch it in a number of poses, analysing how it sits, walks and runs, interacts with its family, or reacts to its foe. Once you have a whole series of sketches to hand, you will be in a position to plan a full-scale painting project which combines them all.

Wildlife comes in all shapes and sizes, from the fine and delicate butterfly to the tall and sturdy giraffe. Choose a style of painting to suit the subject – using subtle and fine watercolour washes for a fragile insect, in contrast to pen-and-ink definitions or richer hues for stronger or more fierce creatures. Masking fluid is an essential ally for wildlife painting, as is a pencil and eraser. This is one situation when underdrawings are essential – they can always be erased when the painting is finished – and masking fluid can be used to define the shape of the animals, and to pick out details.

All creatures great and small
When it comes to wildlife, you don't have to paint every last detail. Sometimes it is enough to capture the essence of a creature by the way it moves, or through its own unique expressions. Have a go at the following three before you set to work on the full-scale project.

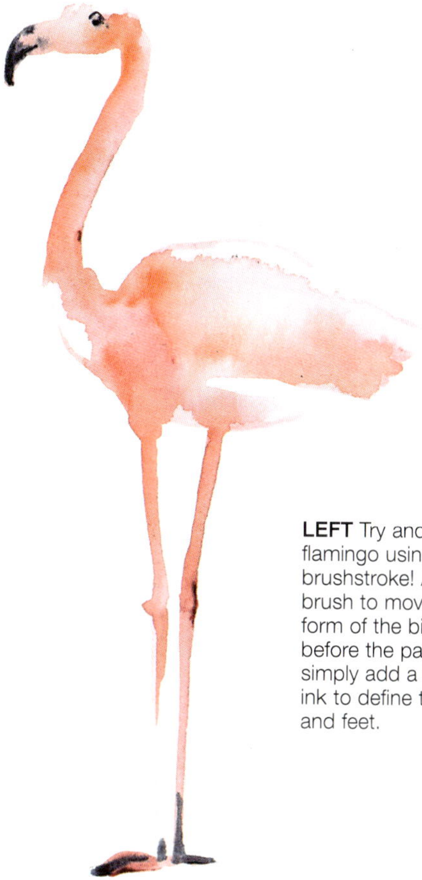

LEFT Try and paint a flamingo using one single brushstroke! Allow the brush to move through the form of the bird, then, before the paint is dry, simply add a touch of black ink to define the beak, eye and feet.

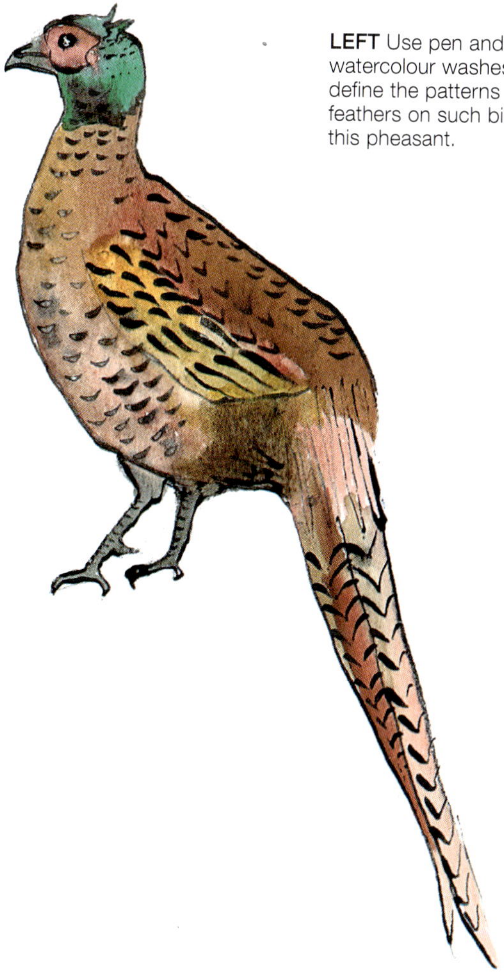

LEFT Use pen and ink over watercolour washes to define the patterns and feathers on such birds as this pheasant.

Helpful Tips

- If you want to keep the outlines of the animals clean but the paint runs, mop up the drips with a cotton bud or piece of cotton rag. If a mark is left behind, cover it up with a little touch of white acrylic paint.

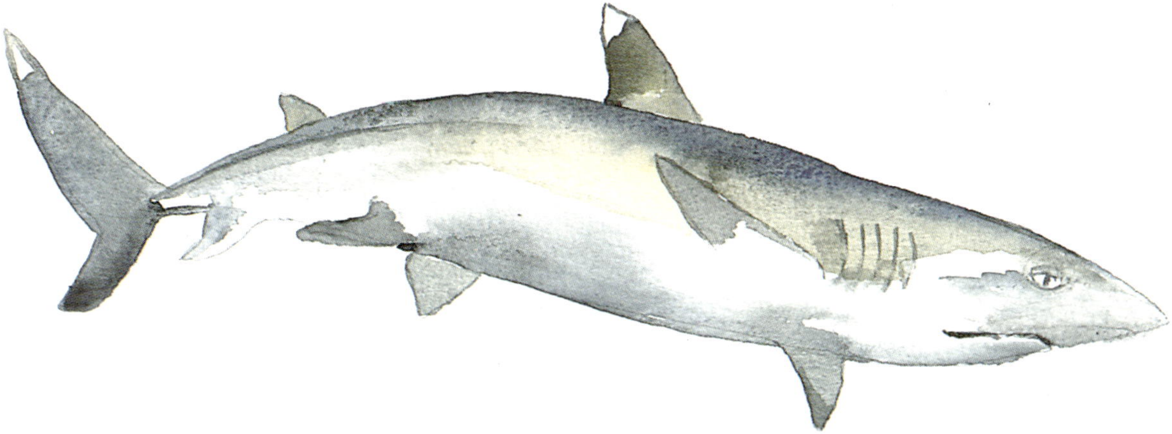

LEFT Mask out the outline of the shark to keep the edges clean. Use variegated washes to reflect its luminosity, and add Chinese white body colour over the top to produce brighter highlights.

Forms through colour
A simple creature such as this tree frog makes a wonderful subject for a painting. Copy the outline shape of the frog on to watercolour paper, then add a patchwork of leaves around it. Mask out the outline of the frog and leave the masking fluid to dry. The leaves should remain quite subtle in tone, painted in simple green mixes that contrast with the vivid pinks and purples of the tree frog itself.

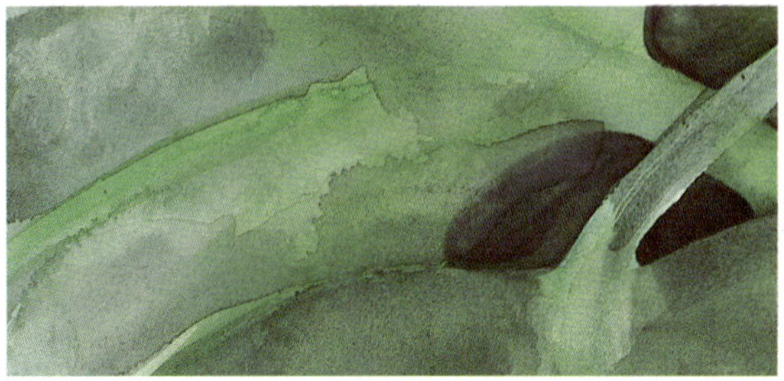

ABOVE Using lots of water and very fluid wet-in-wet washes of Hooker's green and viridian, paint in the general shapes of the background leaves with a large wash brush. The leaves should appear fresh and luscious, so do not overwork the washes, and allow the white of the paper to show through in some areas. Once the washes are dry, refine the details with a finer brush, making distinctions at this point between light and dark areas in the background. Leave the central leaf paler than the others so that the colours do not swamp the frog.

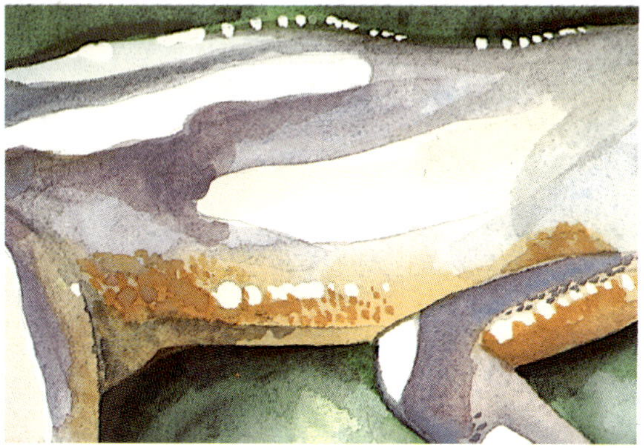

LEFT Try to leave the lighter areas of the frog free of paint, either by masking them out before you start painting, or by avoiding them when putting colours down. If the paint runs into white areas, lift it out with a damp sponge while it is still wet. Leave white speckles or add them with Chinese white gouache around the underbelly, on the nose, and around the eye.

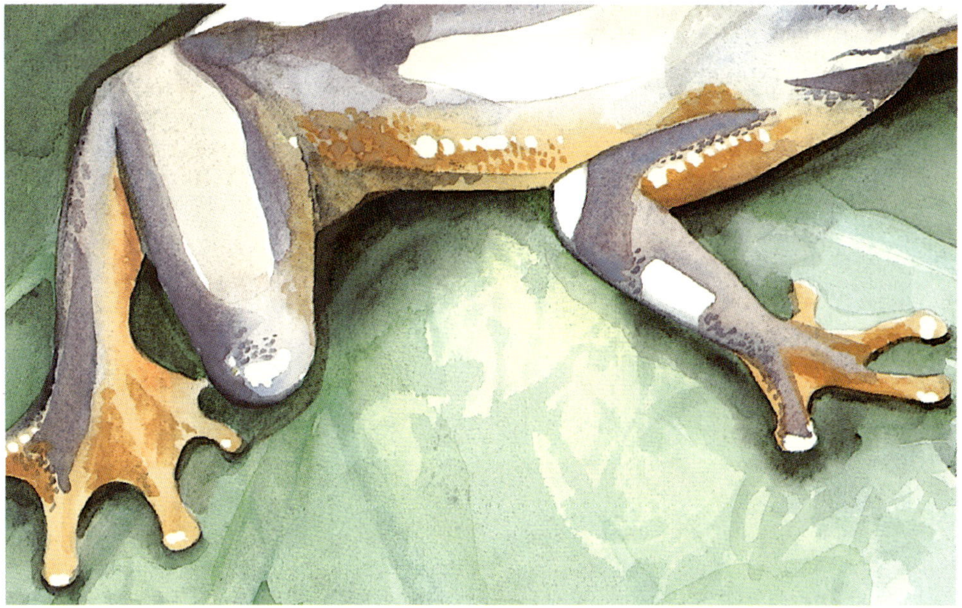

RIGHT Once the leaves are dry, you can start to work on the tree frog. Begin by painting thick pink lines to define the shape of the frog's legs, underbelly and feet. While the paint is still slightly damp, overlay purple lines to add definition to the back and limbs. The two colours should fur together in some places, and stay separate in others.

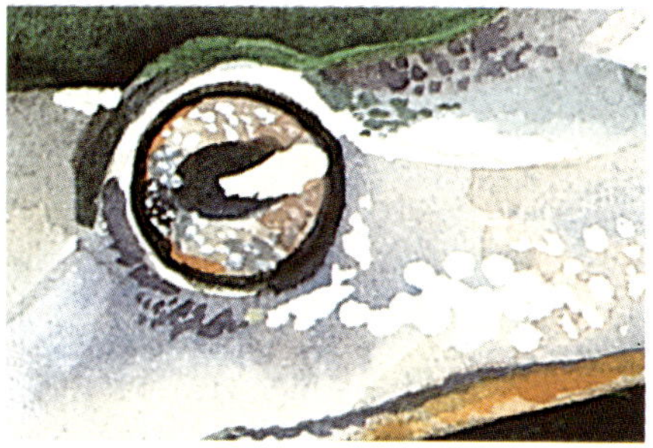

ABOVE Once the painting is dry, refine the details of the eye and mouth with very fine lines of Payne's grey to enhance the frog's expression.

OPPOSITE This simple composition sets the frog in its natural forest habitat. The luscious green leaves enhance the fresh pink and purple colours of the frog. The frog appears to be crouching, which suggests that he may be about to move – or even jump!

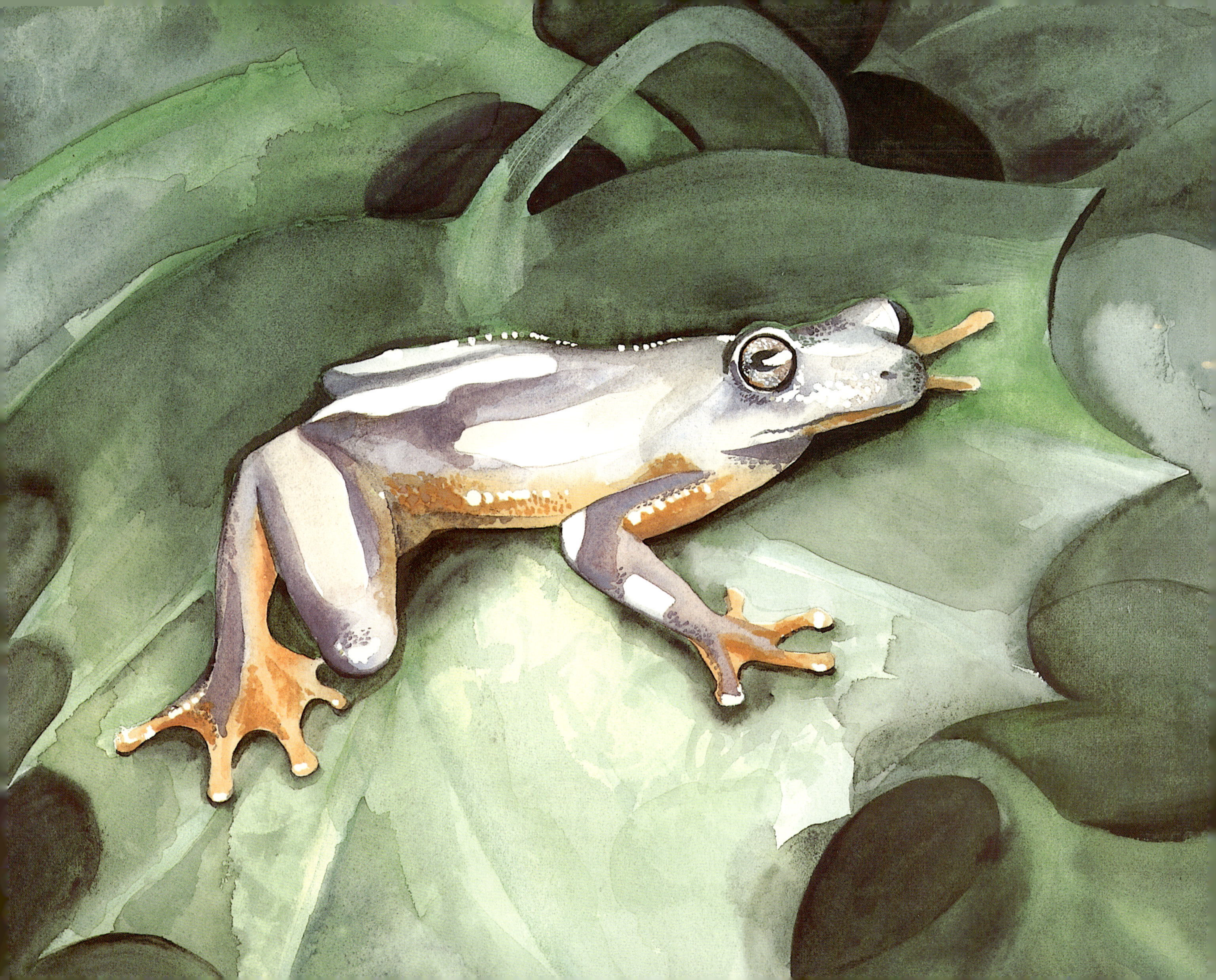

Groups of Figures

Busy Street Scene

In many ways it is easier to paint a group of figures than an individual person. For a start, it is easier to judge proportions if you have more than one object in view, as you can compare and contrast their shapes and sizes. If your group consists of adults and children, the differences in the figures' heights will be readily apparent. If your group of people are involved in an activity that involves a good deal of movement, the differences between their postures – crouching, jumping, bending or standing upright – will produce useful proportion and perspective guidelines. Be aware of the differences between the figures, look out for the negative spaces that exist between them, and concentrate on filling them in. You will find that in so doing, you will simultaneously begin to develop a painting of the group.

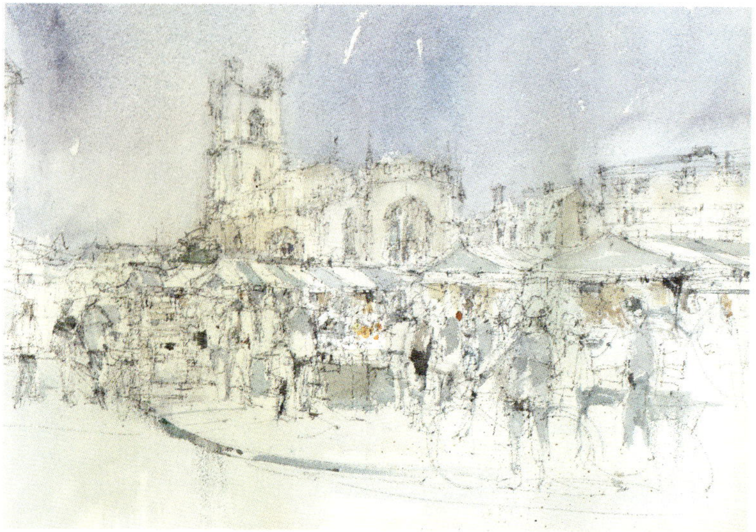

The most obvious mistake that you can make is to try to reproduce a series of individual portraits arranged in group form. You will lose the impression of any relationship between the figures if you try to do this. Think about the group as an entity, and integrate it into its local environment, through the use of colour and tone. You do not have to reproduce every last feature on your figures. It may surprise you to discover that you can leave out almost all details to capture the mood of your group. You may need to use the same colour across each figure's clothing, or to apply the paint with certain types of marks, perhaps short and pointillistic to suggest energy and movement, or long and flowing to suggest a relaxed atmosphere.

In this project, the artist has used line and wash to paint a busy market scene, in which various groups of figures are going about their business. Having put down washes of watercolour to produce a background, the artist then combined pen and ink with watercolour to define details and create a vital composition. When painting out of doors, find a discreet position to settle yourself in and observe your scene objectively before you set to work. What composition will suit your ends? Make a few thumbnail sketches to set the scene, and perhaps make a few quick sketches of people who pass by to focus your attention. Note how you can capture the essence of a figure with just a few lines of paint or ink.

Observing groups of people
Take time to observe goups of figures before you set to work on a painting project. Whenever possible, make thumbnail sketches of them to acquaint yourself with the proportions of one figure against others.

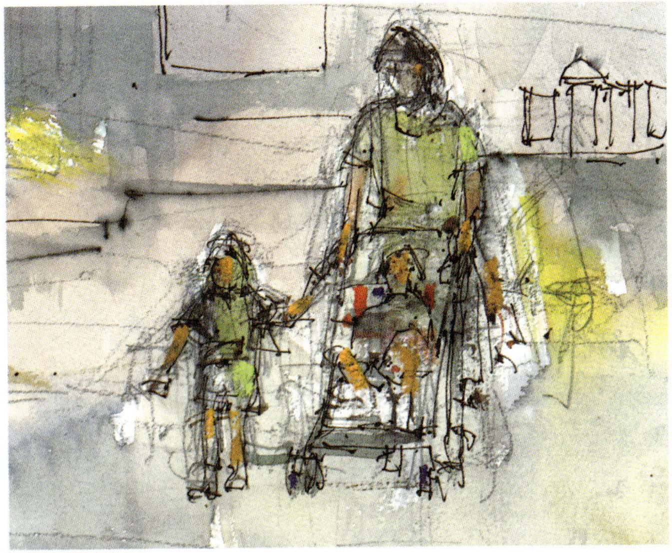

RIGHT Painting a mother with her children will help you analyse proportion.

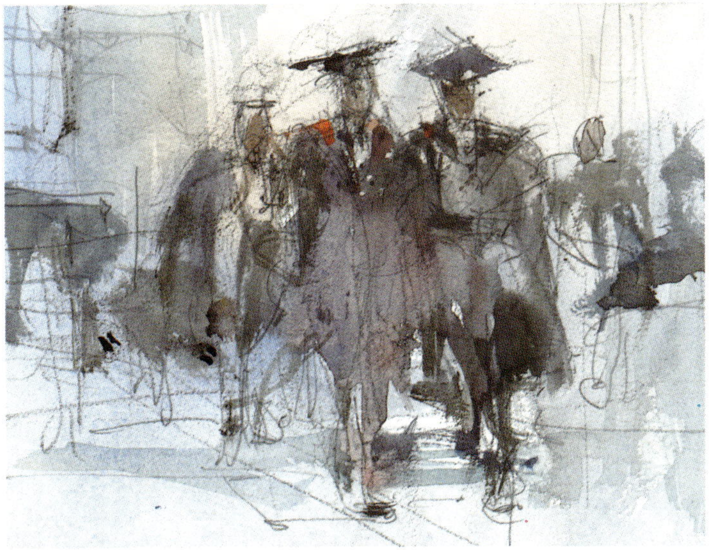

ABOVE Try painting a procession of people to consider perspective changes between shapes.

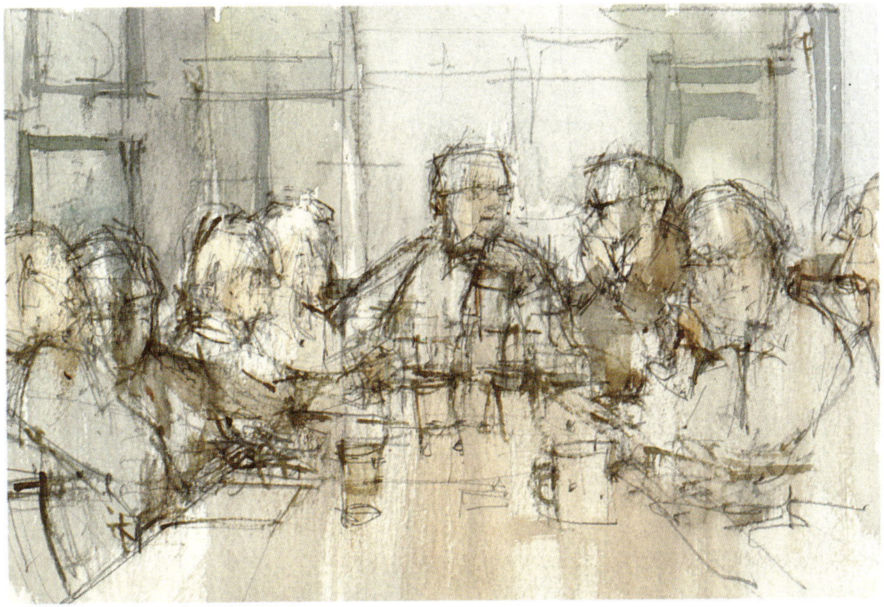

LEFT Tables provide a perfect setting for groups of figures – especially if you want to practise triangular compositions.

Helpful Tips
- Practise painting gradated washes on rough pieces of paper before using quality watercolour paper, as you will not perfect the technique on your first attempt.

Capturing the overall mood
Don't try to capture every detail in a busy street scene – go for the overall impression instead.

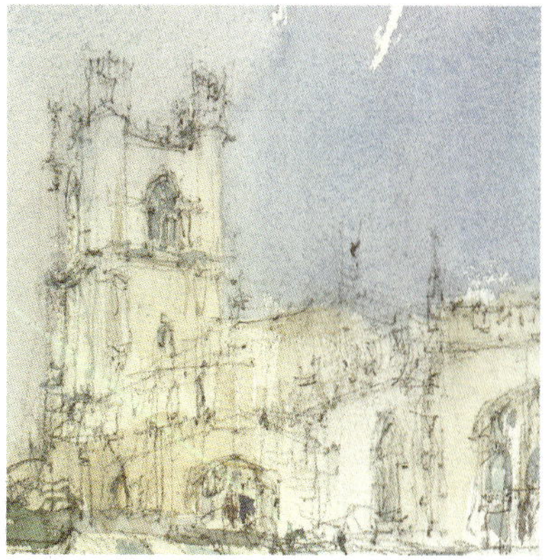

LEFT The church spire dominates the skyline, creating an umbrella for the busy scene below.

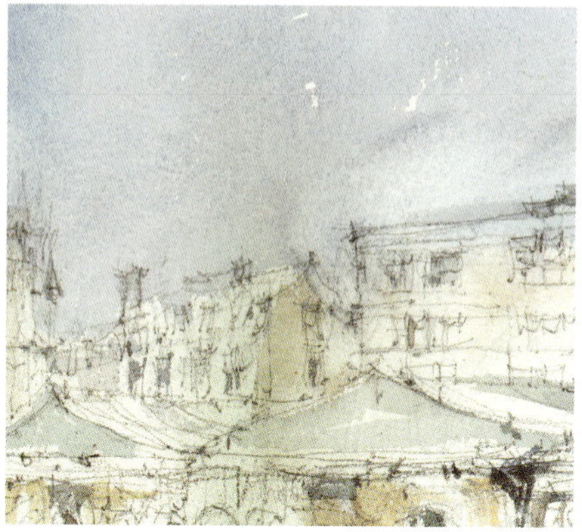

OPPOSITE This painting is composed with only a few colours and pen and ink in order to create structure and enhance textures, using the initial pen-and-ink sketch and a collection of photographs for reference. Note how the viewpoint takes advantage of the angle of the street and the winding road.

BELOW Using pen and ink over watercolour washes, see how you can capture the essence of a group of figures without rendering specific details.

RIGHT Washes of Payne's grey have been flooded into the skyline.

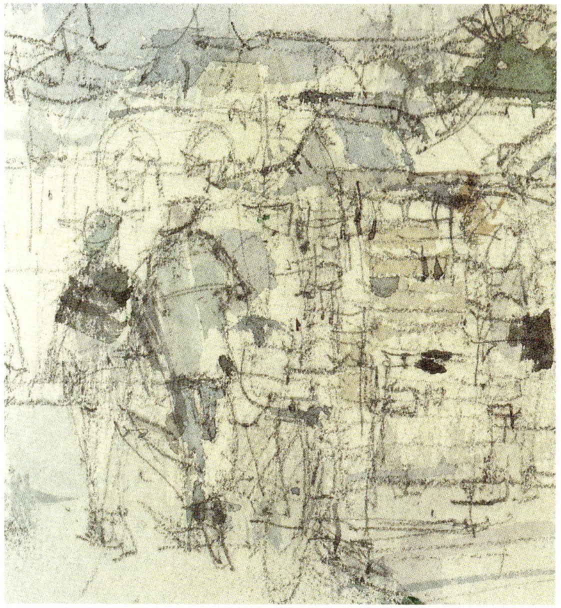

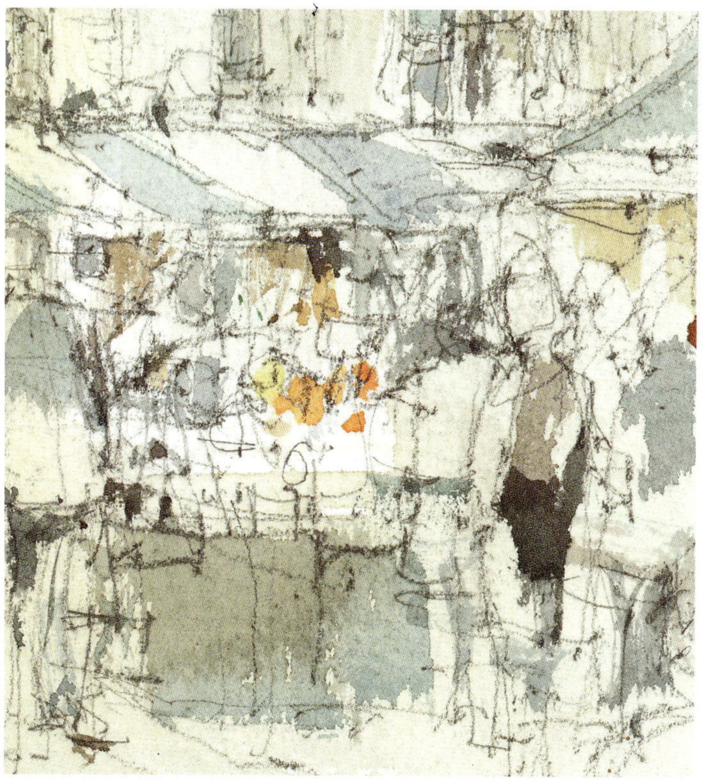

RIGHT The awnings over the market stalls provide structure in a very washy scene.

BELOW Note how loosely the impression of the figures and bicycle have been rendered.

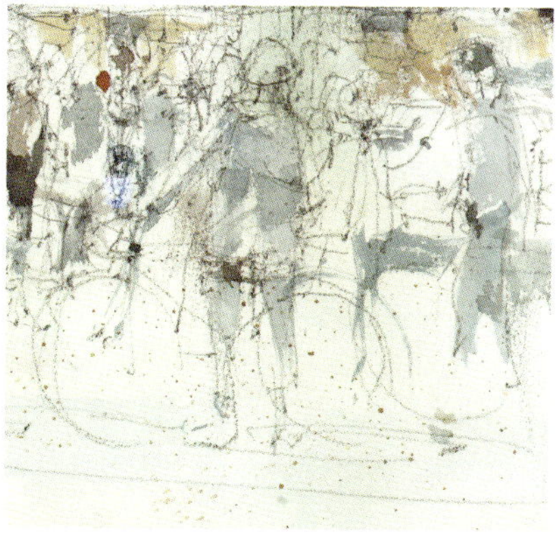

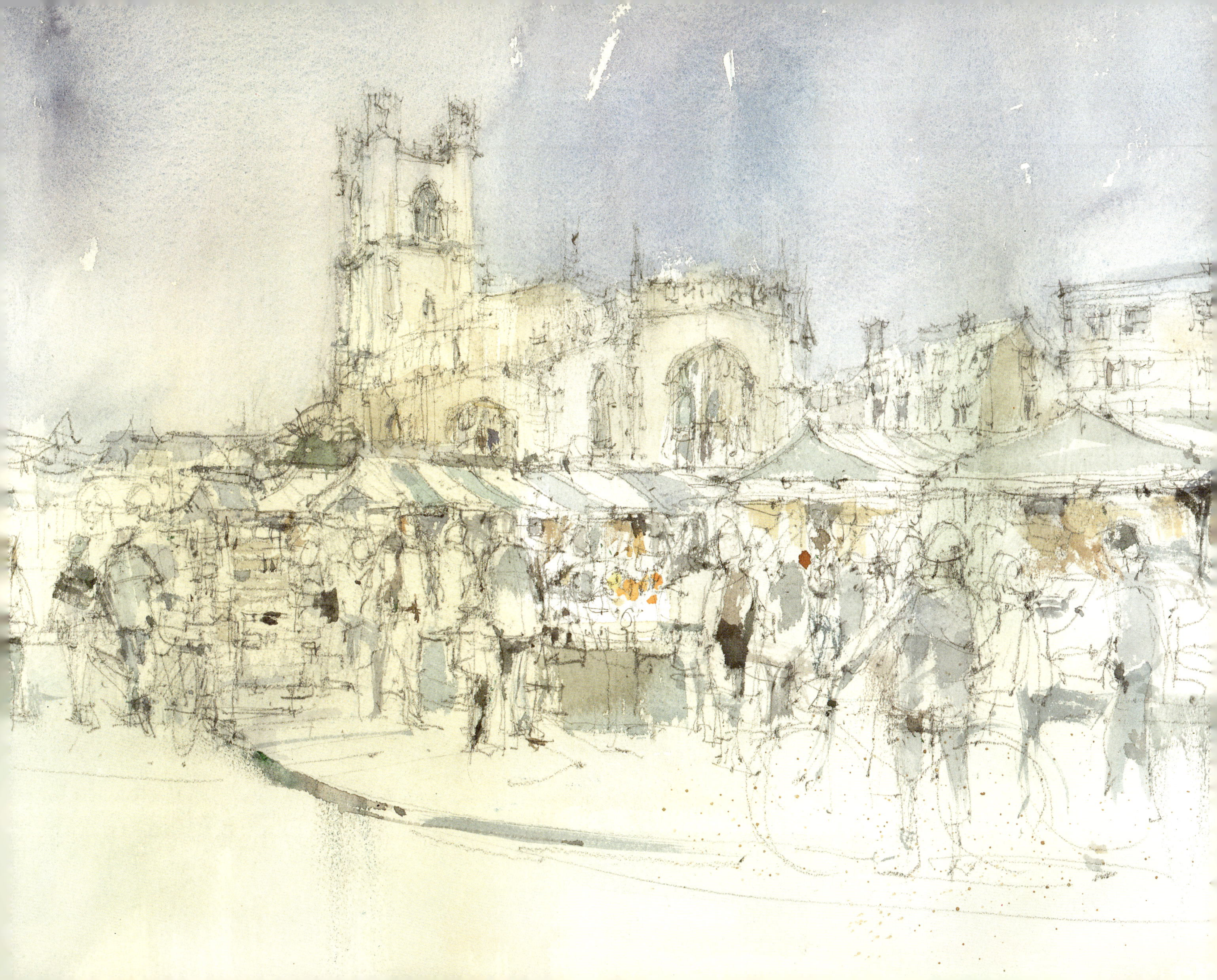

Portraits

Form and Tones

When it comes to painting the head, creative zeal alone will not provide you with enough information to produce a reasonable impression, let alone a likeness. It is a good idea, therefore, to arm yourself with some facts about the physical structure of the head and the methods by which you can capture the physiognomy of an individual in paint, before you begin.

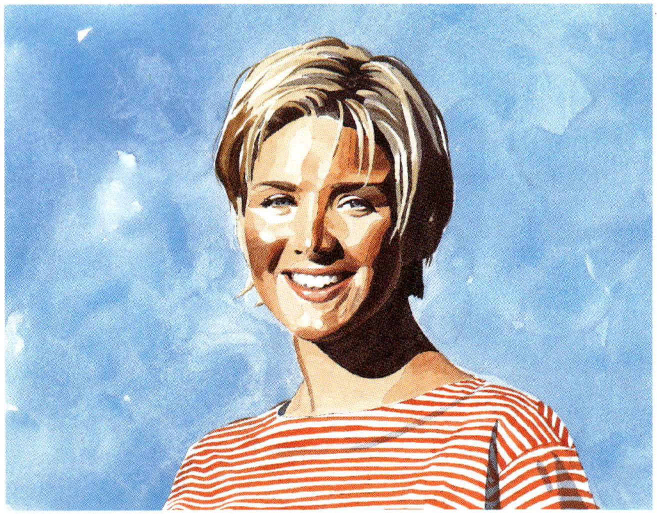

The head is an intricate form, comprised of a series of cavities and protrusions. Beneath the skin is flesh and muscle, and beneath them lies the skull which links all of bones in the head. The only part of the skull that can move is the jawbone and this is set far lower than the back of the skull. Make sure that in your paintings the back of the head is not as low as the chin. The head is perfectly balanced to pivot from side to side and backwards and forwards on the axis of the neck. Don't make the head appear to sit perched on top of a pole – the backbone enters the head at an angle through the centre of the neck, and the neck rises higher at the back of the head than at the front. Rather than sitting on top of the neck, the head should be set into the structure of the neck. Also observe carefully the width of the neck in relation to the width of the head.

A common mistake is to make the forehead too shallow, and the eyes too close together and too small. The forehead takes up at least a third of the face area. The size of the eyes in relation to the actual cavities that they occupy is very small. The eyeballs are set deep into the eye sockets, and are surrounded by muscles covered in folds of skin, as well as by the brow. The cheeks are cavities filled out with flesh. Some people have far more fleshy cheeks than others, and the amount of flesh on a sitter's cheeks will affect the angularity of the face. Don't make the sitter's mouth too small, either. The mouth can be quite wide, and the bottom lip is often far fuller in shape than you may initially perceive it to be.

Watercolour has a natural affinity with human skin. The colour of both is built up through layers of semi-transparent membranes, and in both cases the colour you see is affected by the light that surrounds it. Don't be fooled into believing that skin is pink or brown. It can appear as anything from a bright crimson to a deep purple, a shadowy yellow to a pallid green. To produce three-dimensional form in the face, try to contrast areas of bright light, by leaving the paper free of paint, with areas of more intense colour.

The proportions of the head

Because the head is a difficult form to master, start out by drawing it in pencil to work out its proportions. Make the pencil lines very light so that they will not show through when you add paint over the top. Alternatively choose a pale-toned watercolour pencil to make your underdrawing, as it will melt into the watercolour. Once you have established its form, fill in the skin tones with care.

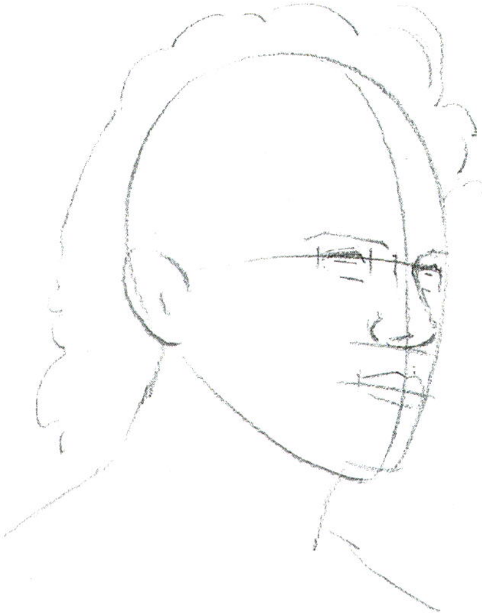

LEFT Draw the head in profile as an egg shape, then divide it into four portions, as shown. When you are on the same eye level as your subject, the eyeline is half way between the top of the head and the bottom of the chin. Don't make the forehead too shallow.

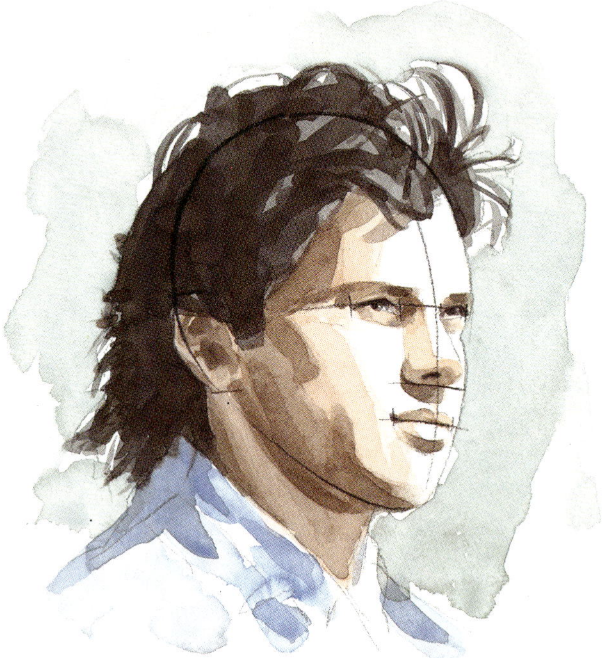

ABOVE Once you have defined the basic structure, fill in the light and dark tones with watercolour and refine details as you build up the colours.

Pale skin tones can be made from colours such as yellow ochre, alizarin crimson and Winsor violet.

For dark skin tones a good mix can be made from burnt umber, cadmium yellow deep and Antwerp blue.

Skin tones often have a slight green tint to them. In such instances, try mixing cadmium orange, sap green and burnt sienna.

For more yellow skins, mix cadmium scarlet, lemon yellow and French ultramarine blue.

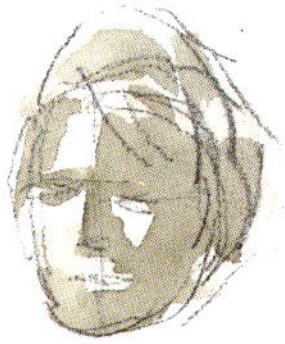

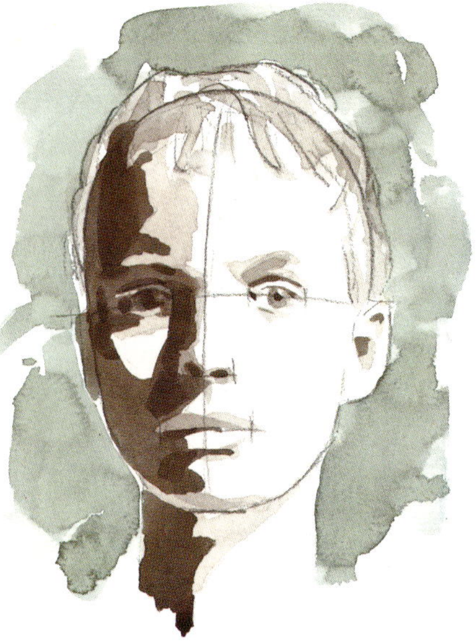

LEFT When one side of the face is in full light, the other may well be in dark shadow. Establish the tonal contrasts with quick tonal studies – you might be surprised by how dramatic the contrast can be.

Modelling with tone
Don't be afraid to use strong tones in a portrait painting – just remember to leave bright highlights to give tonal contrast against areas of strong colour. Use masking fluid to keep bright details clean, and remember to rinse your brush out between each application of paint – any muddy colours will soon ruin a portrait.

RIGHT Note how much paler the skin tone is under the eye than on the cheeks

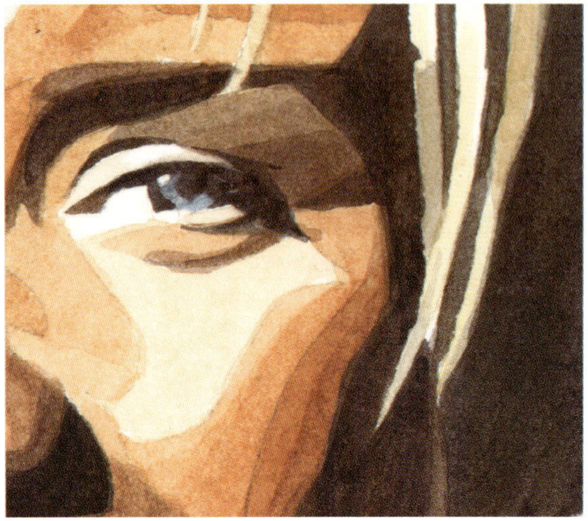

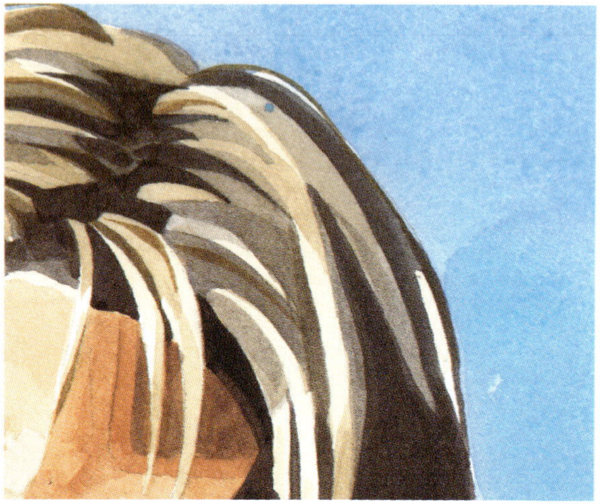

ABOVE Use masking fluid to block out the highlights in hair.

BELOW Use deep orange tones to build up areas of shadow, as here on the cheek.

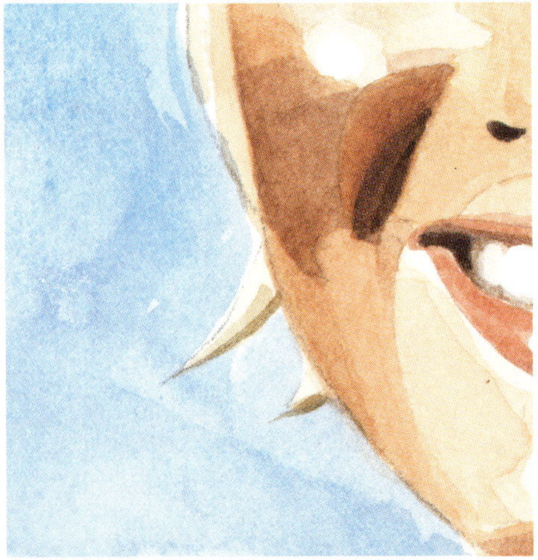

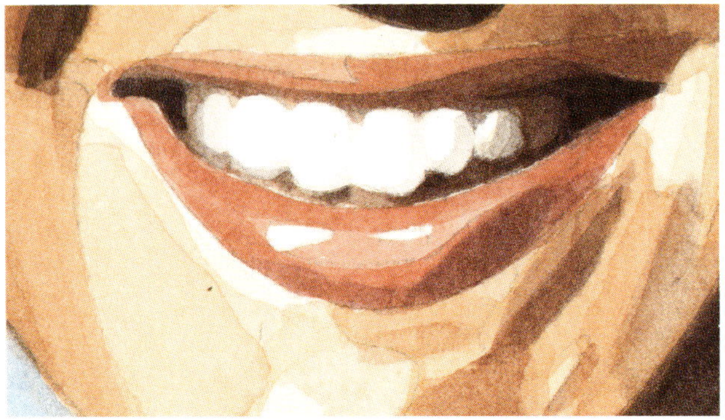

ABOVE Mask out the teeth to keep them bright white, and don't make the lips too bright red.

RIGHT Make areas of deep shadow very dark to produce strong tonal contrasts.

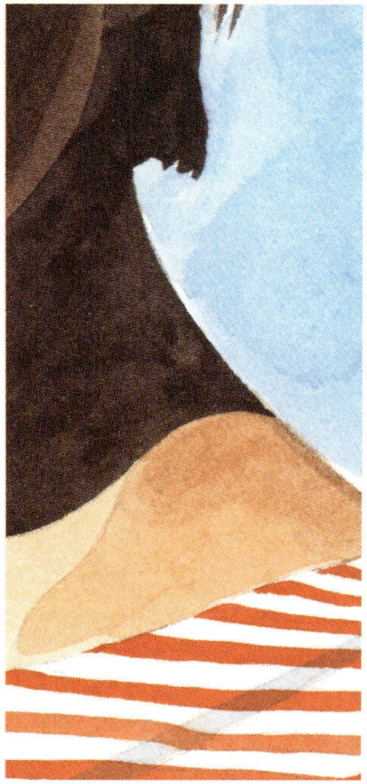

OPPOSITE Strong tones and bright colours give an energy and vibrancy to this portrait. Clear definitions between areas of high and low tone produce a dynamic painting.

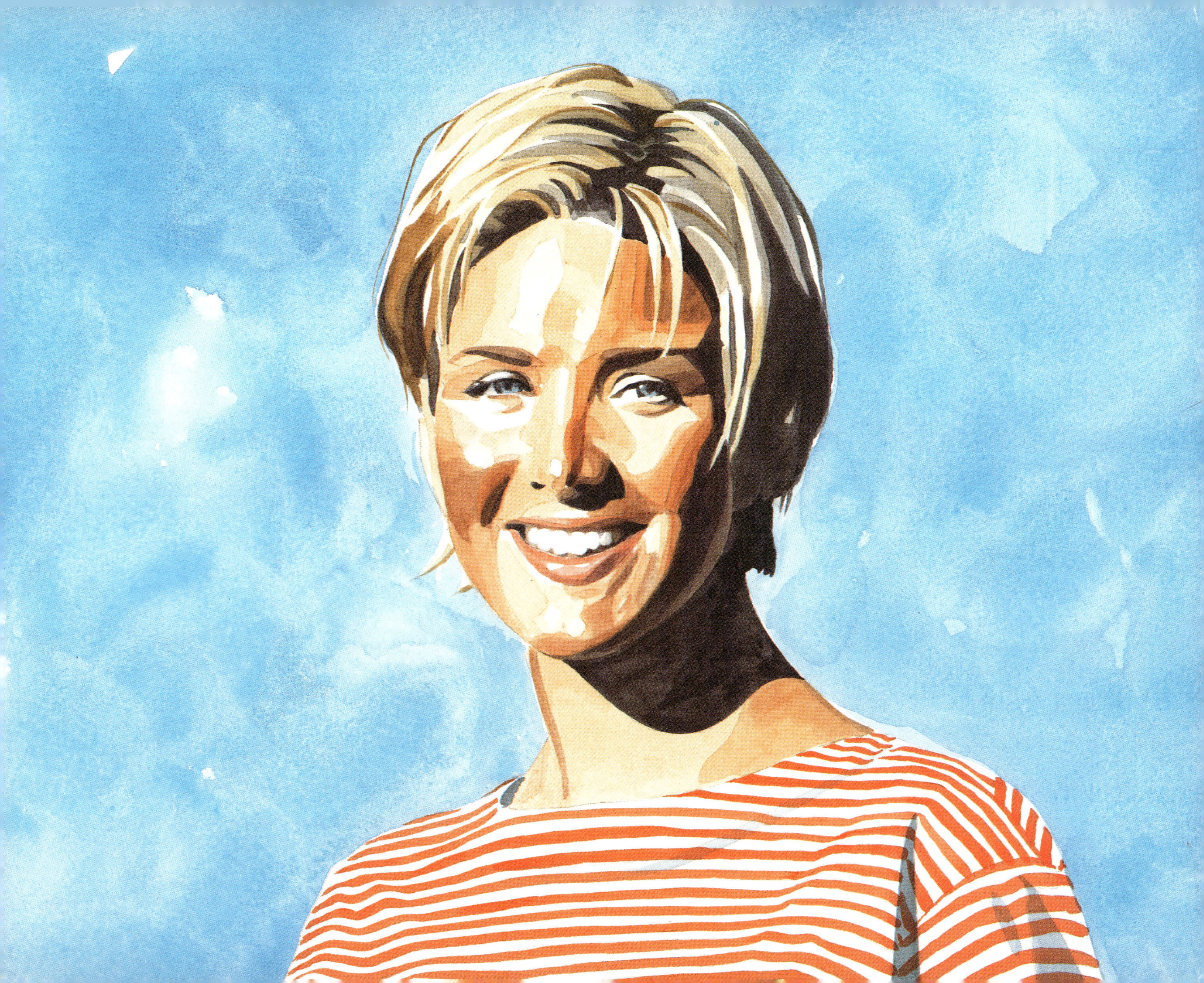

Abstracts

Seeing Objects in a New Light

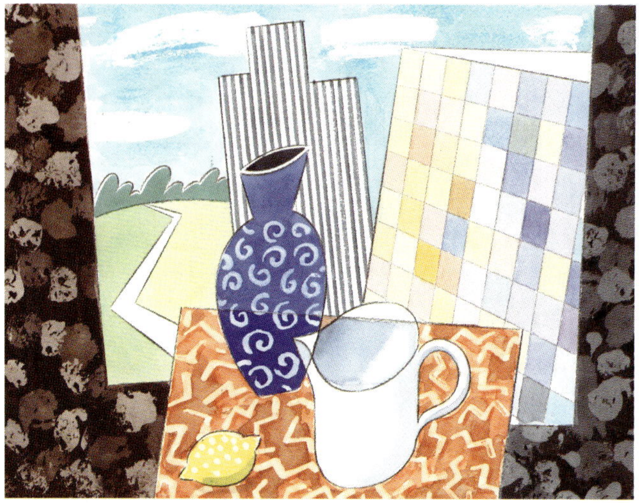

Abstract pictures can be great fun to paint – and will teach you many new things about colours, shapes and lines. Begin by considering objects as shapes and structures rather than as material facts. When you look at any object – be it a tree, a car, a house or a person, you immediately relate what you see to what you are preconditioned to know. Try to break free of that knowledge, and you will start to see objects afresh, simply as shapes, colours, patterns and forms to paint, without the baggage that goes along with knowing, for example, that cars emit exhaust fumes, that they can be driven too fast, that they are a means of transportation. Paintings don't have to reflect the real world – you can paint whatever you like, in whatever fashion suits your mood. There are no hard-and-fast rules.

Colour can be used as a vehicle for personal expression, too. Different hues can be described by the names you see printed on their labels – cerulean, Prussian blue, Hooker's green and so on, but what do these words actually mean to you? It is possible that, before you associated them with paint colours, these words bore no relation to the blues and greens you now see on your palette. Can you think of other ways to describe these colours that might make more sense to you? Perhaps the mood they generate in you would be a good way to begin.

Start off with cadmium yellow. How does this colour make you feel? It is a warm, rich, egg-yolk yellow; it is also a very strong, loud colour that stands out on your paper. Perhaps it makes you feel happy or confident. By contrast, think about lemon yellow. It is a cool, acidic colour, sharp and more recessive than its cadmium counterpart. It is a less inviting and more distant colour. Look at all of the colours in your palette, one at a time, and try to describe them to yourself, governed by the mood they generate. Once you have done this, you will be able to use colours to suggest particular feelings in your work, thus, to a degree, governing the responses of your onlookers.

Shapes can be considered in a similar way. Some shapes are solid, flat and clear-cut. Others are fluid round the edges. Use hard-edged shapes to suggest definite moods, looser edges to represent more uncertain feelings. Lines can be linked to emotion, too, suggestive as they can be of movement. Short dabs appear fast-moving and erratic, in contrast to slow curves that are more meditative to the eye.

Abstract colours, shapes and lines
Break down shapes into their component parts, then add ideas from your imagination into the equation and see what you can come up with! Different colour, shape and line combinations will produce a whole range of ideas. In this project, experiment with lines, shapes and colours, to see just how they make you feel. Once you understand your own reactions to them, you will be able to use them to provoke similar responses in your onlookers.

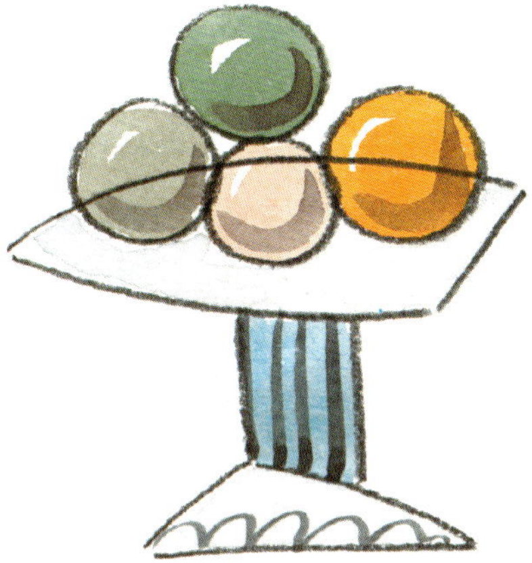

ABOVE This bowl of fruit has become a pattern of overlapping geometric and circular shapes.

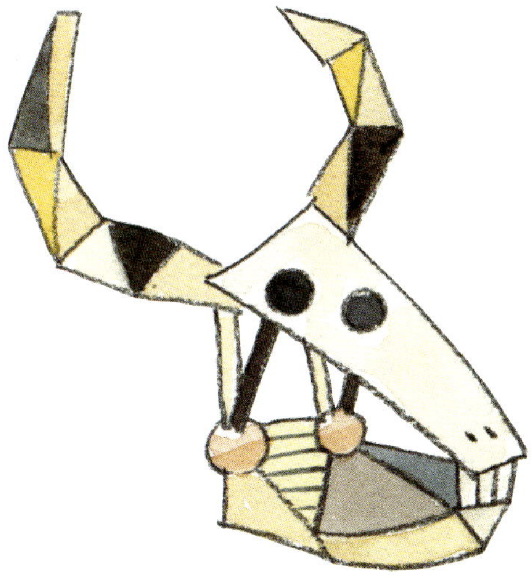

ABOVE This cow's head has been simplified and flattened. Then patterns and shapes have been integrated into the design to create ambiguity.

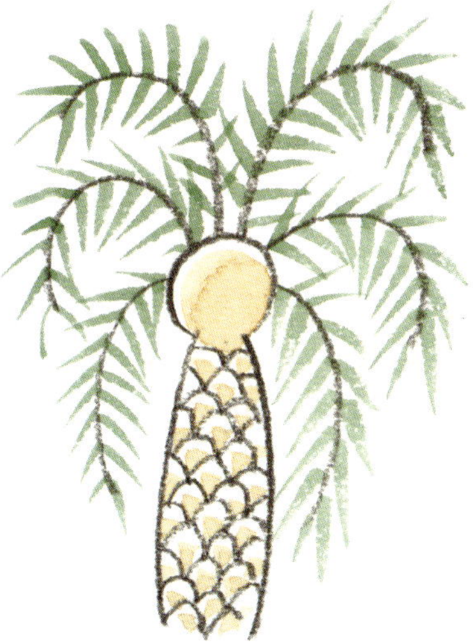

ABOVE This palm tree has been flattened and turned into a decorative motif.

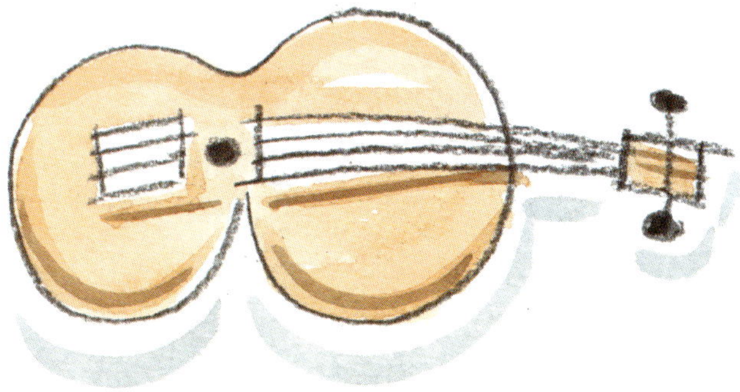

ABOVE The musical instrument is simplified, and the curving grey shadows around it suggest the musical nature of the form.

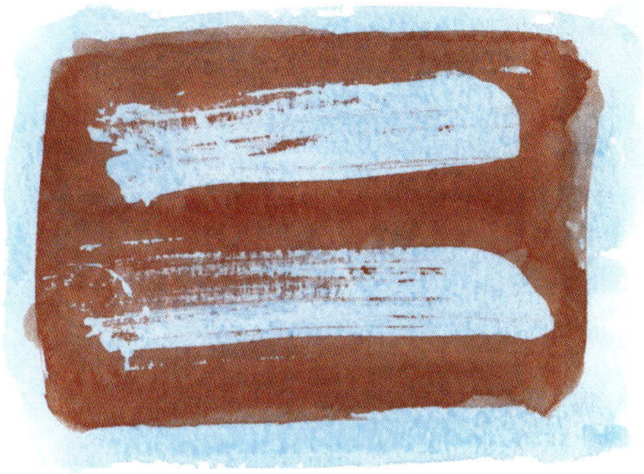

ABOVE Masking fluid is applied over blue paint, and red paint is added over the masking fluid. The masking fluid is removed to reveal a purely abstract design.

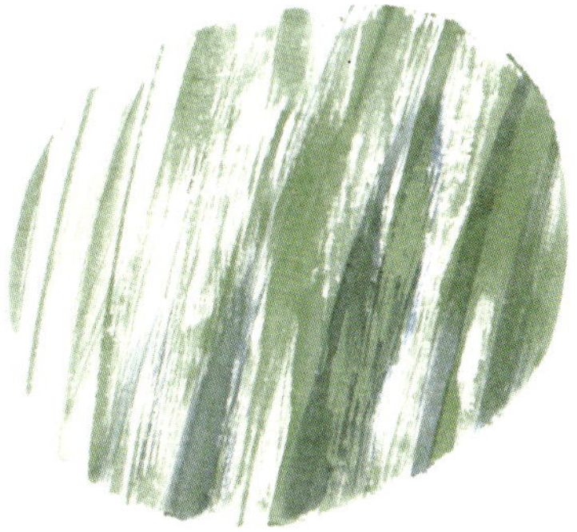

ABOVE Experiment with watercolour techniques to create patterns that are interesting in their own right. Here dryish paint has been applied over a paper mask to produce grass.

Distilling patterns and shapes
Taking a simple arrangement of objects, such as this view out of a window, produce your own abstract painting. Harmony of colour and composition are needed across the picture, but don't worry if the objects don't appear in quite the right order, or look quite as they would do in reality. Experiment with different planes and patterns and see what you can do!

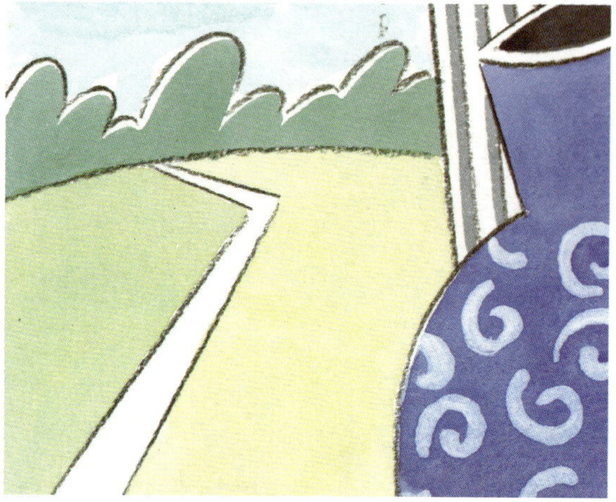

LEFT Pare objects down to their most basic shapes, as has been done with these bushes. The surface of the picture appears very flat, even though a pathway is apparently leading into the distance.

RIGHT Use patterns to produce interesting surfaces and changes in pace across the picture plane.

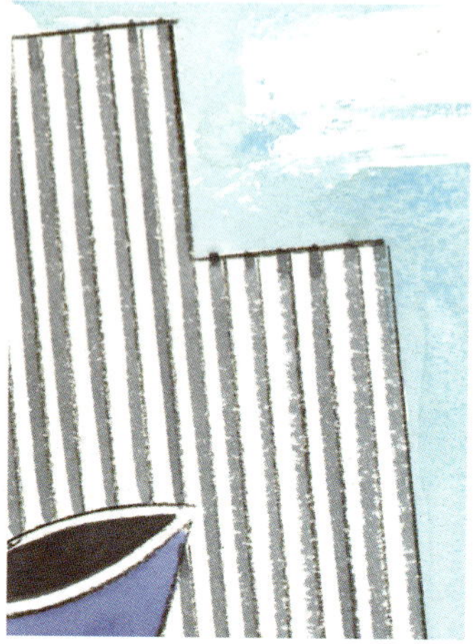

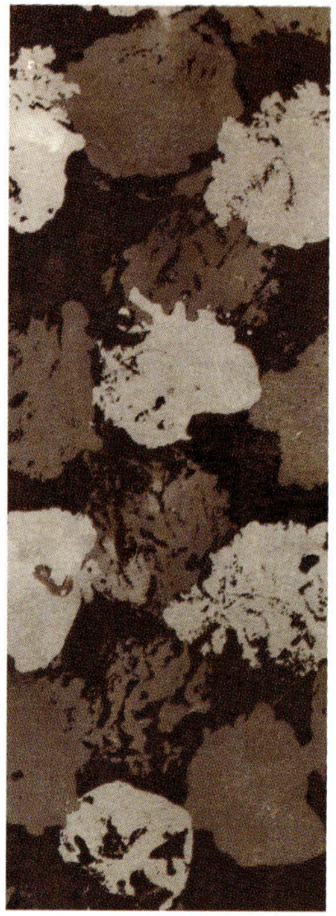

RIGHT Wallpaper provides the perfect subject for interesting abstract pattern-making.

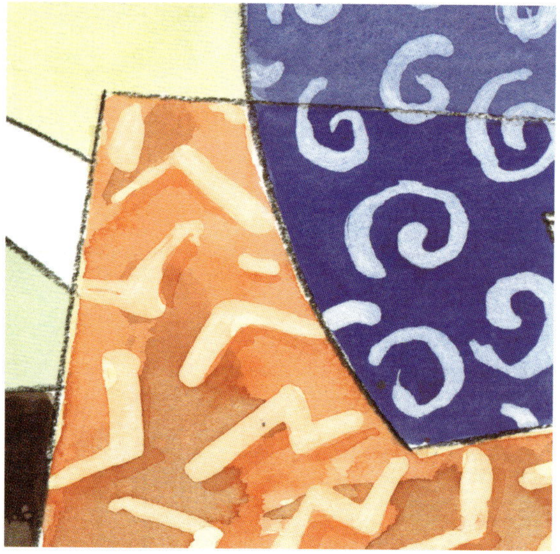

ABOVE Surfaces don't have to be at the 'right' angles to one another. Move them around to create dynamic results. See how the table appears to be falling out of the window.

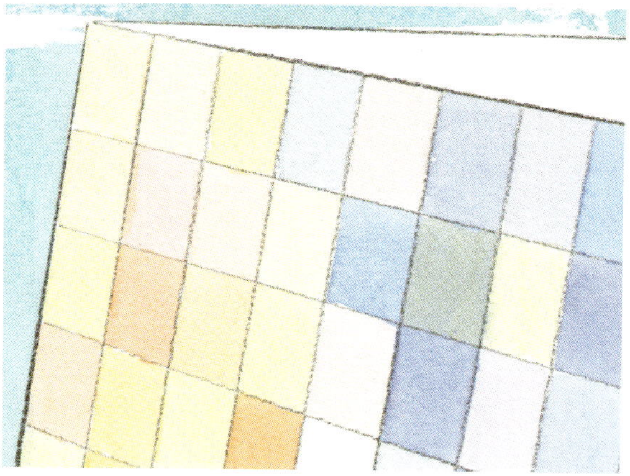

ABOVE Buildings can be represented as simple blocks of colour and shapes.

OPPOSITE The artist has deliberately avoided making the objects in this picture appear three-dimensional. Instead, they all look flat. Although we know that the objects are not flat, a piece of paper is flat, and, after all, that is what you are looking at!

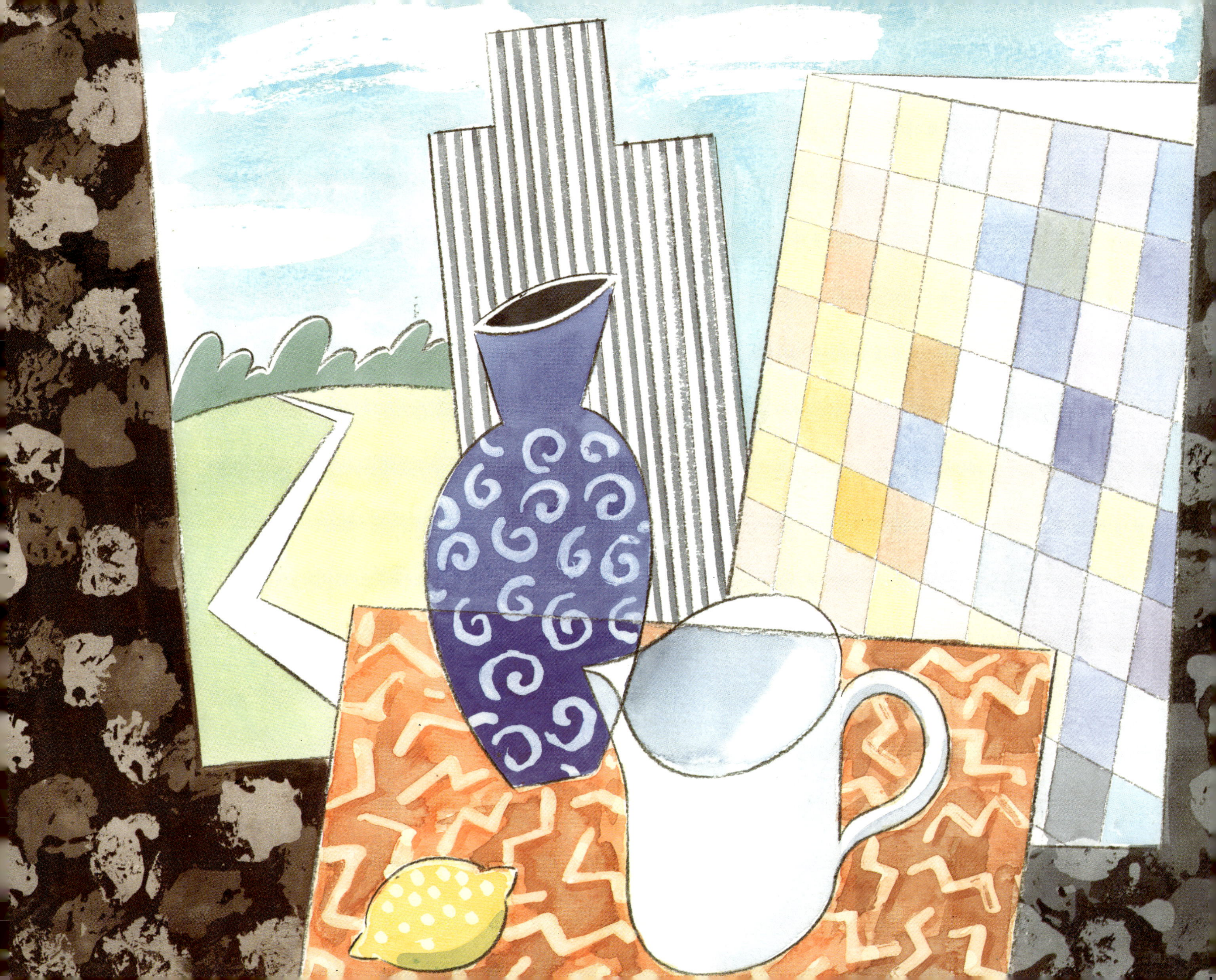

Finding Your own Style

And Making Watercolour Illustrations

Confidence and years of practice are needed before an artist finds the style of painting that suits them. However, every artist has his or her own style, so do have a go at finding yours! You can always recognize a painting by Van Gogh without looking for his signature, and the same applies to Monet and Picasso, even though they continued to change their subject matter throughout their painting lives. The same principle should apply to your own work. When starting out, however, don't try to keep to one style. Experiment with as many different approaches as possible, and a personal style will begin to develop naturally. You cannot force a style; an essential element within its make-up will come from deep inside, and that is what makes it personal.

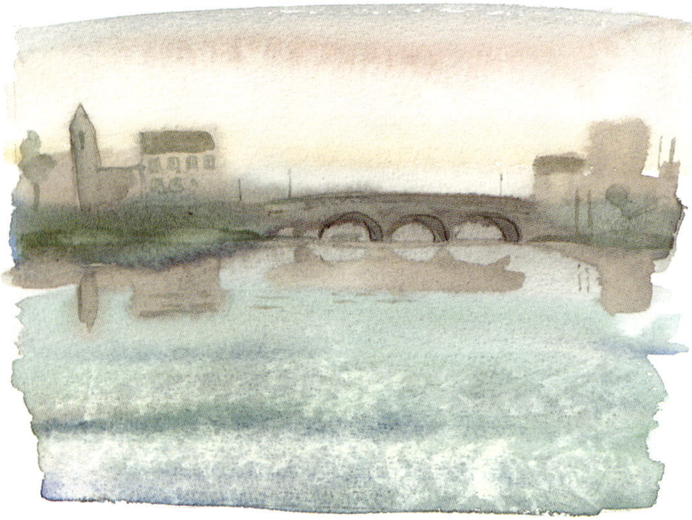

A good way to practise different styles of painting is to look at the works of other artists to see how they chose to approach a particular subject. The portrait is a good theme to contemplate, as there are endless examples to consider, from early primitive pictures to more contemporary experiments. The way you use and apply watercolour paint will affect its appearance, and therefore the style of your pictures. Try painting a face using as many different techniques as you can think of from this book. It should be possible to paint at least ten portraits before you run out of ideas. From these experiments, select the images you like best. Perhaps a consistent style shows through these?

You don't have to paint pictures to hang on the wall. The idea of doing so might even be a little daunting. Rather than exhibiting your work in public, why not start off by painting small vignettes to turn into greetings cards? You could even use watercolour techniques to produce handmade wrapping paper. Alternatively, it might appeal to you to make illustrations for a children's book or to decorate a cookbook. In contrast to artists, illustrators avoid showing off their own style at all costs. In fact, they intentionally conceal it in order to produce pictures that are impersonal. You may want to do the same, especially when making watercolours for illustrations. Watercolour, as you will have discovered, has a mind of its own, so is better suited for one-off pictures than for series of precise illustrations.

One subject – many approaches
Experiment with one subject and see how many approaches you can take. In this case, a bridge has been used as the theme for a wide range of painting projects.

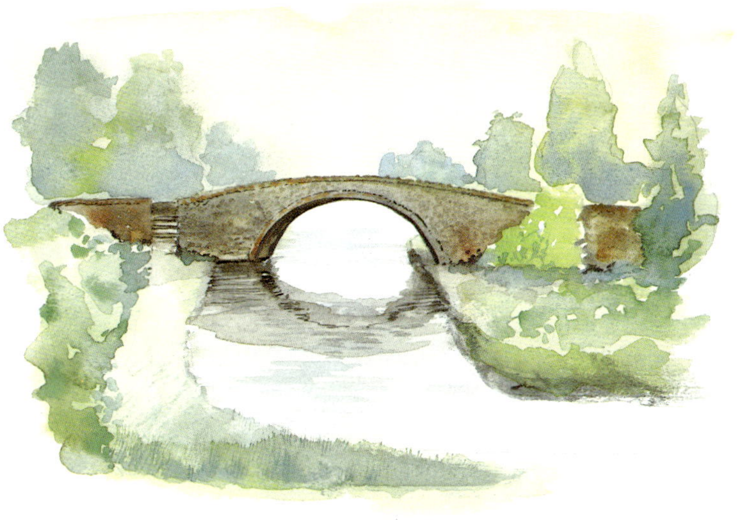

A realistic representation of a bridge in the countryside painted in the middle of the day.

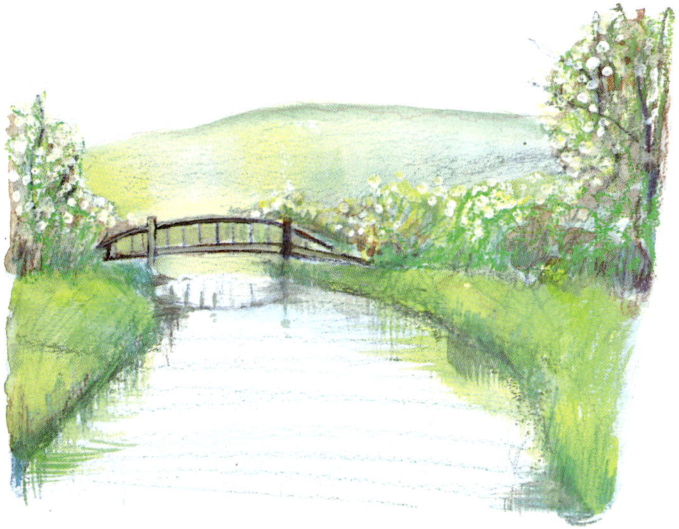

Different media are combined to produce a rich tapestry of shapes and colours in this country scene.

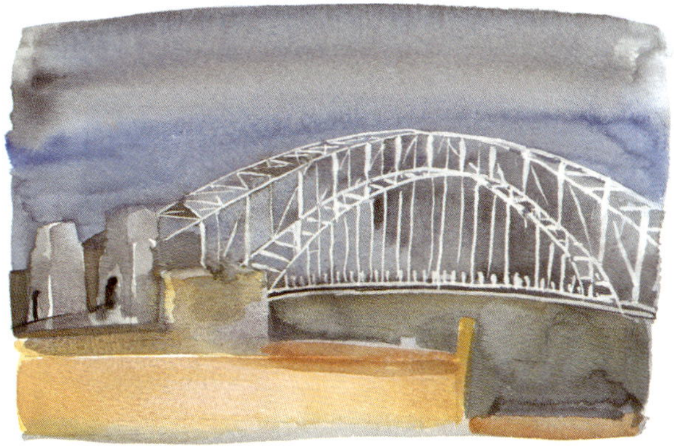

The bridge is masked out against the night skyline.

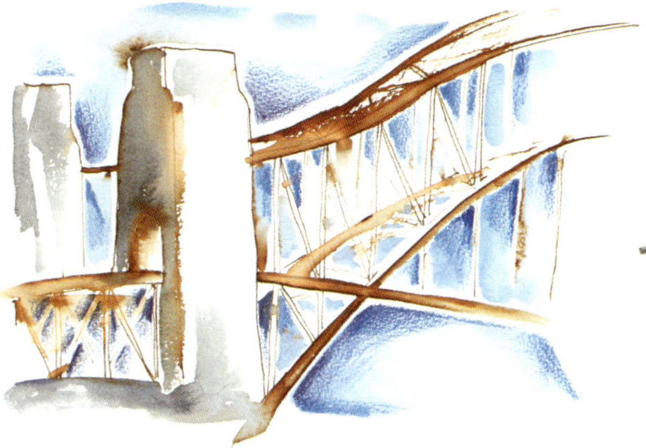

Pen-and-ink lines define this urban bridge in an semi-abstract painting.

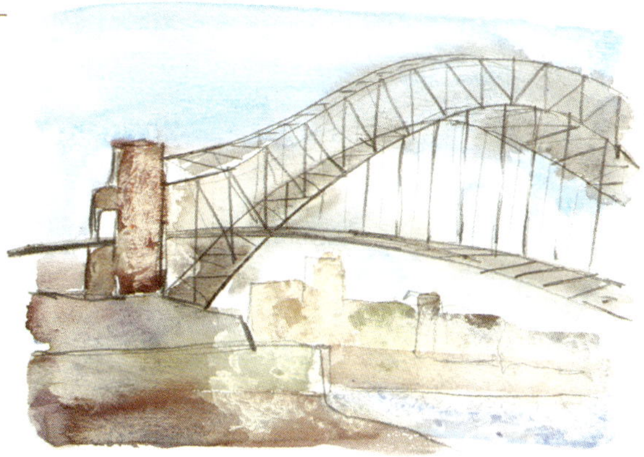

An impressionistic bridge scene, defined by pen and ink over loose watercolour washes.

Designing greetings cards
You can design greetings cards, personalizing them through the use of any motif that will be appreciated by the recipient. Star signs can be a good source of inspiration, as each one will generate a whole new set of ideas for you to work with. Follow these suggestions for Aquarius, the water-bearer, and Scorpio, the scorpion, then try developing your own motifs for the other signs of the zodiac.

BELOW Draw a light plan of your design on to a piece of very rough paper. Paint loose, broken, variegated washes over the design using colours suggestive of water – blues and purples – allowing the paint to melt and flow over the paper quite freely.

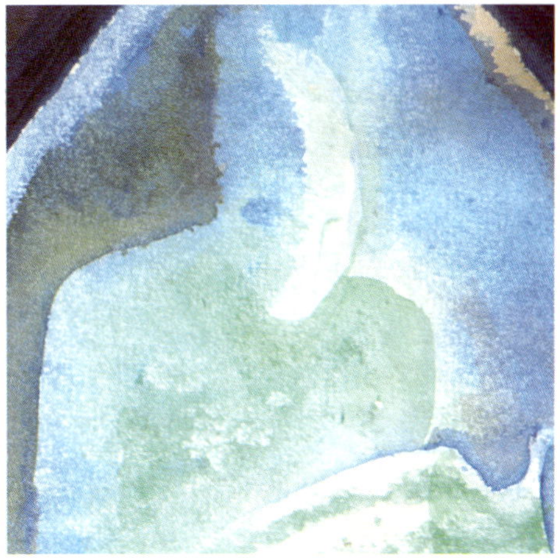

RIGHT Once the paint has settled, lift out and blow the paint around the paper until it conforms loosely to your design. Allow areas of the paper to remain white. Once the colours have dried, overlay details with flat, clean washes of the same translucent colours, defining outlines but making sure you retain the spontaneity created by the loose washes of paint. Cut out the illustration in an arch shape and stick it on to a larger, dark piece of card to give it an interesting border.

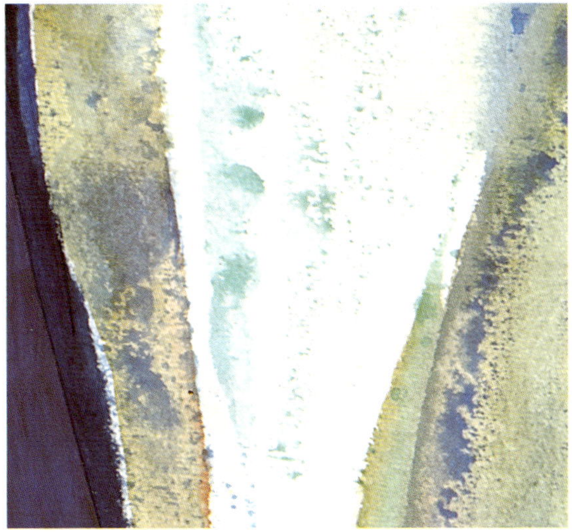

BELOW In this instance, use a smooth (hot-pressed), heavy sheet of watercolour paper, which is very smooth. Mark in the shape of the scorpion with a brown watercolour pencil, and rub over the raised areas of the back and limbs with a wax candle. Paint raw sienna and French ultramarine blue over the scorpion and background in loose, wet, variegated washes. See how the paint pools and settles on top of the smooth watercolour paper.

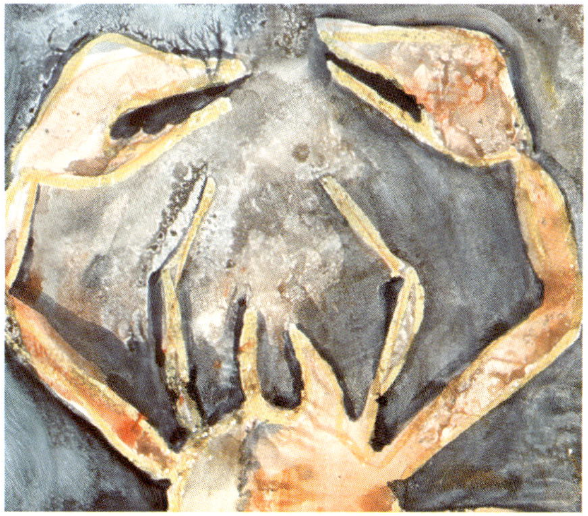

OPPOSITE In the Aquarius motif, the loose, pale blue and lilac washes suggest the flowing water they represent. The wax-resist technique and rich sienna colour combine to emphasize the hard nature of the scorpion.

BELOW The paint will take longer than normal to dry. Leave it until the air has absorbed most of the moisture and the surface of the paint is touch-dry. The wax will have resisted the paint and a change in the surface texture will be apparent over the wax-resist areas. Next, refine the details on the scorpion with a finer brush. Again, cut out the illustration, and stick it on to a dark background. In this instance, the artist has chosen a wash to add further interest and textures to the border of the card.

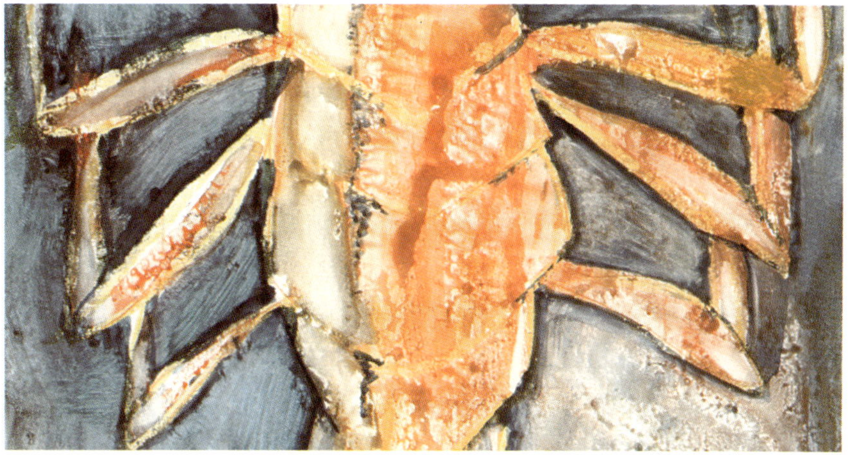

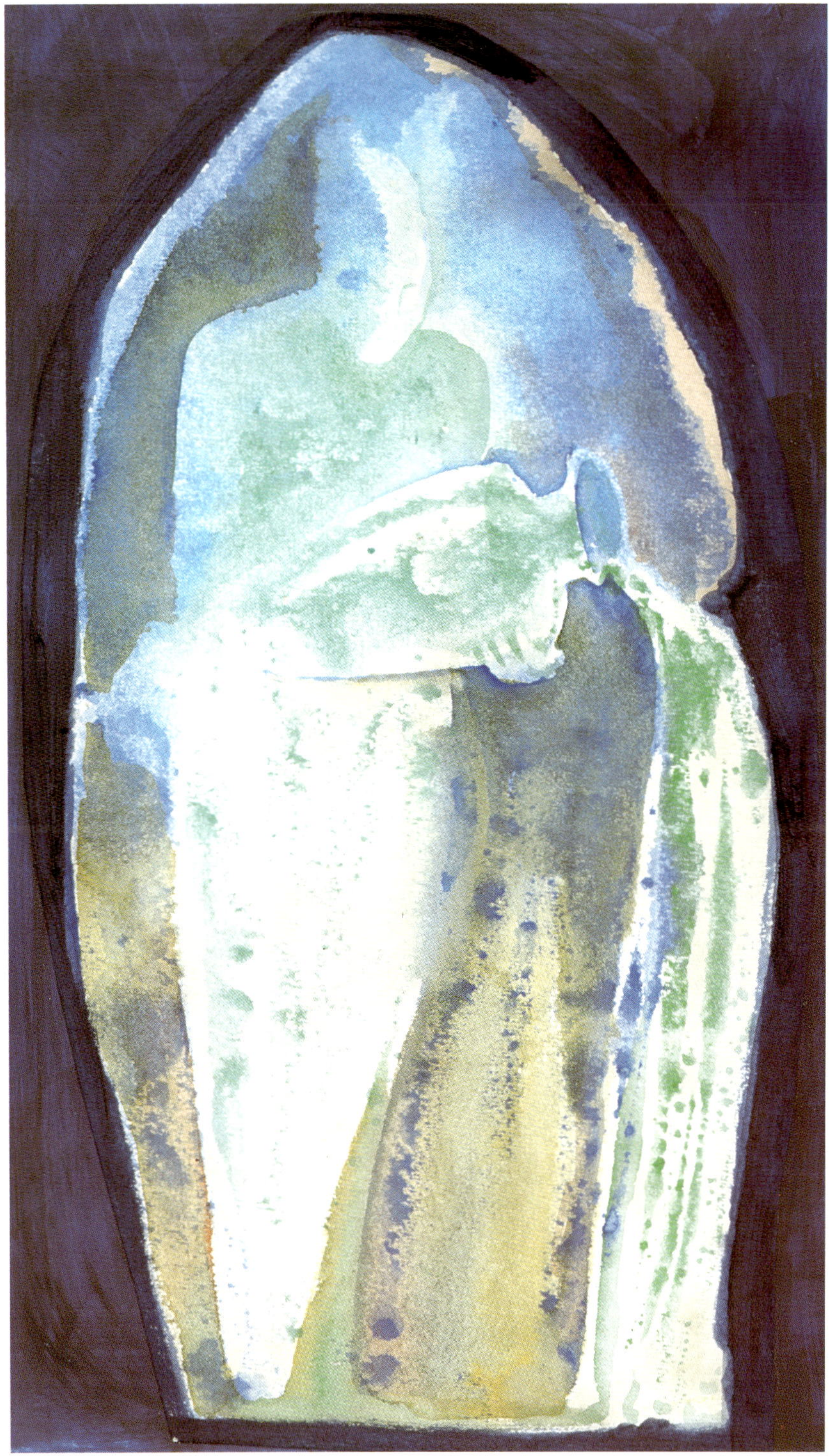

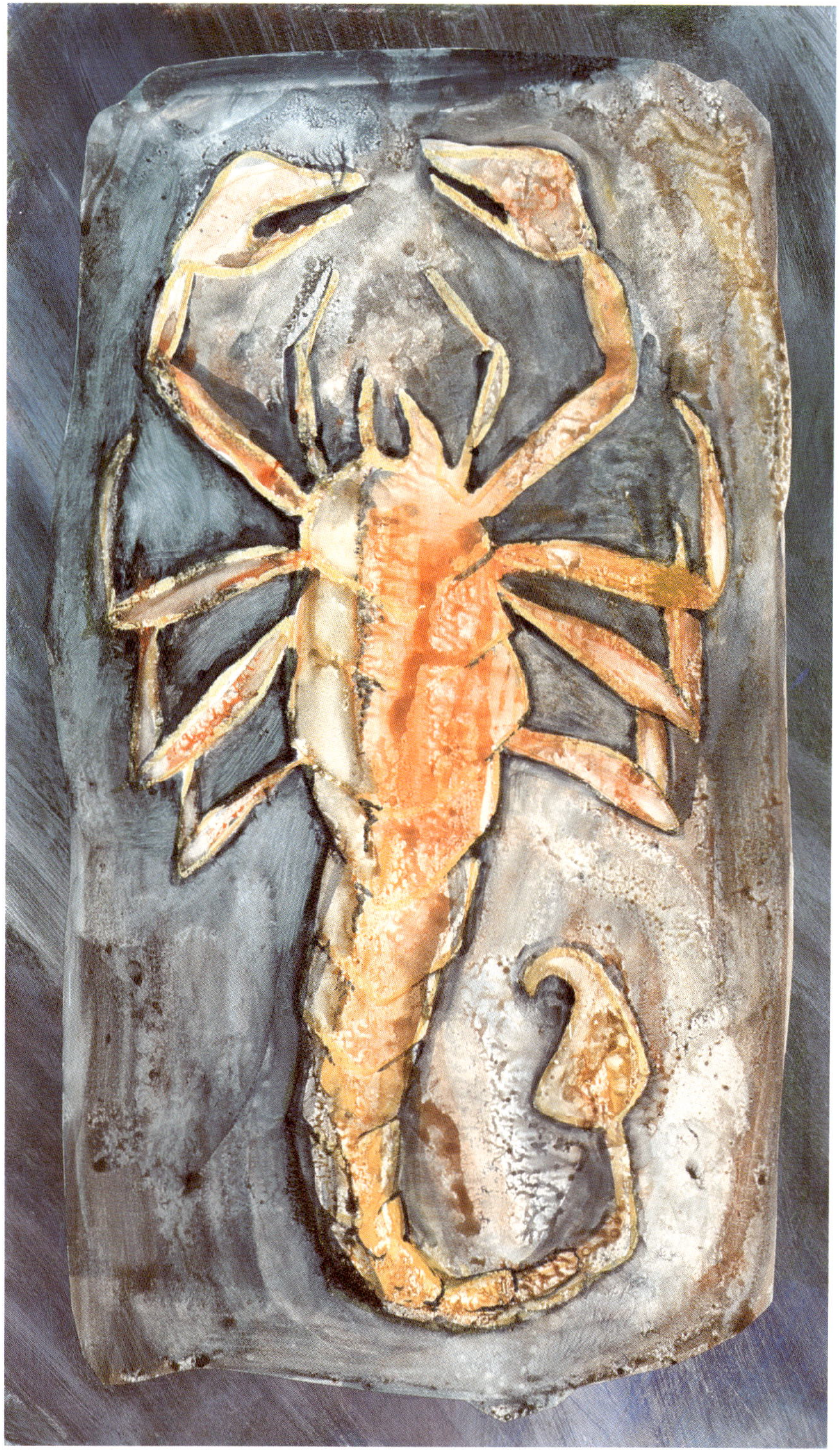

Index